'wisely' pivot a business towards new opportunities in the digital age and definitely a must-read."

—**Jean-Pascal Tricoire, chairman and CEO, Schneider Electric**

"The 'wise pivot' concept is a powerful framework that can shape top leadership teams' decisions around digital strategies and new operating models. With the help of Omar, we used that framework to develop a digital strategy that strikes the balance between growing our core business and shaping new ways of operating."

—**Giovanni Caforio, CEO, Bristol-Myers Squibb**

"We'd better be ready for disruption. I like the strategies I'm seeing for unlocking trapped value and simultaneously reinventing legacy, current, and new areas of a business. I think they could go a long way in helping us—and other companies—get there."

—**John Pettigrew, CEO, National Grid**

"We are facing a period of disruption, the like of which I have not witnessed in my career. It has the potential to obsolete businesses and destroy industries. Even the disrupters are being disrupted!

"As *Pivot to the Future* argues compellingly, traditional strategies are no longer enough. From their own experience, the authors reveal that reinvention must now be a constant, and must address not only the legacy businesses but pivot into new, scalable businesses. This requires organizations to embrace both technological and cultural change, and take bold moves from an outside-in perspective. Change should be measured across three horizons: the old, the now, and the new.

"I recommend this book to those of you who have stepped up to this exciting challenge, understand the magnitude of what is required, and are keen to learn from their peers."

—**Gordon Cairns, chairman of Woolworths Group**
and chairman of Origin Energy

"*Pivot to the Future*—finally—presents a much-needed perspective that reinvigorates tired and outdated concepts of strategy. Instead of building an advantage and defending it, it shows how organizations can release waves of competitive advantage by freeing up trapped value. Instead of innovation for the Next Big Thing, this book shows how innovation plays a role in businesses at every stage. And instead of theorizing, it draws on a real-world journey to figure all this out."

—**Rita McGrath, bestselling author of** *The End of Competitive Advantage* **and professor at Columbia Business School**

"Pivot to the Future helps decision makers break free from traditional, linear thinking and immediate concerns in order to win in the Fourth Industrial Revolution by leveraging disruption rather than fearing it."

—**Klaus Schwab, founder and executive chairman, World Economic Forum**

"The authors succeed in going beyond the theory of disruption—sharing the experiences of those businesses who have successfully pivoted themselves. With case studies and lessons learned, *Pivot to the Future* provides an invaluable tool for reinvention."

—**Luis Maroto, president and CEO, Amadeus**

"The great opportunity of the digital era is to release trapped value from the legacy processes that encumber it. *Pivot to the Future* offers business leaders a much-needed focus on these opportunities, which are often hidden in plain sight. It provides a playbook on how to win— and keep winning—in the digital revolution."

—**Geoffrey Moore, author of** *Crossing the Chasm and Zone to Win*

"Pivot to the Future is timely, insightful, and practical. Just think about the pivot to additive and digital manufacturing that is getting started now, and you'll know how important this book is. A must-read for anyone who cares about the longevity of their firm and their career."

—**Richard D'Aveni, author of** *The Pan-Industrial Revolution: How New Manufacturing Titans Will Transform the World* **and Bakala Professor of Strategy, Tuck School of Business, Dartmouth**

"We no longer live in a world of digital divide. The winner-takes-all markets ahead will create a disruption unlike any other. Winners must make bold and wise pivots required for success. This book illustrates and proves with examples that span multiple industries why incremental innovation is not enough. When the iPhone came out, it destroyed twenty-seven business models and over 10,000 products. THAT is disruption. And that's why we need the kind of advice I'm seeing in this timely book."

—R "Ray" Wang, principal analyst and founder,
Constellation Research, Inc.

"If companies do not learn to innovate and—as Accenture puts it—pivot wisely, they risk irrelevance. But when you combine the ability to pivot with the ability to partner with startups, other companies, universities, and research centers, you're on your way to sustainable growth."

—Francesco Starace, CEO, Enel

"Businesses are experiencing technological and consumer-behavior shifts of unprecedented magnitude, so 'conventional' doesn't cut it anymore. Accenture's leaders clearly get this. But what really counts is that the authors don't just tell us what's wrong, they outline a powerful framework for success."

—Patrick Koller, CEO, Faurecia

"New technologies like Internet of Things, 5G, big data, and artificial intelligence are already leading us into the next industrial revolution, and *Pivot to the Future* helps business leaders to turn these 'disruptions' into opportunities in the intelligence era."

—Yuanqing Yang, chairman and CEO, Lenovo

"When the literature on this subject can hardly keep up with what's going on, it's refreshing to read a succinct work with a unique perspective that cuts to the chase on how companies big and small can not only survive, but really thrive, in these complex, challenging, and incredibly exciting times. The dozens of case studies supporting Accenture's singular vision not only bring this fascinating topic to life, but also underpin and validate the need to pivot where others fear to tread."

—Antonio Huertas, chairman and CEO, MAPFRE

"At a time where business leaders are searching for value and growth, Omar and his coauthors have given us a blueprint of how this can be done by pivoting existing businesses and also leveraging technology and change to pivot to the new. And for those simply seeking a good read, there is a lot of very interesting historical business context and analysis."

—**Alistair Phillips-Davies, CEO, SSE plc**

"Society is being transformed, and it won't stop. Incrementalism no longer cuts it. Ever-evolving digital technologies require a fundamental shift in attitude. Companies must continuously pivot to the new. But as profit windows shorten and one pivot follows the next, the opportunities are vast. Abbosh, Nunes, and Downes explain with some humility how Accenture, where they work, itself learned hard lessons about continuous transformation. *Pivot to the Future* offers deep insight into how to manage the twists and turns."

—**David Kirkpatrick, founder and editor-in-chief, Techonomy Media**

"In this age of lurching change, strategic agility has become the defining signature of the winners. *Pivot to the Future* captures it well. The book is not shy about common missteps CEOs can make and properly emphasizes honing leadership skills to be bold, be courageous, move mindsets, and build teams that execute with a sense of purpose. I saw the essence of the book being discussed by a group of CEOs and many of them commented on how enriched and energized they felt. This book is a must-read for those CEOs who seek to become the disruptors—not the disrupted."

—**Fred Hassan, author of *Reinvent: A Leader's Playbook for Serial Success*, former chairman and CEO, Schering-Plough, and current senior advisor with Warburg Pincus**

PIVOT
to the
FUTURE

PIVOT
to the
FUTURE

Discovering Value
and Creating Growth
in a Disrupted World

OMAR ABBOSH

PAUL NUNES

LARRY DOWNES

PUBLICAFFAIRS
New York

PublicAffairs
Hachette Book Group
1290 Avenue of the Americas, New York, NY 10104
www.publicaffairsbooks.com
@Public_Affairs

Printed in the United States of America

First Edition: April 2019

Published by PublicAffairs, an imprint of Perseus Books, LLC, a subsidiary of Hachette Book Group, Inc. The PublicAffairs name and logo is a trademark of the Hachette Book Group.

The Hachette Speakers Bureau provides a wide range of authors for speaking events. To find out more, go to www.hachettespeakersbureau.com or call (866) 376-6591.

The publisher is not responsible for websites (or their content) that are not owned by the publisher.

Editorial production by Christine Marra, *Marra*thon Production Services. www.marrathoneditorial.org

Book design by Jane Raese
Set in 12-point Dante

Library of Congress Control Number: 2018968130

ISBN 978-1-5417-4267-3 (hardcover), ISBN 978-1-5417-4268-0 (ebook)

LSC-C

10 9 8 7 6 5 4 3 2 1

In memory of our former chairman and chief executive officer, Pierre Nanterme (1959–2019). He was a dear friend, boss, mentor, partner, sounding board, sponsor, coach, and team captain to so many of us at Accenture. He repeatedly broke through the boundaries of status quo. He taught us how to think differently. And, most importantly, he showed us what we could be.

To honor Pierre's legacy, we are donating our net royalties from the sale of this book to l'Hôpital Européen Georges-Pompidou.

To Julien and Aurelien
for their energy, light, and laughter—
budding little leaders already

—OMAR

To the memories of Hilda and Ann,
who always made the most of every situation

—PAUL

To Eric, always

—LARRY

contents

Preface: Becoming an Engine of Continuous and
Perpetual Reinvention, by Pierre Nanterme   ix

Acknowledgments   xiii

Introduction: Reinventing Reinvention   I

PART ONE. Releasing Trapped Value

1   The Trapped Value Gap:
    Turning Disruption into Opportunity   13

2   The Seven Wrong Turns:
    Obstacles to Releasing Trapped Value   41

3   The Seven Winning Strategies:
    Keys for Unlocking Trapped Value   60

PART TWO. The Wise Pivot

4   The Wise Pivot: Discovering Value and Creating Growth
    in the Old, the Now, and the New   97

5   The Old, the Now, and the New: Restarting Growth,
    Accelerating Profits, and Scaling to Win   I2I

6   The Innovation Pivot:
    Concentration, Control, and Aspiration   I54

7   The Financial Pivot:
    Fixed Assets, Working Capital, and Human Capital   186

8   The People Pivot: Leadership, Work, and Culture   212

    Conclusion: Finding Your Brick   240

    Index   245

preface

Becoming an Engine of
Continuous and Perpetual Reinvention

In my thirty-five years at Accenture, I have witnessed firsthand numerous changes, but the greatest are happening right now. The waves of epic disruption that started about five years ago are fueling a digital revolution, which, most agree, stands to be even more significant than the industrial revolution.

Successfully navigating the seas of change is not for the timid. It takes a "rethink" as epic as the disruptive forces. It requires wisdom to strike the delicate balance between maintaining course and speed, creating investment capacity, and continuing to invest in your core business—while at the same time venturing into new business frontiers and profitably scaling innovations to propel growth.

And it takes courage.

Leaders must be willing to fight the urge to prematurely abandon their aging businesses. They must reengage their "cash cows," finding new growth with innovation. And they must become even more ambitious in scaling their emerging businesses. On top of that, they must inspire an entire organization to come along with them as they embrace constant change.

How do we know all of this? Because Accenture faced potentially destructive waves capable of capsizing us and making us less relevant. Our leaders knew we couldn't stand still as a steady wind of innovations swept in. We had to reinvent ourselves.

This book, co-authored by the captain of our own strategies to harness disruption and thrive in the new, Omar Abbosh, along with two of his colleagues, Paul Nunes and Larry Downes, is about realities.

Omar understands change because, with me, he orchestrated the pivot at Accenture, driving us to turbocharge our culture of innovation and perpetual reinvention. Accenture has industrialized these abilities and is passing the lessons along to multiple clients. Their stories are brought home in this book through more than a hundred case study examples that serve as proof that the "wise pivot" is indeed a winning strategy not just for Accenture, but also for businesses that span many industries and geographies.

Let me shed some light on how we learned from experience. In the early 2010s, we recognized that professional services and outsourcing would eventually become commoditized. There were many good players in the market, and we knew we would face big challenges in continuing to differentiate ourselves. Basic technology skills once in short supply were quickly becoming widely available.

So we invested in five up-and-coming digital capabilities with the potential to deliver major benefits to our clients and high growth for us: interactive, mobile, analytics, cloud, and cybersecurity.

But that was not enough. I am an economist by training and temperament, so early on in our journey I developed a new tool to measure the progress of our pivot. We had to develop a way to encourage constant change and know what was working, so that once we became leaders in these chosen categories, we would *continue* leading. We asked again and again one simple question: What is our revenue and growth rate in the "new"? Meaning, for us at the time, our five new capabilities.

By the end of fiscal year 2017, sales in these five areas had increased to more than 50 percent of Accenture's total revenues. By the end of fiscal 2018, they had grown above 60 percent. As we began to experience dramatic growth, we started sharing these metrics with our investors. That way, they could see that as our legacy core offerings began to slow, we were more than making up for them with new sustainable revenue sources. And because we were not disrupted by technology change but were instead fueled by it, we proved our potential to continue growing in the future.

We were building an engine of constant change, investing billions of dollars back into the business and driving the most significant pivot in the history of the consulting and technology services industry. In fact, since 2014 we have hired an additional 154,000 people, grown revenue by $10 billion, and our market value has nearly doubled to above $100 billion.

Accenture's own pivot challenged many core beliefs of our proud corporate culture. But the results speak for themselves. And as Omar, Paul, and Larry make clear in these pages, any business can execute a wise pivot.

To be perfectly honest, I wish I'd had the kind of specific, practical strategies this book offers when I came to Accenture thirty-five years ago. It pulls back the curtain to reveal the how and why of our own wise pivot into the future. And it illustrates that instead of fearing disruption, companies can discover value and drive the new growth needed to pivot wisely and thrive in the digital revolution.

Now it's your turn.

Pierre Nanterme
Former Chairman and Chief Executive Officer
Accenture

acknowledgments

Before we can pivot fully to the future, we must first look to the past, making sure to express the gratitude we feel to those who have given so much to make this book a reality. We have had the help and support of countless clients, colleagues, bosses, mentors, and friends in writing this book. While we cannot recognize them all individually, we are nonetheless grateful to each for all they have done.

Still, there are some we must call out for their unique and outstanding contributions.

First is Vedrana Savic and her exemplary research team at Accenture: Amy Chng, Mike Moore, Babak Mousavi, and Koteswara Ivaturi. We thank them for their years of research, ideation, and thinking on this topic; they have made the book what it is.

We thank Ivy Lee, also at Accenture, who "volunteered" to provide invaluable research in her spare time on many of the company stories chronicled in these pages, as well as priceless editorial help at critical moments; we could not have done it, this time too, without her.

We are also indebted to the top-notch editorial team at Accenture Research. Paul Barbagallo provided invaluable editorial support throughout, and played a critical role in keeping our thinking straight and messaging clear; we are most grateful. For helpful comments, insights, suggestions, and corrections on the manuscript our thanks also go to David Light and Regina Maruca.

We thank, as well, all those at Accenture Research who gave us all manner of feedback, encouragement, and unending support throughout the entire project. Special thanks go to Francis Hintermann (without whose nudge to Omar this book would not have been written), and Barbara Harvey, as well as Josh Bellin, Svenja Falk, Raghav Narsalay, Andre Schlieker, Mark Purdy, Matthew Robinson, Prashant P. Shukla, and H. James Wilson.

For the tremendous support we have received from every corner of Accenture marketing, we thank Amy Fuller and Ginny Cartwright Ziegler, as well as Gwen Harrigan and Jill Kramer. We also recognize Marc Appel, Stacey Jones, Jani Spede, Amy Eiduke, Tourang Nazari, and Allison Tesnar.

At Fletcher & Company, our thanks to Eric Lupfer for support above and beyond the duties of a literary agent.

At Hachette Book Group, PublicAffairs, we thank John Mahaney, whose depth of editing skills were matched only by the depth of his patience. We also express our deepest gratitude to Lindsay Fradkoff, Jaime Leifer, and Christine Marra.

For their wonderful support in bringing the book to market, we thank Carolyn Monaco and Jill Totenberg.

We owe a great deal of thanks to all the fantastic editors and publishers who have helped us to develop components of this book, and to bring those ideas to business audiences. At *Harvard Business Review*, our thanks go to Sarah Cliffe, Eben Harrell, Maureen Hoch, Steve Prokesch, Melinda Merino, and Martha Spaulding. At *MIT Sloan Management Review* we especially thank Paul Michelman, and at the *European Business Review* we are most grateful to Elenora Elroy.

A very special thank-you goes to Tim Breene, retired Accenture chief strategy officer, whose thoughtfulness about strategy and the CSO role preceded us, and whose insights and example inspired us. Omar and Paul are especially grateful for his years of wise and challenging mentorship.

At its heart, *Pivot to the Future* is the story of Accenture and its clients' own wise pivots. These stories are written by teams of incredible people. In the case of Accenture, many, many people have been in the thick of it. Still, we would like to specifically acknowledge Pierre Nanterme, David Rowland, KC McClure, Jo Deblaere, Gianfranco Casati, Paul Daugherty, Bhaskar Ghosh, Chad Jerdee, Mark Knickrehm, Sander van't Noordende, Dan London, Richard Lumb, Laurence Morvan, Jean-Marc Ollagnier, Debbie Polishook, Gene Reznik, Ellyn Shook, Mike Sutcliff, and Julie Sweet.

We are also grateful to the many people who were generous with their time in interviews, who made introductions to people and companies featured in the book, and who helped us in myriad ways to bring it forth. We expressly thank Debra Alliegro, Muqsit Ashraf, Arjun Bedi, Bruno Berthon, Marc Carrel-Billiard, Gemma Catchpole, Chris Donnelly, Stephen Ferneyhough, Piercarlo Gera, Scott Hahn, Louise Howard, Hirotaka Kawata, Jiorgis Kritsotakis, Peter Lacy, Dinah Laredo, Kathleen Leslie, Tomas Nyström, Angie Park, Emilie de Possesse, Kyriacos Sabatakakis, Jill Standish, Bill Theofilou, and Marco Ziegler.

OMAR ABBOSH

Omar acknowledges his family, especially his two boys, who have always put up with his excessively wide-eyed work enthusiasm. Next, he wants to thank his clients over the years who taught him so much about the real-world struggles of leading and who trusted him in sharing the very hard challenges of people, competition, regulation, and more—specifically, Paul Whittaker, Phil Nolan, Steve Holliday, Chris Train, John Pettigrew, and Alistair Phillips-Davies.

Omar could not have developed into the person he is without the trust, coaching, and space given to him by his career sponsors over the years—Gill Rider, David Thomlinson, Mark Spelman, Bill Green, Sander van't Noordende, and Jean-Marc Ollagnier—for which he is eternally grateful.

Omar has been lucky over his career to be accompanied along the way by hundreds of incredible people; special thanks to Kelly Bissell, Scott Brown, Simon Eaves, Dan Elron and the ninjas, Trevor Gruzin, Kathleen O'Reilly, Big Dan Reid, Narry Singh, John Zealley, Stuart Niccol, Mike Corcoran, Kishore Durg, Simon Whitehouse, Beat Monnerat, Silvio Mani, Julie Spillane, Ryan Shanks, Dave "Big Mac" McKenzie, Lisa Dunnery, Dave Abood, Jill Huntley, Anand Swaminathan, Nicola Morini-Bianzino, Ryan LaSalle, Tom Parker, and the awesome, inspiring growth and strategy network.

The people who brought the strategy to life are many, including Atsushi Egawa, Bob Easton, Wei Zhu, Juan Pedro Moreno, Frank Riemensperger, Sergio Kaufman, Anoop Sagoo, Leo Framil, Olly Benzecry, Jimmy Etheredge, Alan McIntyre, Anne O'Riordan, Francesco Venturini, Eric Schaeffer, David Sovie, Matias Alonso, Rachael Bartels,

Billy Smart, Mark Curtis, Olof Schybergson, Glen Hartman, Brian Whipple, Narendra Mulani, Aidan Quilligan, Edwin VanderOuderaa, Steve Culp, Eva Sage-Gavin, Don Schulman, Robert Wollan, Daniel Schwartmann, Jon Coltsmann, Jeff(ers) Doyle, Claire Grazioso, Joel Unruch, Rheka Menon, and Maureen Costello.

Finally, Omar gives special thanks to his boss, Pierre Nanterme, the former chairman and CEO of Accenture, for his wisdom, exigence, and openness to drive change. With his razor-sharp intellect, humor, and pragmatism, Pierre created the best conditions possible to enable our repeated pivots, growing generations of great leaders. Learning from Pierre has been the most inspiring and exciting journey possible; we all miss his presence deeply.

PAUL NUNES

Paul also thanks his family: his wife Joan and their three children, Jonathan, Charlotte, and Michael, Jane Cummings, Jennifer Cummings (for the best accommodations in NYC), Kevin and Julie Mullen, Joseph Nunes, Wendy Heimann-Nunes, and Marcus and Amy Nunes. He also thanks Eric Clemons, William "Doc" Napiwocki, Jim and Lucy Hospodarsky, Mike Cavanaugh and Gong Li, Mike Davis, Tom Davenport, Ajit Kambil, Joe Prendergast, Len Sherman, Rick Stuckey, and all the gang from Week 31.

LARRY DOWNES

Larry also thanks Eric Apel, Rebecca Arbogast, Nancy Bacal, Derek Carter, Shirlee Citron, Peter Christy, Eric Hower, Andrew Keen, Anna-Maria Kovacs, Judy Lasley, Roslyn Layton, Ellen Leander, Blair Levin, Larry Loo, Sarah Loo, Carl Morison, Kevin Morison, Lynn Parks-Carter, Richard Posner, Zhang Ruimin, Hedy Straus, Dennis Summers, and Madura Wijewardena.

REINVENTING REINVENTION

THE CEO OF a large professional services firm might have been slightly amused by the irony of the situation, if the problem wasn't as serious as he had come to realize. He and his colleagues had spent decades advising companies around the world on how to move forward as disruption upended one industry after another. Now, as digital technologies, including broadband internet, cloud services, and mobile devices proliferated, his own core consulting business was getting squeezed on both ends.

From the bottom, high-quality providers in India were offering global customers low-cost outsourcing for application development and other technology services long important to his company's business; and they were starting to move into higher value-add services that directly competed with his company. From the top, hardware giants and software platform providers were leveraging proprietary software products to convert themselves into massive services companies, threatening to interfere with strategic relationships his company had nurtured with senior executives across the Global Fortune 500.

Out on the horizon, gathering storm clouds of emerging technologies, including web- and mobile-based digital technologies and collaborative social media, were closing in quickly and ominously, with the potential to disrupt, well, everything. Economies of scale for technology-based platforms, for example, could soon make it possible for software products to displace large numbers of expert professionals.

Even as the company's existing markets faced stalled or declining growth, new value in emerging technology businesses was being picked off by others. The opportunity was there, and right in the company's wheelhouse. But management couldn't reach it. It was as if the value were somehow trapped.

What was needed was not just a new strategy, but a new approach to strategy: One that enabled the company to make the most of new technologies, turning them from disruptive threats to profitable opportunities. One that would let the company do so faster all the time.

To thrive, the company would have to out-innovate the fastest-moving companies and disrupt its own core business before someone else did it to them.

That potentially disrupted company a few years back, 2014 to be precise, was Accenture, the home of your three authors: Omar Abbosh, Paul Nunes, and Larry Downes. This book originated with Accenture's experiences not only in reinventing itself, but also in reinventing the very idea of reinvention as essential and possible amid constant technological disruption.

To accelerate growth today *and* establish leadership in tomorrow's opportunities, Accenture would need to remake its business. We would need to systematically reinvest in our core assets—including our people, our intellectual property, our culture, and our information systems—all of which were already facing strong headwinds.

Having done so, our key insight was that in the face of predictable unpredictability, a single large-scale "transformation" just doesn't cut it. Reviewing the history of business success and failure over the past half century, we concluded instead that the only solution to continuous and potentially devastating change is constant reinvention, rearchitecting the business in a way that allowed us to pivot from one opportunity to the next, quickly and efficiently.

Specifically, Accenture would need to balance its strategic initiatives around three distinct stages in the business lifecycle: mature products and services approaching obsolescence (the old); today's most profitable offerings (the now); and leading-edge ventures targeted at the immediate future (the new).

We would need to grow profits in all stages, releasing value already there but which had become trapped. We would need to continually pivot the business around a fulcrum of core assets, shifting from one stage to the next, reacting quickly as market conditions changed and technology disruptors emerged—an approach to business value creation we came to call the "wise pivot."

As part of Accenture's own wise pivot, our internal think tank, Accenture Research, conducted more than two years of research on how technology was impacting businesses of all sizes, old and new, across industries and geographies.

We wanted to understand three things: which industries were vulnerable to disruption; how successful companies find their value opportunities; and how leading organizations pivot in response to disruptive change. We also wanted to see how leaders manage to expand growth in legacy businesses while also moving rapidly into new businesses that quickly achieved the scale needed to capture profits.

So far, we've performed economic research and case analysis of over three thousand of the largest companies by revenue across twenty major industry segments, determining both the drivers of disruption and the new strategies leading companies have developed to make the most of them.

In addition, we surveyed or spoke with thousands of executives to gather their perspectives. All that research was validated by hands-on experience working with clients across industries to help them make the kind of strategic pivots we executed for our own business.

Throughout the book, we will be referring to the findings of our research, including insights from detailed case studies and from our engagement with leading businesses. To learn more about how the work was conducted, and to read our latest thinking, please visit our website: https://www.accenture.com/us-en/innovation-architecture -accenture-research.

Our study of the inspiring and sometimes sobering stories of renowned leaders in industries as different as retail, manufacturing, financial services, and consumer products revealed, as in our own experience, that exploiting disruption requires more than just vision.

It calls for, among other things, bold technology leadership driven by senior executives, the creation and acquisition of promising disruptive businesses, and a coordinated process that retrains employees and rebalances assets from one stage of the business lifecycle to the next.

These critical elements are more than just aspirations. They are imperatives that must be translated into new digital-age strategies and executed precisely, using the kind of guerilla tactics favored by disruptive start-ups.

Developing new strategies that unlock trapped value, executing simultaneously in the old, the now, and the new, and repeatedly refocusing the business around a core of old and new assets—these are the elements of the wise pivot.

>

Any business can execute its own wise pivot and turn existential threats into golden opportunities by freeing trapped value. But make no mistake: This is not an undertaking for the faint of heart. In markets driven by continuous technology-based change—increasingly, all of them—one pivot is followed by the next and the next, demanding a strategic approach that doesn't fight the tide as much as it surfs waves of disruption.

The wise pivot crosses businesses and time frames, releasing value already there but currently trapped. Through interconnected, rolling strategies that operate within and between the lifecycle stages—the old, the now, and the new—leaders continually reallocate assets and investments to balance all three. This assures continued revenue from core assets that may be nearing the end of their life and generates profits needed to invest in the future as the business and its people move quickly through the now, and arrive sustainably at the new.

Instead of exploiting core assets—products, customers, and technologies—the wise pivot rotates around those assets, spinning into control rather than out of it:

THE OLD—Even as customers and markets shift faster all the time, sustaining the enterprise still requires intense focus on today's core offerings and the revenues they generate. If you prematurely exit or just plain starve still-viable but mature products and technologies, you forsake additional profits essential for investments in the future. Executives who master the wise pivot apply new technologies to old offerings, restarting growth that can fuel a pivot to the future.

THE NOW—Masters of the wise pivot continue to invest strategically in their most successful products and services with the expectation of accelerating revenue growth and profits even more quickly. Here too, infusions of new technology and innovation can enhance business opportunities and may even lead to new directions for core businesses; directions unforeseen or overlooked in a rush to get to the new.

THE NEW—The wise pivot requires careful planning and insight into the timing of the next disruption. Success may come only after a series of spectacular failures, as was the case, for example, with digital books and digital music services. The key is to minimize your failures, while getting to the new profitably and at scale. The right combination of input technology prices and component availability, along with a commitment and ability to grow rapidly when markets take off, must be made to align perfectly.

In our experience, few enterprises are prepared to embrace the new, even when it's clear the core business is running out of steam. Oil companies know their long-term future will not be based entirely on fossil fuels, but what then? As automobiles become self-driving, likewise, auto insurance companies need to find new things to insure. Each enterprise must find its own route to the new, preserving those aspects of the company's core, such as its culture, that made it successful in the first place.

Even when the path looks clear, pivoting to the new is fraught with obstacles. We regularly hear from leaders of the companies we work with that they lack the resources to invest in the new, let alone scale ventures rapidly, having committed all their assets to maintaining today's core.

Even if sufficient capital can be freed up, inertia may still hold back real change. Today's processes and IT systems, after all, have been optimized, sometimes over decades, to support the core. They are literally hard-coded to implement a strategy perhaps long forgotten. These corporate "antibodies" may unintentionally destroy initiatives with the potential to lead managers to the future. The old wakes up every morning determined to kill the new.

The solution requires a reallocation of resources driven from the top: the CEO, CFO, and other members of the executive team. Consider the courageous decisions of Microsoft CEO Satya Nadella. After previous efforts to compete in social media and smartphones generated disappointing results, Nadella decided to pivot elsewhere.

The company moved from standalone Windows to cloud computing, seeing that as their best route to a new core. To take on fast-growing Amazon Web Services (AWS), Nadella led the company in a number of acquisitions to support its "cloud-first, AI-first" mission. Since the launch of Microsoft Azure in 2010, its commercial cloud business has delivered more than $23 billion in revenue, with a gross margin of 57 percent in fiscal year 2018.

Microsoft recently invested $7.5 billion to acquire open-source software development platform GitHub, further extending its status as one of the world's leading cloud-computing vendors. Microsoft is gearing toward its "next new," building an AI powerhouse with its eight-thousand-employee-strong AI and research division.

As that example makes clear, a wise pivot likewise requires radical approaches to growing new businesses quickly. To truly profit from disruption, an enterprise must be prepared to manage increasingly short windows of profitability, scaling up rapidly as customers embrace the new all at once, then scaling down nearly as fast when demand declines.

To achieve scale quickly, managers need early access to emerging technologies and the relationships to exploit them when the timing is right. To gain needed market and technology insights, the wise pivot relies heavily on experimentation and and early investment. That can take many forms, including internal start-ups nurtured in facilities known as "incubators" or investments in outside incubators sponsored by multiple businesses, known as "accelerators."

Businesses facing disruption have also launched and formalized corporate venture capital funds that give them partial ownership of start-ups developing relevant technologies. But in some cases, the best way to ensure rapid scale in new markets is simply to acquire start-ups that have already developed new products and customer relationships.

Consider the elegant pivot of Dutch consumer products giant Royal Philips. The company recognized in the early 2000s that over the course of a decade or less, LED (light-emitting diode) technology would become better, cheaper, and more sustainable than traditional incandescent lighting—a category Philips helped invent and that had given it a competitive advantage for over a century.

Leveraging the company's old assets in manufacturing, distribution, and marketing, the company made strategic short-term investments in the compact fluorescent lightbulb (CFL)—an interim improved lighting technology—even as it quickly ramped up its research, development, and investments in LEDs. As it sold off the assets of the incandescent business to competitors, Philips was ready to enter the LED market as a service provider, offering one of the first programmable lighting systems based on its proprietary Hue technology.

All the while, the company was investing in and expanding its health technologies business, which ultimately became its new core. Then, after a hundred years in lighting, Philips largely exited the business. It saw its future elsewhere and, thanks to careful planning in its old and now, it had the innovation, finances, and talent to rotate successfully to the new.

Or look at Amazon, which leveraged its success in selling books to successfully enter the e-book market with its Kindle product, despite having almost no previous experience in consumer electronics. Amazon began by increasing investments in key technologies, including storage, display, battery, and networking, that had failed to deliver winning products for earlier, competing readers.

Once these technologies matured enough to be combined in an effective and affordable product, Amazon leveraged its knowledge of the book industry, along with its expertise in retailing and its powerful customer base, to enter the market quickly with a product that finally met consumer needs.

The company was at the same time planning its next "new," finding other uses for the skills, relationships, and technologies it had developed to support its high-volume retailing platform.

Leveraging these core assets, Amazon turned its IT infrastructure into a service for others; first for smaller retailers it hosted on its platform and then, as it scaled up, as the cloud-based hosting business Amazon Web Services. Offering business users convenience and substantial cost savings, AWS exploded into a nearly $20 billion business in the course of a decade.

Finally, consider the wise pivot of Netflix, which began as a DVD-by-mail service for renting movies. Even while the company launched its service—ultimately deadly to traditional rental businesses like Blockbuster and West Coast Video—CEO Reed Hastings was preparing the organization to move to the "new": streaming a subscription-based digital video service over increasingly ubiquitous high-capacity broadband networks.

Capturing and analyzing customer data in the streaming business was in turn an essential pivot to get the company to its next new: the creation of original programming. The inference engine the company built gave it deep insights into customers' viewing habits and preferences, helping jump-start its dramatic and successful entry into its new business as a major video studio, outpacing incumbents that had been producing video content for decades if not longer. In 2018, the company topped traditional and new media company competitors with the most Emmy nominations of any studio.

For Netflix, balancing investments in all three lifecycle stages required delicate and constant shifts in strategy, not all of them executed perfectly. For example, while relentlessly improving the operating efficiency of the still-viable DVD delivery business to sustain revenue as most customers shifted to the streaming service, Hastings tried to separate the two businesses—prematurely, as it turned out. Customers revolted against new pricing plans, and Netflix quickly undid the change.

Likewise, as the streaming market rapidly became crowded with competing products from incumbents and new entrants, Netflix continued to invest in digital compression and other optimizing technologies; it knew its technical platform would be the cornerstone for distribution of its soon-to-arrive original content.

Finally, in today's new, Netflix relies on a deep, data-driven relationship with its more than one hundred million global subscribers. Rejecting the old blockbuster, intuition-based model of Hollywood,

Netflix has applied a scientific approach to developing and promoting original content, scaling it up quickly to keep a growing list of competitors throughout the supply chain continually off guard.

These cases make it clear that the wise pivot doesn't simply balance unrelated investments across the three lifecycle stages of a company's businesses. It discovers valuable synergies between them—some planned, some totally serendipitous.

While building our future AI practice, for example, Accenture discovered innovative ways to automate the tedious and error-prone process of software testing, a key component of our business at the time. These new tools exponentially improved both the efficiency and reliability of the process, improving the performance of our business in the now.

Competitors may have viewed this development as cannibalizing the valuable expertise Accenture had spent decades developing. We saw instead the opportunity to release trapped value growing in an inefficient, expensive, and labor-intensive process that AI was now capable of automating. Rather than wait for others to target that value, we did it ourselves.

Sooner rather than later, we knew, AI would transform testing, if not by Accenture, then perhaps by someone else without a legacy practice to protect. As we worked to pivot our testing experts into other fields, the wise pivot breathed new life—and new profits—into a fading business.

As this last example suggests, mastering a wise pivot requires a constant and courageous rotation through the old, the now, and the new. The new eventually (perhaps quickly) becomes the old, and the cycle continues. Over- or underinvesting in any one stage is a constant risk, one that can prove catastrophic. Leaders must revisit the ratios of investment in each, keeping them in balance in the face of sometimes unpredictable disruption from outside. In effect, they create a triangle of balance, pivoting from one to another.

In the pages to come we will explore in detail the winning strategies of companies old and new that are thriving under constant competitive threat and ceaseless technological change. And we will look closely at the tools and tactics they have devised to sustain growth in an age of continuous disruption.

The key finding of our research is that there is a growing gap between what is technologically possible and what companies actually do with that potential. The mismatch is generating rich stores of trapped value, fueled by continuing improvements in the speed, size, power, price, and efficiency of digital technologies.

Despite this opportunity, in many industries we have studied, the top incumbents are no longer growing profits, even as technology-based innovation is creating vast amounts of new value. Someone else, often a new entrant, is finding and capturing that value.

The wise pivot is driven by a deep understanding of the obstacles that increasingly prevent older businesses from keeping up. It offers strategies for reversing that trend, turning core capabilities and resources from aging assets into engines of faster growth.

The opportunities for discovering and releasing trapped value are great, but the time available to find and release it is growing shorter with each new generation of disruptors. Our research revealed four distinct areas where trapped value accumulates, each attracting different kinds of competitors and new entrants.

How to find and capture that value is the topic we explore first.

part one

RELEASING TRAPPED VALUE

chapter 1

THE TRAPPED VALUE GAP

Turning Disruption into Opportunity

WHAT HAPPENS WHEN new and fast-improving technologies create opportunities to unleash untapped sources of revenue, some of them long trapped by market inefficiencies? As digital components become relentlessly better, cheaper, and smaller, that's a question companies of all sizes and in every industry will need to answer, and almost certainly sooner than they think.

That's because technology is increasingly creating the tools your competitors—incumbents and entrepreneurs alike—are using to build new digital products and services that target and release latent demand and serve unmet needs. We call that potential revenue "trapped value." If you don't get to it before others, you may find not just your future growth disrupted, but today's businesses as well. That disruption may happen quickly or slowly but, either way, it's likely to have already started.

Trapped value to entrepreneurs is like honey to bears. It attracts new sources of capital investment and new entrants eager to experiment in your markets and collaborate with your customers, suppliers, and other stakeholders. They are happy to share the value they release, developing new kinds of business relationships and new approaches to strategy and execution that are upending much of the conventional wisdom of management thinking.

Some good news. From personal experience in our own industry and our work with companies around the world, we know that incumbents can do as good (and often better) a job of releasing trapped value as even the most disruptive Silicon Valley start-up.

The hard part, however, isn't mastering new technology. It is overcoming old plans, processes, and systems optimized for a time when competition was largely static, industry change was slow, and technology improvements were incremental.

To see how, let's begin with an industry whose painful disruption and reinvention has become the stuff of daily headlines.

LOCKED IN AT THE MALL

The last few years have been very, very bad for retail.

Traditional brick-and-mortar retailers, who long claimed immunity to disruption from relatively tiny web-based competitors, are giving up the fight. Bankruptcy filings have set records, including familiar company names such as Sears, Radio Shack, the Limited, Sports Authority, Toys "R" Us, and Payless ShoeSource. In 2017 alone, other venerable brands announced plans to close more than thirty-five hundred store locations.

It wasn't as if consumers had lost interest in shopping. They had simply gone elsewhere.

The obvious disruptor here is Amazon. The web commerce pioneer has quintupled its sales since 2010. It now sells five times as much as Sears, which by 2018 had lost as much revenue since 2007 as Amazon gained. By 2019, half of all US households were subscribed to Amazon Prime, which includes free two-day delivery and original video content streamed over the internet. Overall, digital commerce represents nearly $400 billion in annual sales for the $3.5 trillion industry.

Yet, the fall of brick-and-mortar retail was hardly inevitable. In reality, the industry had over two decades to respond. In 1996, internet shopping was at best a gimmick, but it grew steadily, increasing about 15–25 percent each year. By 2016, web-based commerce accounted for nearly $100 billion in holiday sales. But even then, it was only 10 percent of the total.

Incumbent retailers first denied the risk online sites posed to their business, then tried to mimic them by adding "me too" websites. Fearing cannibalization of their physical stores and offense to suppliers, however, the e-commerce offerings of established brands were always compromised, for example, by offering limited or clearance merchandise, or requiring in-store pickup and return. Prices rarely reflected the lower cost of online service.

What many traditional stores missed was that falling prices for technology and the spread of the internet were creating new opportunities, first and foremost to serve customers more efficiently and more personally. Retailers, however, had for the most part given up on technological innovation. Even the most basic customer service had disappeared amid rounds of cost cutting that left customers feeling frustrated and ignored.

But then, where were consumers going to shop instead? They were trapped in the mall.

That is, until e-commerce companies cracked open the window and heard a thundering chorus of consumer dissatisfaction. Lower prices? Fine. Custom solutions? You got it. Self-service instead of no service? Done.

What distinguished the digital-first retailers wasn't their innovative use of digital technology. It was a relentless focus on making shopping more personalized, convenient, fun, cost-effective, and even socially responsible.

Amazon, eBay, Apple, Zappos, Dell, and others engaged deeply with customers, found out what they wanted, and gave it to them. They added secure payments, video, and other enhancements to their websites. Behind the scenes, they built state-of-the-art warehouses and distribution networks, investing in robotics, drones, and powerful data analysis tools that taught them what customers wanted and when. Products can now reorder themselves through voice-activated smart-home hubs such as Amazon's Echo and Google Home.

As traditional retailers cut staff, dimmed the lights, and left aging inventory on the shelves, web-based sellers continued investing everything they had and more. They added free shipping, easy returns, same-day delivery, targeted promotions, customer reviews, and mobile interfaces. All of this transformed online shopping into a richer experience than getting in the car, driving to the mall, looking for parking, and hoping the product you wanted was in stock and someone was available to take your money and complete the sales transaction.

Online leaders are even experimenting with brick-and-mortar outlets, showing up the incumbents in their own strip malls. Apple Stores, with cashier-free checkout, in-store classes, and the customer service Genius Bar, are consistently mobbed. Amazon is testing grocery stores that automatically charge customers for their purchases when they exit, relying on new technologies, including computer vision, machine learning, and artificial intelligence (AI).

Meanwhile, automated warehouses and the absence of physical locations that need to be leased, heated, staffed, and policed, regardless of whether customers are in the store, made it possible for online sellers to charge less for goods, sometimes much less.

Eventually, web commerce became better *and* cheaper than brick-and-mortar stores, the two catalysts that trigger the kind of disruption that can no longer be ignored. Once the reaction started, it was only a matter of time before the doors began slamming shut at an accelerated pace at malls everywhere.

As Barbara Kahn, a marketing professor and former director of the retailing center at the Wharton School, succinctly told the *New York Times:* "The retailers that get it recognize that Amazon has forever changed consumer behavior. I shouldn't have to work to shop."

Retailing didn't decline so much as it evolved. A constant stream of new technologies, networks, and devices identified and released new value in the form of personalization, convenience, and predictive analysis that consumers and the new entrants happily shared through collaborative applications. And what they each learned from those early experiments led to still more innovation, more technology, and more value.

Much of that value had been accumulating for years, trapped, just waiting for the right technology at the right price to set it free. Yet the incumbents were hardly doomed to sit out the reinvention of their industry. Indeed, they could have studied the very public successes and failures of the start-ups. They could have adapted the innovations that worked. They could have leveraged their long-standing relationships with suppliers, customers, and advertising outlets to fight off the upstarts. They could have turned their ubiquitous physical locations into formidable competitive advantages.

Instead, they adopted customer-friendly technologies haltingly, if not resentfully. And watched as assets slowly and then quickly became liabilities—expensive anchors pulling them into a deadly spiral of diminishing returns to scale as sales volume decreased. Many did little but wait for the end.

The impact on US retailers was especially pronounced, given that floor space per person in the United States was the highest in the world, more than double that of Australia and nearly five times that of the United Kingdom.

Still, a few incumbents, especially those that had themselves been earlier retail innovators, thrived. Walmart notably made significant investments in the internet, including the acquisition of Jet.com and Indian e-commerce highflier Flipkart. Others, such as Dollar General, expanded into forgotten markets, such as rural locations. At the high end, Tiffany is renovating its flagship Manhattan store, leveraging its brand into new hospitality services and creating an updated "breakfast at Tiffany's" at its Blue Box Cafe.

All the survivors are expanding digital offerings and integrating them into their physical locations, turning expensive real estate back into an asset. They are pivoting to new possibilities, enabled by an enthusiastic embrace of technology.

HOW VALUE GETS TRAPPED

The ongoing revolution in retail and other mature industries is a story about what happens when trapped value, simmering just under the surface for decades, is suddenly let loose. Rules of engagement are dramatically rewritten, leverage among ecosystem participants is wrenched in different directions, and barriers to entry suddenly disappear, letting in invaders from adjacent industries and everywhere else.

The release of trapped value can also restart growth for incumbents, expand revenue, and facilitate the move to new markets and new customers that may have seemed too expensive or too distant to serve.

Just when you need to pivot, however, you may find yourselves, like brick-and-mortar retailers, caught in a maturity paradox. After sometimes decades of relative stability in their core business, experienced managers may have little to no experience in thinking big, formulating bold strategies, or anticipating multiple sources of new competition.

Potentially limitless new value is being created in the market, but incumbents are cut off from it. For those companies, that new value is as trapped as they are. Why? Organizations optimized for predictable performance may have long-term contracts that are hard to get out of, with resources intractably committed to a fading business model and internal systems, both technical and human, that hardwire caution over creativity. The assets, supplier relationships, customer base, and human capital you've worked so hard to solidify may prove inflexible, even when it's clear there's both need and opportunity for dramatic change.

In succeeding chapters we will show how any business can diagnose and treat the causes of trapped value and develop the skills to find and release it simultaneously across the three stages in the lifecycle of existing businesses—the wise pivot approach to continuous, sustainable change.

But first, let's understand what we mean by trapped value—why, how, and where it gets trapped—and how to find it.

Trapped value, as the retail example suggests, accumulates when technology makes possible a better experience for customers than what you and your competitors are offering them. It may show up in the form of unrealized revenues for you, lost to missing elements or features of customer service. It also appears as value lost to the customer herself, when she has to do more work than necessary, perhaps due to incomplete product information, inefficient ordering and tracking tools, or generic offerings that don't meet her actual needs.

Within your organization, value likewise becomes trapped when operational inefficiencies that could be eliminated by better automation are left to fester, taking profits straight from the bottom line.

Retail aside, the growing accumulation of trapped value and its potential for disrupting incumbents is not the result of a failure to invest in innovation. Overall, investment in innovation has increased dramatically. The world's one thousand largest companies by revenue grew traditional research and development spending annually by 6 percent between 2012 and 2017, from $361 billion to $465 billion.

That translates to over $3 trillion spent on research and development, technology-based mergers and acquisition, and corporate venture capital, where companies take stakes in start-ups by investing alongside traditional venture fund managers.

While business leaders might think all of that $3 trillion is going toward potentially disruptive innovations, however, in most cases it isn't. Despite prolific investments, most companies are just tinkering around the edges of innovation, unable to achieve any fundamental changes to their business. Much of the spending, it turns out, is directed at incremental improvements. And incremental change is just not enough to seize the biggest trapped value opportunities created by new technologies.

For many companies, becoming the disruptor rather than the disrupted begins with a fundamental shift in attitude toward digital technologies. Rather than seeing them as bolted-on tools for developing a website or enhancing internal systems, you need to integrate them into both your product offerings and your internal operations. You need to design and redesign your interactions with stakeholders by putting new innovations and technologies at the forefront, becoming what we call "digital first."

At Accenture, being digital first means delivering new technology-enabled capabilities to clients around the world, while simultaneously digitizing our internal corporate processes. That led us to build Accenture Interactive, for example, now the world's largest provider of digital marketing services. At the same time, we've also migrated almost all of our internal systems to the public cloud.

Being digital first also drove us to greatly improve our ability to work together as the size of our organization grew rapidly. Our employees around the world connect using a single set of virtual tools, including Skype for Business and Microsoft's OneDrive. Training, document production, project team collaboration, and customer relationship management have all been digitized. Company executives effectively run the business from their smartphones.

Becoming digital first is only the first step, albeit for many companies a big and potentially costly one. It's a necessary, though not sufficient, condition for pivoting wisely.

How does it help? Digital-first companies have a platform for continuous change. As the pace of disruption expands, they can use the platform to pivot faster than their competitors to whatever innovations come next, responding to rapidly changing customer needs and scaling both up and down as markets emerge, explode, and contract.

That kind of flexibility is essential as the digital revolution continues to accelerate. As explained by Moore's law—the prediction by Intel founder Gordon Moore that core computing components would double in capacity, miniaturization, and energy efficiency without increasing in cost—digital technologies have long improved at something approaching an exponential rate every few years.

As a result, everything from cloud storage to genomic sequencing, 3D printers, commercial drones, and basic communications bandwidth has experienced logarithmic declines in price. Between 2001 and 2017, for example, the cost of sequencing a complete human-sized genome fell from $100 million to around $1,000.

Similar cost reductions, applied over an extended yet predictable period of time, have increased the risks and the opportunities for disruption in a growing list of industries. That's because businesses are falling further behind in taking full advantage of digital components that are becoming simultaneously better, faster, and cheaper.

As shown in figure 1.1, the pace of change that technology makes possible and the speed with which that change is being realized are diverging. As the gap between potential and actual value creation widens, more and more of the good that new technologies can do becomes hidden, a latent but intensifying force of future disruption.

Figure 1.1 Technology Change Creates Trapped Value

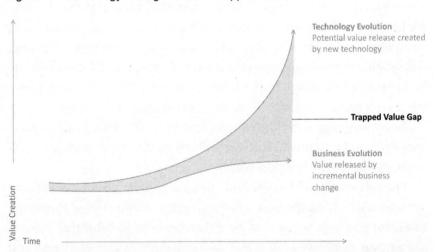

Technology Evolution
Potential value release created by new technology

Trapped Value Gap

Business Evolution
Value released by incremental business change

Value Creation

Time

We refer to that mismatch as the "trapped value gap." The faster technologies improve, the faster the gap widens. And the greater the urgency with which you must adopt new strategies to target and close it more quickly and effectively. Before someone else—competitors, new entrants, or entrepreneurs—does it first.

In digital technology alone, sustained improvement, operating for over half a century, is generating a constant stream of disruption across the economy, including in industries far from the worlds of computing and consumer electronics. We now have nearly ubiquitous high-speed digital networks over wired and wireless technologies, connecting not only people and businesses but also, increasingly, industrial and household objects, keeping everyone and everything in constant communication.

Those networks have also made it possible to decouple computing, applications, storage, and data from having to be physically close to those using them. A fast-growing cloud computing industry has made low-cost IT services readily available, removing many of the constraints that once required every business to develop, operate, and maintain its own unique system.

As more things get connected in more interesting ways, the economics of networks multiply these improvements, making digital technology even more valuable, at a faster pace all the time. Even if the limits of physics is slowing the rate of Moore's law and its effects, it could take businesses a decade or more just to catch up.

To help you shrink that time span, we will, in pages to come, provide real-world examples of how businesses across industries are applying these technologies to release trapped value.

Figure 1.2 gives a short list of some of the new technologies we work with most closely. A somewhat longer list would include data analytics, mobility and location services, artificial vision, natural language processing, encryption, secured transactions, biometrics, autonomous vehicles, drones, and adaptive algorithms.

Though many of these technologies are digital, others are based on advances in materials science, genetics, astrophysics, and even quantum mechanics. Innovation in the manufacture of ultralight and ultrastrong carbon fiber, for example, is revolutionizing the design of aircraft, high-end cars, and even bicycles. Continued innovation will

Figure 1.2 New Technologies

Ten new technologies

Extended Reality
Interactive experience software that blends, overlays, or replaces true reality with virtual ones. Encompasses Virtual Reality, Augmented Reality, and Mixed Reality.

Cloud Computing
Distributed computing model wherein a third party provides Software, an IT Infrastructure, a Platform, or other resources virtually and at scale.

3D Printing
A process of additive manufacturing wherein 3D objects are printed layer by layer. This can enable Rapid Prototyping and innovations in materials, enabling 4D Printing.

Human-Computer Interactions
Sensing technologies that enable more natural interactions between humans and computers, including Gesture Recognition and Brainwave Mapping.

Quantum Computing
In classical computing, a computer runs on bits that have a value of either 1 or 0. Quantum bits can hold much more complex information, or even negative values.

Edge & Fog Computing
Edge and Fog Computing are methods of optimizing cloud applications by taking some portion of an application, its data, or services away from one or more central nodes.

Artificial Intelligence
Algorithms that imitate human intelligence, reasoning, and decision making, and improve over time. New branches include Bayesian and Swarm AI, as well as AutoML, which automates production of AI applications.

Internet of Things
Ecosystem of sensors and analytics that monitor condition and performance of physical assets. New applications include Digital Twins, Smart Dust sensors, and IoT-specific Cybersecurity.

Blockchain
Distributed ledger with timestamped verified changes. Useful applications include asset tracking, document management, payments, and smart contracts.

Smart Robotics
Robots that combine traditional robotic capabilities with sensors, computer vision, and intelligence, which enable new capabilities, such as Collaborative Robotics, Autonomous Vehicles, or Swarm Robotics.

soon dramatically reduce the material's price, making carbon fiber cost-effective as a replacement input for many more applications in transportation, energy, and other industries that can benefit from the material's better performance.

Some of today's other emerging technology disruptors, moreover, cut across industries, multiplying trapped value but complicating efforts to discover and release it. Applications of artificial intelligence are already erasing and redrawing long-held boundaries between work done by machines and work done by humans, a cycle that will continue well past our own lives.

Similarly, low-cost genomic sequencing and manipulation, also driven by the falling cost of computing, are generating uncountable quantities of new raw scientific data, certain to revolutionize health care, pharmaceuticals, agriculture, and industries serving longer-lived populations for decades.

Building off the robustness of the cloud and broadband networks, to give one final example, an industrial-strength "internet of things" (IoT) will connect close to a hundred billion physical items, making possible the constant reinvention of everything from household appliances to transportation to energy production and distribution.

The IoT will also power autonomous cars and the smart roads needed to manage them. Likewise, the cost of LIDAR system components, the technology used by autonomous vehicles to sense their environments, has fallen an order of magnitude in the past five years. Manufacturers predict a price of $500 per vehicle once mass production begins in earnest.

The value potential for just these three technologies is astonishing. Predictions for the impact of AI, for example, suggest a doubling of the economic growth of developed countries between 2017 and 2035, potentially adding $7.4 trillion to the US economy alone.

Not to be outdone, human genomics, which will help identify individual health risks and create customized pharmaceuticals, is already a multibillion-dollar industry. And the IoT is projected to create $14.2 trillion in new value by 2030, contributing a 1.5 percent increase in real GDP growth.

BIG BANG AND COMPRESSIVE DISRUPTION

That's the kind of growing and unpredictable trapped value we're talking about, and it highlights why it's so hard for businesses to quickly and efficiently harness new technologies as they become cost-effective to deploy.

In Silicon Valley and other technology hubs, of course, the search for large pockets of unexploited trapped value is the driving force for investment and entrepreneurship. That's because new technologies generate dramatic expansions of the trapped value gap, igniting the creative spark that brought to life some of the best-known disruptors of the past few decades, including the revolutionary but now ubiquitous offerings of companies such as Google, Amazon, Uber, Airbnb, Apple, Netflix, Microsoft, Facebook, Alibaba, Tencent, Salesforce, Baidu, and Ant Financial.

Together, these and a few other US and Chinese companies make up the most valuable internet businesses in the annual survey of venture investor Mary Meeker. As one measure of the growth of trapped value release, Meeker's top twenty in 2018 were worth a combined $5.5 trillion, an increase of over $4 trillion in just the years since 2013. Nearly all that wealth, in effect the current and potential trapped value these companies have and are expected to continue releasing, was created in the last twenty years.

We reviewed the strategies of many of the companies on Meeker's list in Larry and Paul's previous book, *Big Bang Disruption*, where the focus was on new products and services entering the market both better and cheaper than competing goods from incumbent companies.

Where incremental improvements in technology historically generate the bell-curve-shaped pattern of consumer adoption first described in 1962 by sociologist Everett Rogers, big bang disruptions experience a much more condensed rise and fall, or what we refer to as the "shark fin." It gets its name due to both its ominous shape and the predator-type threat it poses. When an attack happens, it's quickly over. Think of the sudden adoption of smartphone-based navigation apps, which almost immediately displaced stand-alone GPS devices and printed directions.

In effect, technologies that suddenly expand the trapped value gap drive big bang disruption by creating an opening for new entrants and fast-moving incumbents to give consumers something dramatically better than what they currently have. Not surprisingly, consumers who are well informed by social media and user forums about the relative merits of the disruptive offerings tend to abandon the old for the new all at once. (See figure 1.3.)

Figure 1.3 Big Bang Disruption Phases of Market Adoption of Innovation

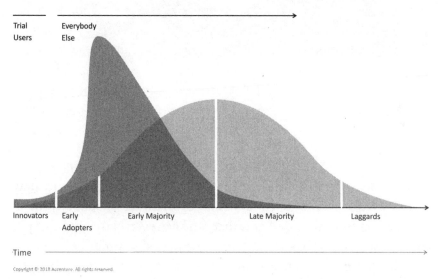

As we describe the success of companies that are pivoting wisely, we'll see many examples of big bang disruption from both incumbents and start-ups.

But there's a second, more pervasive and incidious kind of disruption playing a prominent role in instigating and shaping wise pivots—one that plays out over a longer period of time. It's particularly evident in mature, asset-intensive industries where it may be harder for customers to change from older to newer offerings. We call this second form "compressive disruption," and it is already changing the shape of industries including telecommunications, utilities, energy, materials, health care, finance, automotive, and industrials. (See figure 1.4.)

Why is compressive disruption slower? These industries are each characterized by heavy capital investment or other features, including powerful brands, that give incumbents potent economies of scale. In some cases, substantial regulatory restrictions have the unintended

Figure 1.4 Compressive Disruption

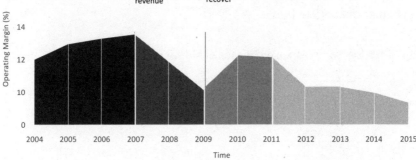

effect of delaying the introduction of disruptive technologies by new entrants. Together, some combination of these factors builds protective barriers around incumbents that can keep even better and cheaper digital disruptors at bay, at least for some period of time.

Still, as trapped value accumulates, disruption occurs, if only just under the surface. Revenue growth may continue in these industries, but profit margins invariably compress as core technologies become obsolete. Once the actual decline in operating margins begins in earnest, there's little you can do to reverse it, no matter how boldly you innovate.

As the release of trapped value accelerates in the final phase of the process, just as with the dramatic introduction of the immediately better and cheaper big bang disruptor, the rules an industry may have operated under for decades are completely rewritten.

Compressive disruption may take longer than the big bangs, but the result is the same: the complete and repeated reconfiguration of traditional industry supply chains, business models, and profit allocation among competitors and other stakeholders, including customers.

The retail story told earlier is one example of compressive disruption. Early e-commerce offerings were not consistently better or cheaper than the in-person experience of shopping, after all. But the technology required to experiment was inexpensive and improving rapidly. At the same time, growing unmet consumer needs that could be served with new technologies continued to widen the trapped value gap further and faster, exerting an almost gravitational pull that drew even more investment and experimentation from those who saw the opportunity.

As in other asset-heavy industries, traditional retailers concluded early on that e-commerce posed no serious threat or opportunity, at least none that could be cost-effectively deployed at scale. Revenue even appeared to grow as the weakest competitors closed down, temporarily boosting market share. Incumbents were left with the false hope that they would be the survivors, serving a consolidated market of legacy customers who neither wanted nor knew how to shop online.

Ultimately, digital-first retailers gained the technology and economies of scale to compete in earnest with the incumbents, triggering the inevitable and irreversible decline that is now clear.

A similar story is taking place in other asset-heavy industries, some more drawn out than others, but always with the same outcome. Whether the result of big bang or compressive disruption, technologies improving at near-exponential rates are generating profound trapped value, enticing venture-financed start-ups and competitors to look for new ways to release and capture at least some of it for themselves.

How do they do it? The first step is knowing where to look.

THE FOUR PLACES TRAPPED VALUE HIDES

Finding and releasing trapped value isn't easy. We analyzed the performance of over a thousand public companies, focusing on two key indicators: current and potential future growth. Current growth, of course, is measured by revenue. To estimate potential future growth, we looked at improvements in the companies' price-earnings ratio, which signals investor confidence in continued revenue expansion.

Only 2 percent of the companies we analyzed consistently improved both current and future growth measures. Why is this percentage so low? We believe there are several reasons, all of them having to do with a failure by business leaders to appreciate the growth of the trapped value gap.

For one thing, executives often overlook opportunities for using new technologies to improve existing and future product and service offerings. Instead, many think of technology solely as a tool for reducing costs. Yet, even in early forms, many of the technologies listed in figure 1.2 can be used to generate improved revenue and profitability.

The cost-cutting mentality also means managers may evaluate technology opportunities solely within their own business. But trapped value is also building up outside your business where, indeed, the opportunities for current and future revenue growth may be even more attractive.

Within an industry, value is often trapped because an outdated infrastructure serves perhaps hundreds of companies, reducing the incentives for any one of them to invest heavily in more efficient technologies. Doing so, after all, would benefit competitors as much if not more than it would the company spending the money. That's the roadblock that has, since the dawn of the internet revolution, long stalled infrastructure change in mature and often regulated industries. Think of energy generation and distribution, or commercial banking.

A third source of trapped value lies with consumers, who may suffer from insufficient technology investments by the companies they buy from through poor customer service, high prices, and stagnant offerings. But in traditional industry supply chains, consumers have few opportunities to express their collective preferences, let alone exert the leverage needed to get producers to respond. So trapped value accumulates as a kind of latent demand.

Even more trapped value accrues across economies or, indeed, on a global scale. Technologies exist that could improve the living conditions of people in the developing world, and generate vast revenues in the process, but few executives train their focus on such broad markets.

Billions of people, for example, lack access to basic human needs, including clean water, as well as reliable energy and communications. And, collectively, the impact of unsustainable environmental practices imposes costs on every living thing, but does so in a way hard for any one company to translate into an opportunity.

There's also a fundamental truth about trapped value that is anathema to traditional ways of doing business. Our research showed that consistent value release requires companies to give away much more value to others, including customers, suppliers, and ecosystem partners, than they keep for themselves, perhaps by as much as a ten to one ratio. So if your approach to innovation investment is limited to opportunities where you can retain all or even most of the value you create, you're ignoring the biggest opportunities.

Releasing value for others may seem off-putting, until you realize how wide the trapped value gap already is. Simple digital payment systems using mobile devices, for example, have enabled new services, including ride sharing, advanced gaming, and basic banking for low-value transactions, which previously required buyer and seller to be in the same place at the same time, cash in hand.

In our retail example, similarly, e-commerce released value trapped in the form of inflated prices, inconvenient or poor service, and an overall customer experience that was growing more unpleasant as compressive disruption necessitated catastrophic cost cutting.

That's why even the most successful e-commerce companies continue to give much of their value back to customers rather than investors. These companies may have astronomical market capitalizations, but that number largely reflects the confidence investors have in the potential for future disruption—and future profits.

A willingness by incumbents even to consider such a strategy is unlikely when executives see profits within their industry as a zero-sum game: a fixed pool to be competed over in small increments (what authors W. Chan Kim and Renée Mauborgne in their book *Blue Ocean Strategy* would call a red ocean versus a blue ocean strategy). They focus instead on increasing margins for a small market when they should be targeting new revenue in a much bigger market—increasing the pie rather than fighting over tiny differences in the size of their slice.

The spread of network technologies—and the economies of scale that make them so powerful—means future opportunities are fundamentally shifting from competition to collaboration. You need to think of yourself as a partner, not a competitor, doing business in a broad, collaborative ecosystem rather than in a narrow industry supply chain.

Even consumers can be part of these ecosystems, whether by sending electricity back to the grid from their solar panels, or allowing data about the operation of their smart devices to flow up the supply chain in the emerging internet of things.

How big is the new pie? Just comparing the current value and future value of the thousand public companies in our study, Wall Street thinks the answer is enormous. For 2016, analysts assigned 42 percent of the total valuation of these companies to future value they expect the companies will actually deliver. That means nearly $14 trillion, up from $8 trillion in 2000.

In your own quest to release trapped value, start by looking to the four interconnected sources: the enterprise, the industry, the consumer, and society as a whole. (See figure 1.5.)

Figure 1.5 Where Trapped Value Resides

Four Levels of Trapped Value

SOCIETY
Value trapped in failure to engage in profitable partnerships to solve societal issues, such as the need to recycle electronic waste.

CONSUMER
Value trapped in underused private assets, such as vacant homes in popular tourist areas.

INDUSTRY
Value trapped by lack of cooperation and investment in shared infrastructure, such as charging stations for electric vehicles.

ENTERPRISE
Value trapped in limited use of digital technologies (such as smart meters) with power to transform business models.

Let's consider each in more detail.

ENTERPRISE—When evaluating new technologies, many managers focus solely on their potential for disruptive innovation. In doing so, they fail to recognize the technologies' potential for improving the mundane parts of their current business, which might yield substantial cost savings and process improvements. Such changes reduce what economists call "transaction costs"—inefficiencies that take the form of bureaucracy, incomplete information, and outdated processes.

Enterprise trapped value also accumulates when an economic opportunity is visible, yet cannot be released by existing business models and capabilities.

You might see others, especially new entrants, using disruptive technologies to dramatically improve the efficiency of business processes or to rapidly introduce innovative new products and services. But your business may be unable to respond quickly, held back by outdated rules and procedures, a corporate culture that doesn't encourage innovation, or IT systems and other technology that haven't kept up with competitors.

Value can also be trapped in the day-to-day management of core activities. Artificial constraints on how you delegate authority, budget for technology initiatives, and manage relationships with internal and external stakeholders may raise unintended barriers. You might see great opportunity to automate high-cost activities by applying AI, for example, but feel restricted from doing so by labor contracts and regulations.

Generating other efficiencies might require closer collaboration with end-users. Given the right digital tools, including interactive websites and easy-to-use apps, your customers may be willing to take on some of your expensive service functions, such as order entry, tracking, and answering questions from other users. The problem is that you may be cut off from your customers by intermediate supply-chain partners—including agents, resellers, retailers, and service professionals who jealously control access—making collaboration or even direct interaction impossible.

Releasing trapped value at the enterprise level, finally, often requires a combination of improved business processes and more efficient technologies. Apparel manufacturers, for example, are deploying new robotic technologies that can rapidly learn new tasks. Nike, in conjunction with its manufacturing partners, can produce a shoe "upper" in thirty seconds, with thirty fewer steps and up to 50 percent less labor. Adidas, similarly, is working with Carbon, a company that offers 3D, or "additive" manufacturing technology, to "print" shoes personalized by the consumer, cutting the traditional design process from months to days.

INDUSTRY—Trapped value accumulates at the industry level when technologies that could improve the entire ecosystem chiefly benefit only a small number of industry players, leading to stalemates and holdout problems, or what economists call "coordination costs."

Here, disruptive technologies create opportunities for improvements, perhaps enabled by new platforms and an extended ecosystem that connects more stakeholders. Consider streaming music service Spotify, which allows independent artists to upload their music directly, bypassing the exclusive and inefficient supply chain optimized for physical media such as records and CDs. Spotify shares 50 percent of revenues and 100 percent of the royalties these artists generate—far more than they would get from a label, assuming they could get access to one.

Because incumbents often lack agility, new entrants may establish new rules for the industry, or create an alternative supply chain that excludes existing competitors.

Tesla, for example, is leveraging its expertise in electric vehicles to disrupt energy storage with its Tesla Powerwall. The Powerwall, an in-home rechargeable battery, will allow consumers to store and access energy generated by solar panels in their homes rather than returning it to the existing electrical grid.

Homeowners can then enjoy lower energy costs and protection from outages, but in the process they will be disrupting the core business of electric utilities. This is likely to occur even more quickly than predicted if, as expected, the early users are also the heaviest consumers of power.

Or consider the complex supply chain of the automotive industry. Traditional carmakers dominate the personal transportation market because of high capital costs that allow them to leverage economies of scale and an extensive distribution network. But a combination of emerging technologies, including electrification, autonomous driving, connectivity, and the sharing economy, has the potential to release enormous trapped value, challenging the incumbent business model in the process.

Cars, after all, are a vastly underutilized asset. Even though American households spend more on transportation than food, their cars remain parked 95 percent of the time. Emerging car-sharing businesses, including on-demand services such as DriveNow, as well as ride-shar-

ing companies such as Uber and Lyft, release the trapped value of surplus availability. Industry estimates predict that car sharing combined
with autonomous technologies will slow the annual growth rate for
vehicle sales, with the new entrants capturing 40 percent of the profits
in a redefined industry.

CONSUMER—Consumer trapped value exists when customers bear excessive costs that could be reduced by available technology. That includes their time and energy as well as their money; things like going
to the store themselves, rather than having goods delivered. It also
includes goods they own that are underutilized, as when homes sit
idle when they could be rented out. Released trapped value at this level
goes by the economic term "consumer surplus."

Opportunities to find and release that value can be staggering. Take
for example, most internet businesses, where consumers enjoy content,
software, and other services without paying anything beyond agreeing
to have their interactions analyzed for more accurately targeted advertising. Our research estimates the release of trapped value in internet
services has been over $1.5 trillion as of 2016, growing over 10 percent
annually since 2007. Much of that value comes in the form of information goods that can be infinitely reproduced at no added cost.

Releasing consumer trapped value in particular means sharing
much, if not most, of it with the consumers themselves.

Consider online marketplaces for lodging, car-sharing, and other
technology-driven innovations that improve the utilization of consumer-owned assets (including intellectual capital such as expertise).

Once you buy your house or car, whoever sold it to you may have
little incentive to help you get the most use out of it, even when new
technology makes it easy to do so. For them, helping you may seem
counterproductive, perhaps because your sharing that asset may mean
reduced sales of new inventory for them.

The trapped value, however, may be much larger than the current
industry's existing revenue, with plenty to be allocated between the
consumer and the industry. When incumbents ignore that opportunity, new entrants rush in. Airbnb is estimated to have released $20
billion in user revenue between 2010 and 2016; earnings that would
otherwise have been left on the table. The company itself, meanwhile,

earned $2.5 billion in revenue and $100 million in profit during the same period.

Alibaba and eBay, likewise, earned a combined $140 billion between 2004 and 2014 by facilitating transactions between consumers eager to buy and sell new and used goods for which there was previously no low-cost, easy-to-use global market. The liquidity the online platforms created released nearly $1.4 trillion in value, most of it literally trapped in garages, attics, and storage lockers. (See figure 1.6.)

Beyond underutilized assets, consumer trapped value can be released by addressing unmet needs that translate to productivity and quality-of-life gains—often difficult to measure but unmistakable when you experience them yourself.

Examples include technologies that shorten wait times or reduce errors, including Amazon same-day delivery, apps that allow fast-food customers to order by phone and skip the line, or rich media websites that make it easier and less unpleasant for consumers to self-service rather than navigate through a company's phone tree.

Other value may be lurking in products and services consumers may simply not know they want until they are made available, at which point it becomes unthinkable to live without them. Smartphones included cameras as an afterthought. But having a single device that integrates photography and video with connectivity through social networks including Facebook, Instagram, and Snapchat has unleashed profound value for users even as it decimated the stand-alone camera market.

SOCIETY—Finally, societal trapped value accumulates when commercial activities fail to create benefits that would aid everyone, what economists call "positive externalities." These might include reduced pollution and carbon emissions, improved education, safe food and drinking water, and health and wellness.

Simply improving communications channels among residents of a community, for example, can improve the livability of a neighborhood, releasing trapped value in the form of increased property values. Even relatively simple bulletin board and email alert systems, such as Nextdoor, and UrbanSitter, which can dispatch a qualified caregiver within minutes, strengthens ties between neighbors.

Figure 1.6 Trapped Value Unlocked by Innovation

Using technology to release trapped value...
eBay and Alibaba.com unlocking $1.4tn

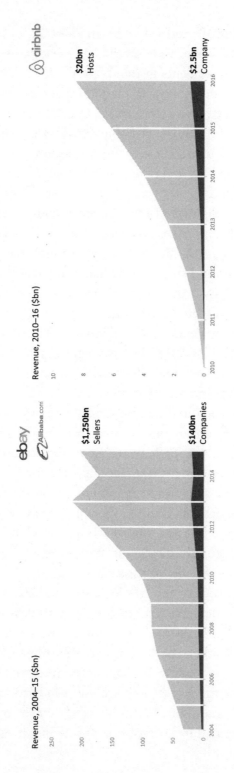

Revenue, 2004–15 ($bn)

$1,250bn
Sellers

$140bn
Companies

...to disrupt mature industries
Airbnb unlocking $22.5bn

Revenue, 2010–16 ($bn)

$20bn
Hosts

$2.5bn
Company

Source: eBay Press Releases, Market Watch; AirDNA Research, Airbnb Press Releases, CBRE Group Research.

Piggybacking off platforms created for other uses can also uncover societal trapped value. Ride-sharing services, created with younger, on-the-go urban residents in mind, are finding additional growth by helping seniors and those with disabilities get around without having to drive, allowing more people to age in place in their own homes.

This additional release of value provides enormous though unquantifiable and intangible benefits for seniors, including improved quality of life and the ability to stay active in the community, and unleashing profound trapped value lost to nursing homes.

Our research discovered a few superstar companies that have found ways to identify and release trapped value across all four levels, often using the same combination of disruptive innovations. (See figure 1.7.)

Chinese gaming giant Tencent identified trapped value in inefficient and untrustworthy financial networks, leveraging its existing relationship with Chinese consumers to add electronic payment capabilities that now generate $1.3 billion in revenue for the company. In just a few years, China's mobile payment market has grown to over $5.4 trillion in transactions, fifty times the size of the equivalent US market. Of that amount, Tencent processes nearly 40 percent, while Alibaba, which got into the game sooner, handles over half of the traffic. China's traditional banks, meanwhile, barely register.

Consumers also benefit from these applications, generating six hundred million payment transactions daily, many in small amounts for essential daily activities such as buying food and transportation.

Another Tencent application, the wildly popular WeChat communications service, releases industry trapped value by giving foreign firms a way to communicate and transact with Chinese consumers who might otherwise be inaccessible to them.

For Chinese society as a whole, Tencent's banking application has leveraged low-cost technology, including smart devices and broadband networks, to offer basic services to millions of lower-income consumers who would otherwise have no access to financial services. With two billion people worldwide unserved by traditional banks, the company is showing the way to both inclusion and profitability.

California-based Illumina has likewise outgrown its peers in both the value generated by current operations and investor expectations.

Figure 1.7 Releasing Trapped Value

	ENTERPRISE	INDUSTRY 	CONSUMER	SOCIETY
Tencent 腾讯	Tencent's fastest-growing businesses are payments, cloud services, and digital-content subscriptions (video subscriptions were up 85% in 2018)	WeChat provides an e-commerce platform for foreign firms—95% of global luxury brands sell over the platform	WeChat Pay is a function within WeChat, Tencent's messaging app that is used by more than 1 billion people	Meets demand of global unbanked; M-payment in China is 50x the US market
illumina	Pioneers in advanced genome sequencing, accountable for over 70% of the market	Setting up an "App-store" for DNA informatics, supplying Healthcare providers with easy access to tools	Central role in reducing sequencing costs from $100m to $1,000 (with target of $100), enables consumer genomics	Deploying technology to cattle breeding to meet global food demand
	Since 2000, Starbucks has grown its store locations by 12% compound average growth rate (CAGR)	Partnered with Spotify to provide premium streaming for its baristas, as part of its strategy to build a "next-generation music ecosystem"	Launched an online idea submission portal, My Starbucks Idea, which has gathered more than 100,000 consumer suggestions	Donated more than 1m meals to foodbanks, from its leftover and unsold products

Source: Fortune, 2017; Starbucks website, 2018; MarketWatch, 2018; Business Insider, 2018.

Founded in 1998, Illumina's main business is gene sequencing. Early estimates suggested the cost of decoding the human genome might be $3 billion, but the actual price fell to just $300,000 with the 2006 release of Illumina's first device. Then, in 2014, Illumina introduced the HiSeq X, which does the job for just $1,000.

Even with a 90 percent share of the market, Illumina continues to release trapped value, with its latest innovations expected to push the price below $100.

Meanwhile, the company, with revenues of $2.4 billion in 2016, is growing the size of the overall pie, staking a claim to new markets it is helping to create. In 2015, for example, Illumina spun out its subsidiary Helix, which makes DNA-based insights and their benefits more accessible, tapping latent consumer demand for personalized services and products.

For $80, Helix can sequence key components of a customer's DNA using a sample of saliva, creating an individual profile. Customers can use their profile in a variety of ways, including to learn more about their genealogy or acquire a tailored health and fitness plan from third-party providers in Helix's app store. App providers release more trapped value, trading access to Helix's customers and their data for a share of their revenue going back to Illumina.

Or consider coffee juggernaut Starbucks, which has found ways to use digital technologies to grow in-store revenues at an annual rate of 12 percent since 2000. It has also invested in what it calls a "next-generation music ecosystem," partnering with Spotify to integrate music into the company's own app.

Starbucks also actively collaborates with its twenty million mobile consumers, supporting an online suggestion box that has attracted more than a hundred thousand submissions for improving the company's offerings. Finally, the company reduces food waste and improves the lives of those most in need. Since 2016, it has donated more than ten million meals to food banks from its unsold but still-edible food products.

Each of these innovations separately improves Starbucks' bottom line. But taken together, they amount to a full-scale assault on trapped value, much of it reflected in the company's balance sheet as improved brand value, goodwill, and other intangibles.

Investors have responded to Starbucks' release of trapped value with a dramatic increase in the company's market capitalization, which nearly tripled between 2011 and 2017. Of Starbucks' $79 billion valuation in 2018, well under half is explained by current earnings. The rest reflects investor confidence that the company can continue to grow revenues and profits by releasing even more value going forward.

THE CASE FOR A PIVOT

As these examples suggest, companies in very different industries are successfully deploying innovations that target a growing supply of trapped value. And the opportunities to find trapped value are increasing, even as the technologies to release it are becoming more accessible and cost-effective. In the chapters that follow, we'll show you how you can apply the strategies of these trapped value leaders to your own business, using the wise pivot approach.

There's no time to waste. As the trapped value gap expands, it is driving the global reinvention of every economic sector and every industry. No business is immune. As the old joke about the two campers who hear a bear rumbling around outside their tent puts it, you can't outrun the bear. But if you get your shoes on fast enough, you can still outrun the other camper.

Despite what might have been decades of relative industry maturity, you can't escape the gravitational pull of disruptive technologies. In industries already remade by the digital revolution one or more times, as well as those whose high entry barriers kept them largely immune until now, big bang and compressive disruption have found your campsite.

You've no doubt seen the signs of change in your own business. Static supply chains are breaking apart, reforming as dynamic ecosystems that engage every stakeholder, including customers. Legacy products and services, some of which may have enjoyed a century of dominance, are being replaced by innovations driven by digital technologies. Barriers to entry, whether created by incumbency, high infrastructure costs, or regulatory controls, are crumbling and collapsing. Competitors are finding new partners and new investment models, jump-starting their pivot to the new.

In that new business reality, textbook approaches to strategic planning are simply too slow, incremental, or serial in nature to work. One-time "transformations" buy you at best only a few years before the next wave of disruptors engulfs the market. Focusing on a single disruptive product, hoping for one big hit, leaves you without the infrastructure or expertise to launch a series of innovations to satisfy ever-shorter waves of customer demand. Doubling down on one or two market segments risks losing everything, as better and cheaper alternatives draw the most profitable customers away, gradually or suddenly.

As the trapped value gap expands, the opportunity is there for you to close it, leveraging your own innovations, expertise, intellectual property, corporate culture, and human capital to gain rather than erode competitive advantage.

Critical to understanding what we call the wise pivot, however, is the realization that you don't have to attack the gap all at once. There's no need to abandon your core assets, resources, and products prematurely. Instead, as we'll see, you need to leverage them to generate more revenue, applying new technology to restart stalled, older products and accelerate the development of newer ones. Then you'll invest that revenue in building the next generation of your organization, scaling rapidly with new offerings based on even newer technologies.

Disruption, in other words, is no longer a once-in-a-career problem to be dealt with. It's a constant cycle. In every industry we studied, an expanding trapped value gap between what is possible and what is available is appearing and reappearing with greater frequency.

That translates to new opportunities and new imperatives to remake your business and your industry again and again. To pivot wisely and repeatedly, the skills we'll describe for finding and releasing trapped value will become an integral part of how you do business, a core tenet of your organization's mission.

Before we get to the how-tos, however, we need to pause to explore some of the do-nots.

chapter 2

THE SEVEN WRONG TURNS

Obstacles to Releasing Trapped Value

TRAPPED VALUE RELEASERS are companies that consistently find innovative ways to target and unleash trapped value accumulating at the enterprise, industry, consumer, and societal levels. In subsequent chapters we'll describe the new strategies they use to speed up the reinvention of industries, create dynamic ecosystems, and attack global environmental and social problems. First, however, we need to pause for a reality check.

Despite their having recognized the opportunities for value release, most of the businesses we studied simply weren't ready to embark on a wise pivot journey. Leaders were committed to current technologies, products, and markets. In public companies, managers had been trained to put the needs of Wall Street analysts over those of customers. Organizations were rigid, with brittle IT systems and employees focused on refining and reinforcing skills to satisfy outdated and limited career paths.

Many of these limitations, as we learned in Accenture's own reinvention, stemmed from business practices that worked perfectly well when market change was slow and the behavior of competitors was more or less predictable. The problem is that when technology-driven disruption comes calling, these behaviors quickly mutate from virtues to vices.

Before engaging your own wise pivot, then, it's important to understand the changes in direction some companies make that unintentionally stop them from recognizing and releasing trapped value, or what we call the "seven wrong turns."

By way of a cautionary tale, consider the dramatic rise and tragic fall of music and media retailing giant Tower Records. Tower emerged from a single location operating out of the back of a drugstore in 1960 to dominate the global music retailing business by the late 1980s. It was the disruptor of its age.

Yet in 2006, the company dropped suddenly from a peak of two hundred stores in fifteen countries and over $1 billion in annual sales to liquidation, after having seen its revenues grow every year since its founding.

The conventional wisdom about the collapse of Tower pins the blame on the unexpected explosion of digital music distribution, first illegally by Napster and other online exchanges, and later legally by Apple's iTunes and streaming services such as Pandora and Spotify.

But the emergence of digital music distribution was far from the company's only challenge. It simply exposed how poorly designed and managed Tower had been all along.

The company expanded into new countries on a whim, borrowed recklessly, and channeled all decision making to famed CEO Russell Solomon, who notoriously ignored the advice of his longtime CFO and creditors. Solomon had no strategic plan, taking pride in a seat-of-the-pants operating philosophy.

In short, Tower had no mechanism for responding to significant market change, let alone to an existential threat to its business model from advancing digital technologies. It was, to use a term from the music industry, a "one-hit wonder."

The company was no company at all, really. Rather, it was a single, well-timed idea: to create an enormous, lavish retail space for music fans to hang out in, staffed by young, energetic salespeople who were even bigger audiophiles than the customers. Tower simply surfed atop a last great wave of baby-boomer-inspired growth in recorded media that began in the 1960s, but which was already showing signs of fatigue well before the internet changed the industry forever.

Yet, the very behaviors that sealed Tower's fate were celebrated at the time. Solomon was a visionary, a maverick who understood the music market and built a company devoted to its employees and customers. Tower's growth stimulated consolidation of inefficient and unfriendly local record stores, justifying its rapid expansion. New technologies, including CDs and DVDs, were growing the market for high-quality physical media and stimulating rapid replacement cycles, encouraging a strategy of accelerated expansion.

Meanwhile, the true solution for growing trapped value, digital distribution, was becoming better, cheaper, and faster by the day, just waiting for someone without Tower's obsession with physical media and a superior in-store experience to show up.

Beyond audiophiles, it turned out, average music consumers wanted songs more than albums, and resented the constant upgrades of media and artificially high prices charged for the latest products. They also wanted to hear from a much wider range of styles and independent artists, who couldn't be accommodated in the inefficient label-centric supply chain for which Tower served as retailer.

A gap was building between the anytime, anyplace music experience users wanted and the well-laid plans of record companies determined to dictate both tastes and technologies. It took only access to the internet and a little bit of software for college student Shawn Fanning, creator of Napster, to expose the growing resentment of music consumers and under- or unpaid musicians. When the legal dust had settled, it was technology companies, not record labels or retailers, that took up the challenge to redress the imbalance.

Tower was doing everything right, in other words, until suddenly it was doing everything wrong. When the time came to pivot to digital technology, a new source of trapped value with tremendous potential, management decisions that seemed to fit every business school dogma instead pushed Tower into a corner with its equally stunned record producer partners, unable to move in any direction but down.

A GROWING TRAPPED VALUE CRISIS

Tower's collapse was so dramatic it became the subject of a documentary movie. Still, the company is hardly alone as a business that abruptly ended in the face of underestimated technological change and the growth of trapped value in its industry. Even disruptors can be victims, as consumers anticipate the next generation of innovation and don't get it fast enough, opening the door to even-newer entrants, or other companies listening more carefully.

When accumulated trapped value reaches a crisis point, it may take little more than a start-up experiment with new technology—a Napster, an Uber, an Airbnb—to expose it and make its eventual redistribution inevitable.

Incumbents who build management and organizational barriers that filter out actual customer needs when those needs don't fit the current business plan are certain to stumble when the Band-Aid is suddenly ripped off. If they aren't ready with their next innovation and the flexibility to pivot to it, they risk getting caught not only with nothing to replace shrinking revenue, but also with all their resources committed to the now-faded product. Total and rapid collapse is often the result.

The reasons for these dramatic failures have been a focus of our research for some time. We reviewed some of the causes, for example, in our recent *Harvard Business Review* article on reinvention and the difficulties companies have in finding their "second act."

What we found is that for venerable incumbents and once-shining start-ups alike, the problem isn't simply that new technologies make them obsolete. The music business might have become more chaotic, but there was little doubt that consumers were still willing to buy recorded media, even as they began to shift their preferences to digital products like Apple's iTunes and the paid subscription services that followed.

The tools the incumbents needed to reinvent themselves not just once but continually were readily available.

So why couldn't CEO Solomon find ways to refine and revitalize his core business, at least enough to generate the capital to invest in nascent digital music technologies? What stopped Tower, with its powerful global brand earned with a passion for music it shared with its devoted customers, from leading in the next incarnation of the entertainment industry? How did the energy and expertise of its youthful staff simply go to waste? And why did it fail so quickly when confronted by its first real challenge?

All too often, the explanation for business flameouts is the growing gap between the value new technologies make possible and the shrinking percentage of it the company's existing structure can capture—an expanding chasm of trapped value. Executives see a bright future where their business continues to lead, but just can't get to it. Often, they can't even take the first steps.

Why not? In many cases, the answer has little to do with the disruptor and everything to do with the basics. The company has failed over time to embrace business fundamentals, so dazzled by its own success in the market that it never gets around to institutionalizing its values into a business culture that balances innovation and sustainability. It may have no financial controls, too much debt, or inadequate systems for hiring and retaining the best human capital.

As with the slow then sudden collapse of Tower and other retailers in the face of growing consumer adoption of e-commerce, the disruptor simply tapped on the door, exposing a business that had become little more than a Potemkin village that promptly falls to pieces when challenged.

Our research reveals an even deeper, indeed ironic, cause for the hollowing out of disrupted businesses. In many cases, the lack of resiliency results tragically from senior management doing everything "right." Or at least right from the standpoint of popular management theories.

Whether it's pursuing "shareholder value," operating under a "lean" structure, embracing "design thinking" or "agile" development, or spinning off next-generation R&D in hopes of overcoming an "innovator's dilemma," the enterprises least able to release trapped value are invariably those most rigidly committed to business school approaches to strategy and execution. Even if the academic methods once worked, they can't hope to adapt to a world where disruptive technologies come calling faster and more urgently every day.

Different errors yield different pathways for value to become trapped. Some businesses become so focused on serving yesterday's customers, for example, that they fail to capture a new and often larger market segment emerging quickly from other demographics or other geographies. Or, having gone public, founding entrepreneurs find their culture usurped by a manic focus on quarterly earnings, foregoing the kind of innovative thinking that made them successful in the first place.

In mature industries, including financial services, utilities, and transportation, the root cause of trapped value is often an unhealthy relationship with regulators. After a long period of intensive oversight that might include rate setting and new service approval, the entire supply chain becomes subservient to the regulator—in effect, their only real customer. When disruptors break down barriers that long kept out new entrants, management is lost. They've forgotten, if they ever knew, how to compete.

What is even more common in our experience is a simple failure to execute. Even new companies are becoming quickly saddled with the kind of bureaucracy that plagues many incumbents, diluting a culture of rapid execution that first made them successful.

Value becomes trapped, in other words, because today's market leaders are hardwired to pursue incremental gains within today's industry structure and the core technologies that underlie it. Even with a clear path forward, management can't change the organization's trajectory. They're stuck in their ways, committed to their own gradual and then sudden demise. They've become brittle. They're unable to pivot, wisely or otherwise.

This sclerosis is often the direct result of professional management that emerges or is brought in to run successful, fast-growing businesses. Operators can quickly lose touch with customers and product and service offerings. A growing distance between management and the front line can make leaders hesitant to really change the business— to shake things up—for fear of not understanding the full implications, and potential unintended consequences, that might result.

They are not like founders, as we will see, who inherently have a hands-on, detail-oriented approach to execution. Professional managers can easily acquire a laissez-faire style that can look like complacency, but actually represents a loss of speed and agility.

The resulting accumulation of trapped value will only grow more acute with the accelerating pace of technological disruption and the increased speed with which new innovations penetrate markets, the phenomena we referred to earlier as big bang and compressive disruption.

These volatile industry changers are in turn the result of two big-picture economic trends: the near-instant consumer adoption of new products in a growing number of markets and the rapid obsolescence of digital goods. Let's look briefly at each.

NEAR-PERFECT MARKET INFORMATION—As anyone with a smartphone knows, the time between introducing a new product and its adoption by most of its eventual customers has grown dramatically shorter. This instant saturation began in consumer goods and software products, but has now spread to digitally enabled durable and even industrial goods. Buyers either show up all at once or never.

In part, that's because digital technologies have lowered the cost for buyers to learn about and evaluate new offerings, what economists refer to as "information costs." The spread of information through social media and other digital channels has dramatically lowered these costs, allowing consumers to quickly and effectively evaluate potential purchases.

We call this phenomenon "near-perfect market information." Buyers are now entirely informed about your product, including what other users like and dislike about it, at launch (and in some cases even before). Everyone who wants the product will adopt it immediately. The rest of the hoped-for market never arrives, waiting instead for the product to become better, cheaper, or both, often from a new entrant.

In 2016, for example, Tesla presold nearly 400,000 Model 3s in the first two weeks of its highly anticipated unveiling, most in the first three days. That didn't mean, as it might have once, that there were armies of additional buyers waiting in the wings. Most had simply showed up at product announcement.

The pace of new orders slowed dramatically by week three; by mid-2018 the company reported only 450,000 net reservations at the end of the first quarter. Filling orders will take time (shipments didn't begin until 2017), but that is simply backlog, not new demand. Indeed, some analysts are estimating as many as 25 percent of customers demanding return of their deposits.

New market realities can catch even digital-first companies off guard. Consider the dramatic rise and fall of Pokémon Go in 2016. In July, game developer Niantic had the hit of a lifetime with its launch of the first augmented reality game, where players could "find" and "capture" digital creatures that appeared randomly on the screens of their smart devices, superimposed on real-world camera views.

For a brief period, it seemed, everyone in the world was playing the game. In its first week, 7.5 million players downloaded Pokémon Go, peaking in just one week at 28.5 million playing for an average of 1.25 hours a day. But the excitement only lasted a few months. Ten weeks in, the game had largely run its course. In one week alone, Pokémon Go lost 15 million players.

By the end of the summer, the beast hunters were largely gone, along with about $6.7 billion in value for Nintendo, which co-owns the characters licensed to Niantic. Imagining that the $35 million of in-game-revenue players had spent in the first month would continue and even grow, investors added $23 billion to Nintendo's market capitalization in early July, which fell back to earth by August. Niantic has yet to find a replacement game with anything close to the adoption of Pokémon Go.

DIGITAL OBSOLESCENCE—The second economic force, as the Pokémon Go example highlights, is the rapid obsolescence of digital goods, which are a core component of a growing range of products and services across industries. As noted, continued improvements in the price, performance, size, and power utilization of digital components, often fed by increasing returns to scale, lead to ever-shorter cycling of new versions and new innovations.

As more products and services embed digital technology, the speed with which consumers and businesses replace pretty much everything is now determined by the chaotic pace of technological change rather than the orderly evolution of industry standards.

Put these two trends together, and you have the recipe for accelerating accumulations of trapped value and the kinds of existential crises that increasingly occur in the gap.

Tower Records may be an extreme example, but even the most respected and successful companies in the world rarely survive their first crisis, whenever it arrives. The average life span for companies on the Standard and Poor's 500 has fallen from sixty-seven years in the 1920s to only fifteen years today. As many as three-quarters of companies on the list in 2020, according to Yale professor Richard Foster, will be companies unheard of in 2010.

Big bang and compressive disruption are spreading rapidly to industries largely untouched by the first wave of internet technologies. The internet of things and 3D printing stand poised to disrupt manufacturing, while genomics, agronomy, drones, and low-cost sensors are converging to reinvent agriculture. Car companies and insurers are already grappling with a near future that will include electric and autonomous vehicles. And professional services companies, including Accenture, are wrestling with commercial applications of applied artificial intelligence and its potential impact on knowledge workers.

THE SEVEN WRONG TURNS

We have identified seven common management mistakes that explain why so much trapped value continues to go unreleased by incumbent businesses. Many of these errors are the result of generations of executives following management best practices. Each is aimed at solving a particular problem, but either fails to take into account its impact on the long-term health of the organization, or simply doesn't scale fast enough as the pace of disruption increases.

MAKING THE COMPANY TOO LEAN—The American entrepreneur and author Eric Ries's advice for start-ups, codified in his book *The Lean Startup,* is to start selling as quickly as possible a minimally viable product and then iterate rapidly based on intense customer interaction and feedback, using low-cost channels including social media.

While the lean approach has found great favor in both new and old enterprises, companies fail when they devote all their resources to a single product. As market saturation occurs faster all the time, the capacity to generate new products has become more important than the specialized expertise needed to create just one, no matter how enthusiastically customers embrace it.

Focusing every resource on one product, even after it's clear customers have tired of it, leads to trapped value within the enterprise, where talented developers and smart entrepreneurs miss out on the chance to innovate with the next wave of new technologies.

If the market has simply moved on and is waiting for the next innovation, investing core resources in the repeated iterations and course corrections the lean methodology demands solves the wrong problem. Before demand saturation occurs, management must organize a new team to begin the cycle from scratch. If not, the company becomes caught in a death spiral of striving to continually better serve the incremental needs of a dwindling number of once-enthusiastic customers. The business survives, if at all, as an acquisition by a more diversified company, often at a fire-sale price.

Consider lean methodology acolyte Groupon, which continues to pivot around its core innovation of "social shopping," in which consumers leverage scale to negotiate discounts from merchants. Despite strong indications that enthusiasm for social shopping is fleeting, Groupon has remained singularly focused on proving the concept, methodically tweaking its interface, acquiring its failing competitor LivingSocial, and perhaps unwisely expanding group buying into travel.

Meanwhile, a failure to attend to basics has led to ballooning operating expenses and run-ins with the SEC over embarrassing accounting errors both before and after going public. Since its IPO in 2011, Groupon had lost over 70 percent of its value by mid-2018, with sales falling every year since 2014.

It isn't just strict adherents of the lean philosophy that risk missing the market forest amid obsession with existing customer trees. TiVo, which first popularized the digital video recorder, was hailed as a disruptive innovator when it debuted in 1999. It quickly became synonymous with video on demand: to record a program for later viewing was to "TiVo" it. But the company has since been surpassed by internet-based streaming applications that broke the pay-TV model more fundamentally, including Netflix, Hulu, and Amazon.

TiVo continued to make incremental improvements to its boxes and to license its technologies, but the company is near the end of life for many of its key patents. Despite a 2016 merger with entertainment software company Rovi, TiVo has lost two-thirds of its value over the last five years. It has outsourced hardware and retail sales, and recently dismissed the possibility of more acquisitions.

The instant saturation problem is even more acute in the cut-throat jungle of smartphone apps, where a failure to prepare for potential new value created by continued improvements in technology often spells the end of the enterprise. Developers frequently become anchored to product development focused on the wrong problem.

Consider Zynga, the wildly successful game developer of hits like FarmVille, which only barely survived the rapid rise and fall of its sketching and guessing game Draw Something. The game jumped to sixteen million players in a matter of weeks in 2012, only to fade quickly over the next few months as the company belatedly scrambled for a replacement. Though revenues have improved recently, the next big hit has proven elusive.

While many of these examples come from start-up companies, the urge to go lean also affects older and more asset-intensive enterprises. In the communications, utilities, and financial services industries, the trend has been to outsource R&D and engineering. In doing so, however, companies often shed their innovation muscle as well, exacerbating the risk of disruption.

CREATING A CAPITAL STRUCTURE BUILT TO FAIL—One area where lean does pay off is in corporate finance: having as few investors as possible for as long as possible, and avoiding crippling debt. A deeply leveraged capital structure only works during times of extraordinary growth. If markets contract, even modestly, traditional creditors quickly become anxious, encouraging or even forcing retrenchment at the precise moment renewed investment in innovation is critical to survival and future expansion.

With short-term creditors knocking loudly at the door, value becomes trapped at the customer level. Users see the potential value that could be released in the next wave of innovation and slow their buying in anticipation. A downturn may not signal a need to economize, in other words, so much as it indicates the need to accelerate development of next-generation innovations. Without the funds or the freedom to ride the next wave, the company risks being left behind in the eddy, exacerbating rather than solving a credit crunch.

Tower Records, for example, had long relied heavily on debt financing to fuel expansion, at one point topping $300 million. The heavy burden of serving that debt put extraordinary pressure on the company's finances; pressure that couldn't be relieved as record sales plunged in the early 2000s.

After losing $10 million in 2000, Tower lost nearly $100 million the next year. Creditors, predictably, pulled back hard on the reins, cutting off any hope of a reinvention by investing in nascent online services. The company filed for bankruptcy in 2004, leaving creditors with 85 percent of the company and $80 million in debt forgiven.

Or consider big-box children's retail giant Toys "R" Us, which shut its doors for good in 2018 after filing in 2017 for bankruptcy protection. Though the headlines inevitably focused on the company's inability to compete with better and cheaper online alternatives, including Amazon, the seeds of its sudden collapse were sown much earlier, and had everything to do with unsustainable debt.

As part of a 2005 buyout by private equity investors for nearly $7 billion, the company loaded up on cheap debt, which it continued to refinance until the financial crisis of 2007–2008 began. By the time the company filed for bankruptcy, it was paying $400 million a year to service a $5 billion debt, much more than it was spending on its stores and computer systems.

Beyond capital, brittle enterprises often take on other long-term encumbrances before they need to, limiting future flexibility. For established companies, future liabilities including multiyear leases, debt-financed equipment purchases, and lengthy outsourcing contracts may severely constrain management's ability to shift course.

While start-ups generally don't have many of these problems, they often incur excessive operating expenses, including catered lunches, generous leave policies, free daycare, and office space leased in high-end properties. Proportionately, these costs are just as dangerous, especially when markets change suddenly.

High-flying commercial drone software start-up Airware, for example, burned through over $100 million in venture financing between its launch in 2011 and its sudden shutdown seven years later.

Where did the money go? The company changed strategies recklessly, at one point trying to build its own drones before shifting to playing the role of industry consultants. They acquired other start-ups and even launched their own drone-specific investment fund.

As the company's founders acknowledged, Airware's software was consistently too sophisticated to work with available drone hardware. Faced with the choice of preserving cash while waiting for the industry to catch up, the company instead built a series of expensive workarounds, refusing to compromise its ambition to be state of the art.

As one ex-employee told the TechCrunch website: "They had a knack for hiring extremely talented and expensive people from places like Google, Autodesk, there was even SpaceX and NASA alumni there. They spared no expense ever."

LOSING YOUR HEAD—Whether in tech start-ups or in new product development hatched inside corporate incubators, best practices often force innovators out of leadership roles too quickly. Outside venture investors and internal venture boards give visionary entrepreneurs considerable freedom to run their organizations, sometimes haphazardly, until a successful product is launched.

But once there are real customers, investors and corporate overseers quickly push for experienced management, or "adult supervision," to take over day-to-day operations. Founders, like Yahoo's Jerry Yang and Twitter's Evan Williams, are often sidelined into engineering roles they find constraining. Without the means or encouragement to continue innovating, they soon quit, often to launch their next start-up, taking their most trusted colleagues with them.

The leadership problem then becomes acute for the company or department left behind, a problem that arrives earlier all the time as the trapped value gap widens ever faster. Experienced managers end up focused on improving the original product, often the target of sudden competition from new entrants with ready access to newer value-releasing technologies and no commitment to the original disruptor's business model, which may have outlived its usefulness.

Companies without their visionary leaders may feel they have little choice but to double down on their existing tactics. In doing so, they increase their chances of being stranded when the market moves on. Absent its founders, for example, Yahoo failed in efforts to find new ways to capitalize on its search engine or diversify elsewhere.

Consider instead what Google did. After experienced CEO Eric Schmidt had stabilized the core search and advertising product, the company's board recognized the risk of becoming reliant on unsustainably explosive growth in one product. So they brought Google's original founders back into leadership positions, igniting an even bolder approach to innovation than they'd had before.

Apple, likewise, famously returned Steve Jobs to the helm for a second and even more glorious incarnation of the company after his seasoned replacement failed to launch the products consumers wanted.

Yahoo, on the other hand, struggled with a succession of inwardly focused strategies aimed at transforming the business without really listening to what users wanted. When these efforts failed, investors forced a sale of the company to Verizon in 2017 for $4.5 billion, a steep decline from Yahoo's peak market value of $125 billion in 2000.

Yahoo had for many years dominated internet search, but never regained momentum after Google captured first place in 2004 and never let go. At the time of Yahoo's acquisition by Verizon, Google was worth over $640 billion.

MANAGING TO WALL STREET—Public investors, and the research analysts who advise them, can be even more conservative than the creditors that hold corporate debt. Beloved start-ups that go public too soon find themselves stymied by investors who say they want more disruptive innovation but who pummel the company's shares and management when profits don't show up fast enough.

Mature companies, likewise, may be constrained by legacy Wall Street analysts whose focus on day-to-day performance often misses the deeper disruptive trends and technologies unraveling the industry. Efforts to capture growing trapped value are postponed as investors furiously rewrite the script for the company's last strategy, initiating a sometimes fatal loop.

Management teams at companies including Snapchat and Blue Apron are already struggling to balance a dynamic strategy with public demands after recent and possibly premature IPOs in 2017. Both companies have since experienced the departure of key executives and a substantial drop in stock price.

And while many factors contributed to the difficulties of business-networking pioneer LinkedIn, which went public in 2011, the company's repeated failure to generate the kind of revenue Wall Street expected led to a collapse of its stock price five years later. That made

LinkedIn an attractive takeover target for Microsoft, which believed it could, and largely has, restored LinkedIn's lost luster.

Adjusting strategy to appease shareholders can quickly threaten the very mission of a young business, to everyone's disappointment. When handmade-goods pioneer Etsy went public in 2015, then-CEO Chad Dickerson limited retail investors to a $2,500 stake, hoping to ensure the company's social and political missions would continue to take priority.

But after two years of ballooning costs and confusion among Etsy's artisanal sellers over a decision to allow manufactured goods on the site, activist investors forced Dickerson out, along with 8 percent of Etsy's staff.

Etsy has since given up its status as a socially conscious "B Corp," and a promised reincorporation as a public-benefit corporation is unlikely. Though professional management has improved both revenues and the company's stock price, increases in Etsy's commission have alienated some producers, and more experimental initiatives were killed off. Instead of helping Etsy burnish its brand and make it possible to rapidly scale the business, going public early may have hurt the company more.

Compare Etsy to Amazon, whose CEO Jeff Bezos takes pride in spending only six hours a year on investor relations. The company works hard to educate analysts who would rather see short-term profits than new businesses that include drone-based delivery, Amazon Echo, Alexa, and other major investments in the internet of things.

Though Bezos and his management team consistently reinvest the company's revenue, they do so in the service of creating even more value going forward. Imagine the trapped value left behind if instead Bezos had simply optimized and iterated around his successful online bookstore, as traditional investors might have preferred.

RELYING ON LUCK—In an era where new products and services are quickly built out of combinations of interchangeable hardware and software components, a growing number of companies have achieved private and sometimes public valuations in the billions of dollars in record time. These "unicorn" prices seem based not on investing fundamentals, but simply on the fervor of early user enthusiasm and the promise of revenues to follow; the result of near-perfect market information generating winner-take-all success.

Whether by a start-up or an incumbent, launching a product that proves to be a big bang disruptor can leave leaders feeling invincible. Too often an ex post facto history is written that makes the enterprise's successful but largely accidental popularity seem like the result of prescient management decision making—a dangerous delusion.

Worse, a cult can build around the CEO of the company. Mistaking popularity for genius, the CEO stops listening to customers or learning from his or her mistakes, becoming sidetracked with keynote speeches or weighing in publicly on the events of the day. Managers with little autonomy simply wait for the latest pronouncement rather than concentrate on analytics. Success breeds failure.

Twitter, which ended its first day of public trading at a value of $14 billion, has since struggled to find revenue and maintain the kind of growth Wall Street expects given its valuation. New features, including promoted tweets, polls, and long-form posts annoyed many longtime users, who used the company's own service to complain. Management, meanwhile, became something of a revolving door, with key executives and engineers leaving.

User growth has also slowed, though recent cost cutting in compensation, R&D, sales, and marketing, along with revenue growth from new features, has allowed the company to turn the corner into profitability.

Managers who mistake a high valuation for genius may also cripple an elegant product design with all the bells and whistles they wisely left out of their first offering, alienating the devoted customers who launched them into the spotlight in the first place.

For example, after winning Best of Show at the annual Consumer Electronics Show in 2014 with a prototype-stage virtual reality headset, start-up Oculus was acquired for $2 billion just months later by Facebook.

But design excesses delayed the company's first commercial product until 2016, and the resulting price of $800 for a fully configured unit depressed consumer enthusiasm.

Products developed in the interim by HTC, Sony, and Samsung outsold the much anticipated Oculus Rift in its first year, leaving Oculus with just 4 percent of total sales. Sales of virtual reality hardware over-all have become sluggish, with consumers skeptical about the technol-ogy's capacity given excessive early hype.

This was by no means a failure of the idea of virtual reality and its potential to unlock massive trapped value at all four levels. It was a failure of confusing insight about the market for the superpower to shape that market in the future.

SERVING REGULATORS, NOT CUSTOMERS—When products that are si-multaneously better and cheaper quickly undermine an established market, stunned incumbents increasingly turn to their longtime reg-ulators, hoping to derail the insurgent or at least buy more time. In industries as different as financial services (fintech), aviation (drones), hospitality (Airbnb), and health care (genetic testing), incumbents first lobby for outright bans of the disruptors.

When consumers fight back on behalf of the disruptors, the regula-tors fall back to hastily crafted and often crippling new rules, designed with little to no understanding of how the start-ups' products or ser-vices differ from those of the incumbents. Ironically, the result is often more trapped value at the societal level, with innovations designed to use technology in ways that improve quality of life for a wider popu-lation needlessly slowed or skewed into less-productive trajectories. A dream deferred means, in this case, potential value unrealized.

Governments are also becoming more concerned about the poten-tial social costs of the information revolution, and in particular the impact of a few powerful companies that collect and use consumer data to fuel free online services with advertising. That concern, how-ever, is translating to new regulations that may unintentionally favor larger companies that can afford the high costs of compliance. In 2018, for example, the European Union implemented an expansive new law, the General Data Protection Regulation, threatening enormous fines for companies experiencing data breaches or involved in misuses of consumer data.

In the first six months after the law went into effect, however, there was strong evidence that the regulation had inadvertently increased the already strong market share of Google, Amazon, and Facebook in online advertising. At the same time, the average investment in

European start-ups saw a dramatic decline as markets considered the high costs of compliance and the risk of life-ending fines for new companies.

As that example suggests, start-ups must now engage legal counsel much sooner than was ever thought necessary, diverting critically scarce resources away from building the company to dealing with city councils, public utility commissions, and legislative hearings. Around the world, companies like Uber, Airbnb, and other sharing economy enterprises are engaged in pitched battles for the right to do business at all, let alone to do so without taking on the regulatory legacy of incumbent hotels and transportation companies.

For start-ups, the focus on regulators carries hidden risk. Disruptors desperate to stay in business can quickly develop the same dependency on regulators that stalls incumbents. Start-ups suddenly have lawyers and advisors, feeding a new cautiousness. They too come to believe they can use the law as a barrier against next-generation innovators. They may win the regulatory battle, but in doing so lose their momentum and, perhaps, the once-potent sympathies of their customers.

ANTICIPATING CUSTOMERS WHO AREN'T LIKELY TO SHOW UP—The winner-take-all phenomenon means that customers for disruptive products and services all show up at once, sending confusing signals about future sales and the market's appetite for follow-on products. As Tesla is learning the hard way, consumers use social media and other electronic channels to signal when a new product is a must-have, leading to a sudden rush followed quickly by silence. There's no longer Everett Rogers's relatively gentle bell curve of adoption. There's only the shark fin.

Consider the smart watch, a product that is effectively a wearable smartphone. Apple attracted one million pre-orders from American customers in 2015 on the first day of availability for the Apple Watch, at a relatively high price point. Smart watches, however, don't seem to have the same kind of frequent replacement cycle that smartphones and tablets do, driven by new features, new looks, or new hardware. Although Apple is now the leader in wearable technology, sales have cooled overall, and many early leaders have declined or disappeared.

Unfortunately, companies with big initial success often read enthu-siastic early sales as a sign of future growth. Anticipating more cus-tomers and new market segments, managers conditioned to the bell curve commit costly resources to expanded production and distribu-tion for follow-on sales that never come. They hire customer service staff, build production and distribution facilities, commit to market-ing campaigns and sales channels, and invest in high-cost dedicated IT networks—all to support products no one wants by the time they're done.

Or worse, they produce vast inventories that quickly become un-sellable at any price. Game developer THQ, which experienced great success in 2010 with a drawing tablet for the Nintendo Wii, went on to prematurely commit to versions of the tablet for other game platforms.

But the launch of the Apple iPad soon after suddenly shifted con-sumer demand to stand-alone drawing applications separate from game consoles. THQ continued to manufacture its tablets anyway, eventually warehousing 1.4 million unsold units. The company was forced into bankruptcy, and never recovered. After the fact, THQ's new president, Jason Rubin, confessed: "I'm not sure how that happened."

Whether resources and inventory are overbuilt or purchased rather than leased, investments made to support scaling up turn into trapped value when it becomes time, sooner rather than later, to scale down.

>

In succeeding chapters, we'll show you how to avoid each of these wrong turns and replace them with real-world strategies that release trapped value rather than generating more of it for new entrants and competitors to pick off. Let's start by replacing seven bad ideas with seven good ones.

chapter 3

THE SEVEN WINNING STRATEGIES

Keys for Unlocking Trapped Value

THE SEVEN WRONG TURNS can waylay even the most visionary leaders and keep them from releasing trapped value accumulating in the industry they seemingly know so well. After overcoming those temptations, your next task is to chart a course that places you ahead of competitors and start-ups eager to seize the opportunity before you do.

How to do it? Sometimes, oddly enough, the best starting point is to take a step backward, grab the nearest blunt instrument, and start swinging.

SMASHING THE INVENTORY, SAVING THE COMPANY

Creative destruction became quite literal in 1984, when Zhang Ruimin, a thirty-five-year-old Chinese official with little experience in business, took over as manager of a failing appliance factory in provincial China. The company had been through several general managers in just a few years when Zhang decided just to run the place himself. He began reading everything he could find on good management, even having books by his favorite author, Peter Drucker, translated for him.

Zhang was appalled by the state of the plant. Production was falling and money was short. Morale was so low that workers had to be reminded not to eat, sleep, or go to the bathroom on the factory floor.

Not surprisingly, product quality was also low. Early on, customers came to the factory to complain to Zhang that new refrigerators were being delivered already broken.

In those days, supply was so sparse that some Chinese companies could turn out shoddy or even nonfunctioning products and still sell them to an emerging middle class. But Zhang decided to do something radical. He and an unhappy customer went through the stock room and found seventy-six defective units—20 percent of all finished goods. He ordered the refrigerators placed in the factory's courtyard. Then he took a sledgehammer and, to the horror of the assembled workers, destroyed every one of them.

It was a seminal moment: the dawning of a relentless customer- and quality-focused, innovative culture that would eventually make Haier Group Corporation the largest home appliance manufacturer, first in China and then worldwide.

Rather than continue to serve a both literally and figuratively broken market, Zhang decided to sacrifice some of today's revenue to secure tomorrow's much larger opportunities. He set out to remake the brand around superior quality, a move that required a total rethinking of strategy, operations, and organization.

What Haier needed most, Zhang realized, was first to bridge a vast technological divide that existed between the loss-making business and its major global competitors. To achieve that goal, Haier partnered with a leading German manufacturer, Liebherr, to modernize the factory and instill in its workers a previously absent sense of pride and ownership.

Crossing that initial technological divide laid the groundwork for several more reinventions. Over the years, Haier has executed a dizzying series of acquisitions of weaker competitors including, in 2016, GE Appliances. At the same time, the company has won multiple international quality awards, cementing Zhang's status as a cult figure in China. To this day, superior performance at Haier is rewarded with a plaque featuring a golden sledgehammer.

Under Zhang's leadership, Haier has continued to evolve. With each subsequent pivot in strategy, he has narrowed a fast-growing trapped value gap, driven less by his competitors than by fundamental economic and technical change. As middle-class consumers emerge around the world, Haier is there to serve them. As new technologies reset what is possible in product design, manufacturing, distribution, and customer interaction, Haier is first to adopt them.

As rival home appliance manufacturers in China caught up and improved the quality of their own products, for example, Zhang relentlessly pushed Haier toward superior customer service. And as those competitors became more consumer-focused, Zhang was already reinventing his business again, focusing on complete flexibility by reorganizing the workforce into hundreds of small business units, or "microenterprises," that operate like entrepreneurial start-ups, funded by Haier and others.

In every case, Haier first closed a technology gap, then closed a business gap. It was the first company in China to adopt modern manufacturing technology, for example, and then to work with entrepreneurs inside and outside the company to diversify by introducing new and improved products with the latest features. Haier fully embraced social media to form direct relationships with consumers and engage them in the design of new products.

Today, the company is busy reinventing itself again, this time as a software-driven leader in the fast-growing internet of things. It is harvesting information collected from the appliances it sells, data that Haier believes will become more valuable than the devices themselves.

"We cannot expect to smash refrigerators every day," Zhang said years later, reflecting on the fridge-demolition episode. "But actually, I think about doing it every day."

NEW STRATEGIES FOR VALUE RELEASE
IN AN AGE OF DISRUPTION

Haier and its inexhaustible CEO are one of a kind. Still, Zhang's fearless leadership demonstrates both the need for, and the tools available to, unlock trapped value in even the most challenging markets and ossified industries. Haier's constantly changing structure and strategy keep its competitors off balance, rendering them, to use Zhang's colorful phrase, "stunned fish."

More importantly, Haier's thirty-five-year-long revolution proves that in the face of a growing trapped value gap, sustainable growth requires executives who can continually pivot around a fulcrum of evolving core assets, shifting from one future vision to the next. And they must do so with increased velocity as market conditions change and technology disruptors emerge faster all the time.

This chapter begins our journey to the wise pivot, by looking at the new strategies employed by companies that consistently unlock trapped value faster than their competitors.

In subsequent chapters, we'll explain what it takes to infuse these strategies into every fiber of your organization, executing one pivot after the next as technology pushes the trapped value frontier further out.

For now, to appreciate the potential in releasing trapped value, let's see what Zhang Ruimin's efforts have done for Haier. With seventy-five thousand employees and annual revenue of $35 billion, Haier has consistently delivered year-over-year growth of as much as 20 percent. It has remained the world's largest retailer of household appliances for the last nine years, with over 10 percent of the global market. From 2005 to 2015, enterprise value grew by 25 percent, and investments in new ventures generated $2 billion in market value.

The Haier brand is widely respected both inside and outside China, with its CEO regularly invited to speak on leadership and strategy at such prestigious events as the annual Global Drucker Forum, honoring Zhang's hero.

With every reinvention the company—working with customers and other stakeholders—remained laser-focused on targeting and releasing trapped value across all four levels. As it shared more and more of that value with consumers, its industries, and society as a whole, the company became a giant in its own right.

Trapped value releasers like Haier have adopted new strategies, ones especially well-suited to continual change. These new strategies replace the shop-worn categories of an older generation of thinking regarding competitive advantage. It's no longer enough, if it ever was, to pursue a single goal with generic names such as "cost leadership," "differentiation," and "focus." Now companies must embrace digital-first strategies, targeting those that best fit the needs of customers rather than the preferences of the planners.

Rather than operate and measure performance solely on a quarter-to-quarter basis, value releasers reorient every function and every employee around a commitment to the care and feeding of core resources, including technology, customers, stakeholders, and broader social values. They manage the business as an integrated portfolio, looking for superior overall returns over a sustained period of time.

Collectively, we call our digital-first approach the "seven winning strategies." While few companies in our study adopted all of them, value releasers successfully pursued at least one or more. And they did so not just once, but continuously.

These winning strategies are the turning points of a wise pivot. Practiced consistently and fearlessly, they are the keys that unlock trapped value. They take the organization off a tried and true path that may have worked for decades, but which everyone now agrees is certain to fail, likely sooner than they think, in the face of inevitable and persistent disruption.

In this chapter, we'll explore examples of each of the winning strategies in detail. First, let's introduce them briefly:

- **TECHNOLOGY PROPELLED.** Mastering leading-edge technologies that enable business innovation.

- **HYPER RELEVANT.** Knowing how to be—and stay—relevant by sensing and addressing customers' changing needs.

- **DATA DRIVEN.** Generating, sharing, and deploying data to deliver new product and service innovations safely and securely.

- **ASSET SMART.** Adopting intelligent asset and operations management to run businesses as efficiently as possible, freeing up capacity for other innovative efforts.

- **INCLUSIVE.** Adopting an open and transparent approach to innovation and governance that embraces a broader range of stakeholders.

- **TALENT RICH.** Creating modern forms of workforce management (flexible, augmented, and adaptive) to gain competitive advantage in fast-changing markets.

- **NETWORK POWERED.** Harnessing the power of a carefully managed ecosystem of partners to bring the best innovations to your customers.

Which of the seven winning strategies will unlock trapped value for your organization? In part, the answer depends on the nature of that value. In our study, some organizations were able to achieve value release with just one of the seven. Others combined several, while a few applied all of them. Some focused their attack on value trapped in their own enterprise or industry; others reached for richer sources locked inside problems that plagued customers and communities, but for which no good solution was previously available.

Figure 3.1 maps the new technologies most often used by the companies in our study to the winning strategies they best support. Of course, as we'll see in the examples that follow, in some cases the right combination of older technologies works just as well.

TECHNOLOGY PROPELLED

Technology-propelled companies are led by senior managers who personally advocate for and drive the adoption of new technologies, investing in those that improve the innovation process itself, and creating a robust infrastructure that safely and securely facilitates external collaboration. They recognize that for the other six winning strategies to work, their organizations must become leaders in adopting the new.

Indeed, at every technology-propelled company we reviewed in our study, such as Haier and here at Accenture, the CEO is the company's chief technology booster. The CEO provides not just the resources to invest in unproven technologies but, just as important, communicates to every employee the need to think and act boldly and creatively, to develop new applications with an expansive view of the users of the future and their needs.

Figure 3.1 Technologies for Executing the Seven Winning Strategies

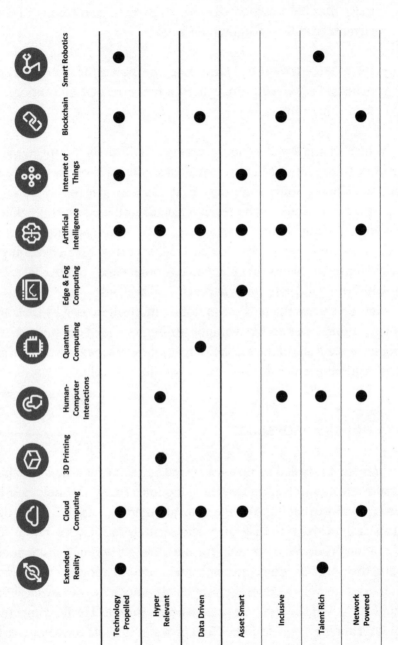

Former Accenture CEO Pierre Nanterme, who led the company's reinvention as a digital-first enterprise, underscored the importance of new technologies by using them himself. To support our global organization, for example, we've invested in the latest communications tools, including holography. Nanterme had been an avid user of these tools since 2016, seeing them as a way to communicate effectively across time and space without losing the personal connection.

But be careful here. Embracing a technology-propelled strategy places extraordinary pressure on already strained IT departments, pressed as they are to support ever-more internal and external users with a growing backlog of new requirements. The need for fast IT solutions may encourage short-term hacks to existing systems and other myopic decisions that compromise an open, extendable, and robust systems architecture.

A broken technology infrastructure is the principal side effect of the first of the seven wrong turns—of sacrificing sustainable business-building in service to the false virtue of running a "lean" organization, or following too religiously the quick-iteration model of agile systems development.

While those are often superior approaches for individual projects, applying these techniques to core technology infrastructure assets is a recipe for disaster. It can leave you with brittle, aging, and disconnected systems that don't communicate with each other, let alone with outside stakeholders.

Many of the enterprises we studied start out their wise pivots with IT systems that have been bandaged, bruised, and otherwise compromised over the years, as short-term fixes and patches were made without considering the integrity of the overall architecture.

Each of these hacks—linking files rather than building a database, bolting new front-ends onto unmaintainable systems, running incompatible versions of the same software for different parts of your organization—contributes to what software developers call "technical debt."

We view the problem more broadly, and refer to it as "technology debt." Technology debt is based on more than just the sunk costs of hardware, software, and code. It is a measure of the inefficiencies, duplicate processes, and extra work created by relying on an outdated or out of control technology architecture.

Technology debt represents a key source of trapped value at the enterprise level. Erasing it may require considerable renewed investment just to untangle the mess, let alone develop your technical infrastructure into a strategic asset. If left to fester long enough, technology debt may leave you IT bankrupt, with systems that are unfixable at any cost. We saw several examples where parent companies disposed of subsidiaries just because the cost of repairing outdated and broken technology became too onerous.

How does technology debt lead to enterprise trapped value? For one thing, as your IT infrastructure ages and more features are added to legacy systems, technology debt accumulates in the form of growing fixed operating costs, diverting investment from innovation and new capabilities. Over time, the cost and technical challenges of connecting and updating disparate and patched systems may become overwhelming, foreclosing the kind of strategic innovations characteristic of technology-propelled organizations.

Businesses born before the internet era generally face greater technology debt than newer or "digitally native" competitors. No matter how well maintained and updated older systems may be, they are inevitably less adaptable than systems designed for the kind of distributed, extendable, and scalable use internet technology makes possible.

Indeed, digital natives often avoid the risk of stale systems altogether by leasing applications, capacity, and infrastructure from cloud service providers, including Amazon Web Services, Microsoft, Google, Salesforce, and SAP. These providers offer one-stop shopping for IT independence, all at an increasingly attractive price.

The scalability, flexibility, and modularity of AWS's component-based IT systems, for example, are key assets fueling Amazon's ability to outperform incumbent brick-and-mortar retailers—a competitive advantage the company now rents out to over a million other businesses, most of them small- and medium-sized enterprises that could never afford, let alone maintain, the state-of-the-art technology AWS provides.

The same could be said for relatively new digital powerhouses, including Netflix, Uber, and Airbnb. Their nimble IT infrastructures are central to their ability to disrupt older competitors in entertainment, transportation, and hospitality, respectively.

So to become truly technology propelled, step one is to erase your technology debt and commit to the kind of IT discipline that ensures you don't accumulate it again in the future.

For established companies, that means moving as quickly as possible to decouple older, monolithic systems and convert them to smaller, modular components. Techniques for achieving that goal include building application programming interfaces (APIs), migrating to cloud-based platforms, and shifting to microservice architectures that structure applications as a collection of loosely coupled services and real-time "data lakes," which allow you to store all your structured and unstructured data in one place.

These techniques leverage essential parts of core IT assets without limiting current or future agility. Decoupling also has the virtue of providing incumbents the flexibility of cloud computing while building on the enormous wealth of information in a company's existing data warehouse, accumulated through systems built for another era.

Manage your transition right, and you extend and enhance core IT assets even as you position yourself for the future, moving from an organization weighed down by its infrastructure to one that is technology propelled—fueled rather than stalled by its digital assets.

Consider the experience of UK insurance broker Towergate, which has grown significantly in the past two decades. The company has completed nearly three hundred acquisitions. These additions have brought onboard new businesses that greatly expanded the company's knowledge and expertise, making it possible to serve customers with niche and specialized insurance products.

That kind of growth, however, came with severe IT headaches. New brokers brought their own IT with them, resulting in a highly fragmented internal environment. There were multiple telephone systems, different types of hardware, and numerous versions of Windows and other software. There was no IT help desk. Maintenance breakdowns regularly incapacitated the business, sometimes for days at a time. Towergate's technology debt was growing. Eventually, it came due.

"It was like a museum of IT," Adrian Brown, the company's COO, told us. "You name it, we had it."

Towergate's out-of-date and unstable patchwork of IT systems, applications, and processes threatened customer service, employee collaboration, and innovation capabilities. Worse, without a strategy for systems integration, the risk of accruing more technology debt ran dangerously high.

The repeated shutdowns prompted Towergate to commit to a complete IT modernization project, including the migration of all their systems to the cloud. Networks, data centers, end-user computing, and support were all reinvented in one of the most comprehensive technology reboots the financial services industry had ever seen.

Begun in 2016, the project was completed in just over a year. You can well imagine how difficult a year that was. The company reduced the number of IT applications it supported from over twenty-five hundred to just over two hundred, installed new networks at a hundred sites, and became the first insurance firm to store all its data in the cloud, eliminating two-thirds of local servers and substantially reducing system outages.

The overhaul also helped Towergate's bottom line, generating a 30 percent reduction in costs, or about $5 million in annual IT savings.

Towergate's customers are the real winners. With an integrated infrastructure, information can now move seamlessly throughout the business. Towergate can provide new services on demand, creating better experiences for customers and employees. For the future, Towergate's new modular architecture ensures the company can integrate new acquisitions and chart a path for even more growth.

Technology-propelled companies don't just focus on technologies that make the enterprise more efficient, however. They also look for IT investments that can stimulate future innovation.

Lucasfilm, for example, the Disney-owned producer of *Star Wars*, has created a "digital backlot." This virtual archive provides easy access to production assets regardless of their source, allowing them to be cataloged and repurposed for future projects, including films, games, and theme parks. The company's creative staff saves time, focusing more on storytelling and less on reinventing the light saber.

A creature needed for 2017's *The Last Jedi*, for example, could be sketched by a concept artist, then built as a physical puppet. Once the design was finalized, the puppet was 3D-scanned, touched up, and approved as a production asset. At that point, the asset could be exported to the digital backlot as a file. When the creature was later needed for a Hasbro toy or a character in a game, it could be easily reused and kept consistent at the same time.

Sometimes the sharing goes the other way. For the film *Rogue One*, Lucasfilm partner Industrial Light & Magic borrowed some assets that game developer Dice had built for the popular video game *Star Wars: Battlefront*.

HYPER RELEVANT

Hyper-relevant organizations collaborate with customers during the innovation process, personalize customer interactions, and develop products and services that revolve around customer experience.

Let's start by acknowledging a pervasive problem. Your customer retention strategy probably relies on "buying" loyalty with rewards, rebates, or discounts, an approach popularized during the 1980s with airline and other frequent customer programs. But that tactic comes at a high price and very little benefit. It commoditizes your brand and gives away profits to consumers with little in return. At the same time, ironically, it does little or nothing to secure loyalty—quite the opposite. You're simply training customers to look for a competitor with a better giveaway.

Little surprise, then, that the loyalty era of marketing is waning.

Instead, in the new world of digital competition, deep data collection, and advanced analytics, consumers are buying because of a brand's relevance to their needs at the moment, needs that smart producers can glean, shape, and customize with ease. Today, you need to serve customers in an instant, offering precisely the right product and service at the right time. Hyper-relevant companies don't sell things. They sell, as authors B. Joseph Pine II and James H. Gilmore put it, experiences.

One global car-rental company in our research, for example, has developed a real-time approach to generating customized offers to customers as they complete a reservation. A data analytics tool proposes offers a customer is most likely to accept. Customers who refused an offer in the past, for example, might be presented a different kind of promotion, even if the alternative is less profitable for the company but more likely to be accepted. The company understands that a promotion is only as good as the customers' willingness to act on it.

As this example suggests, hyper relevance requires access to detailed customer behavior data, and the analytic tools to make sense of it. More than that, you need to engage in a long-term relationship with customers rather than simply selling them one thing or another. You and your customer need to learn about each other, and customize products and services accordingly.

Hyper-relevant companies are not just suppliers, in other words. They are an integral part of their customers' lives, embracing their values as well as their needs. So a hyper-relevant strategy requires deep, digitally enabled interaction and, ultimately, collaboration with consumers, even when that means, as it does for companies like Haier, coordinating millions of interactions across different channels, social media platforms, and interest groups.

Our study found that companies releasing value through hyper relevance collaborate directly with customers during the innovation process itself, using insights gained from the interactions to personalize user responses, whether that means simply acknowledging their contribution, actually building products to their precise specifications, or anything in between.

Mobile network operator Sprint, for example, built an AI-driven "chatbot" that uses information provided by customers looking for support to guide the conversation just as a human would do. Customers know they are talking to software, which hands the conversation over to more experienced humans when its abilities are exceeded. Still, the chatbot quickly learned how to help customers looking to upgrade devices, tapping potentially rich new markets.

That kind of consistent and persistent interaction enables hyper-relevant organizations to predict customer needs even before the consumer realizes she has them. It's not just about understanding customers better. Hyper relevance means forming a lasting and healthy relationship with them, one that emphasizes trust and security, especially regarding sensitive or personal information.

CVS Pharmacy, the retail brand of CVS Health, provides a good example of this new approach. The company is moving away from merely filling prescriptions to investing in technologies that will help it develop long-term relationships with its customers, working together to improve health outcomes. Focusing on current customer "pain points" yielded simple but effective innovations that improve today's retail experience, including a customized prescription labeling system, home delivery, and the ability to update insurance information just by texting a photo of a new insurance card.

As a hyper-relevant company, CVS's driving principle is to adopt the health aspirations of its customers, building on the trusted relationship most patients already have with their pharmacist. They have fully embraced consumers' health care goals to evolve from reactive sick care to proactive self-care. Store layouts devote retail space to nutrition, sleep, and immunity products. The company is also experimenting with lower-cost telemedicine solutions for optometry and audiology.

Today, these technologies facilitate sending personalized reminders to refill or take medications. But in the future, consumers will be offered solutions personalized to their specific genetic makeup. By working with these new technologies now, CVS is positioning itself to offer future hyper-relevant solutions in everything from supplements to skin care.

DATA DRIVEN

Data-driven companies discover insights and make recommendations. Future demand is predicted by analyzing multiple data sources and deriving behavioral insights to influence customer behavior.

Becoming a data-driven enterprise can be a double-edged sword, however. You only have to spend a few minutes reading your news source of choice to know we face a global data crisis. Faster and cheaper digital technologies have made it possible to collect, store, analyze, and reconfigure so much new information that it's nearly impossible to measure either its scale or its value.

On the one hand, new data sources and the technology to manipulate them have led to essential new services, including social media, user-produced video content, and the emerging internet of things, all of which have and will continue to enrich the lives of billions of users worldwide.

On the other hand, all that cheap technology has led to some remarkably poor data hygiene practices by companies old and new, as well as government agencies, all of which have experienced embarrassing and dangerous data breaches and other leakage. In some cases, valuable trust in familiar brands, built over years or even decades, has been lost in a matter of days.

Consumers and citizens respectively bear much of the cost of an epidemic of information misuse—everything from identity theft to a general loss of personal privacy, misinformation, the decline of public discourse, and anxiety over growing "addiction" to our mobile devices and favorite apps.

The net result is a lot of unhappy users. Lawmakers, taking notice of the growing discomfort of their constituents, have begun passing new laws in an effort to put the data genie back in the bottle—efforts that in some cases may only succeed in making the problem worse, costing users still more inconvenience, discomfort, and lost opportunities.

Data security breaches also threaten your brand, operational capacity, proprietary information, and other intellectual property assets. These are key sources of value and need to be protected—treated as the uniquely networked, renewable, and sustainable assets they actually are, rather than simply as data. That means taking an end-to-end view of security across the company and adopting the latest security hardware, software, and business practices to protect it.

Still, avoiding innovations that use information for fear of potential damage to your relationships and brand leaves too much trapped value accumulating in padlocked data warehouses. That's a lost opportunity eventually ceded to more nimble competitors who manage the risk of data security problems in order to make competitive use of information. In fact, one of the major advantages incumbents maintain over new entrants is deep, industry-specific data they have carefully collected, sometimes over decades. They shouldn't waste it.

Data-driven organizations commit instead to a long list of best practices, including responsible data design, information security, transparency, and proportionality. For example, they collect only data they actually need. They let users know precisely what they plan to do with it. They share the value they earn from its use, and jealously guard it from external and internal misuse, criminal or otherwise.

As is the case with technology-propelled organizations, data handling policies must be communicated from senior management, and enforced throughout the organization. No exceptions, no shortcuts. At many companies, unfortunately, those imperatives are more often aspirations than realities. Three-quarters of senior executives we surveyed agree that safe data-handling practices must be embraced by the entire organization, though most admit that for now their own cybersecurity remains a centralized function.

With security and trust risks properly managed, the upside of becoming data driven is tremendous. The more data you collect, the more your products and services improve, attracting more customers and deepening relationships with those you already have. That in turn improves future products and helps predict and shape future demand.

Data analysis, increasingly driven by applied artificial intelligence, likewise creates a virtuous cycle that helps to identify looming competitive threats and new partners who can help defend profits. The more data you have, the more you can create competitive advantage, building a protective information barrier around your business.

A leading technology here is advanced analytics: data processing tools that generate recommendations to improve decision-making processes. These tools are being augmented with AI techniques, including machine learning—along with simulations and data visualizations—that help users in many industries. In manufacturing, analytics can predict future failures down to the level of a single component part, and when they might happen.

Rigorous data-handling practices not only protect consumers and your brand, but also your own bottom line. Consider data-driven Chevron, the world's third-largest publicly traded oil producer. The company is spending over $5 billion annually on production in its shale basins, approximately a fourth of its annual capital spending. It is using drilling expertise developed on its offshore wells to improve the efficiency of the company's onshore horizontal operations, in which a single well is drilled across the length of an oil field.

Chevron's data-driven approach leverages a proprietary database of over five million well attributes, supplemented by processing-intensive analysis of petrophysical properties such as porosity (the measure of void space), water saturation, permeability, and density. The insights the company has gained reduce the time to drill a shale well from twenty-seven days to just fifteen, even for the new longer and more complex wells.

Or look at South African insurer AllLife, the first company in the world to offer whole life coverage to people who are HIV-positive. In a country where nearly 20 percent of the adult population is living with the AIDS virus, the company now has more than a hundred thousand such policies.

How does AllLife insure the "uninsurable"? The company collects detailed customer profiles and uses the data in conjunction with outcomes from other people it insures to personalize recommendations for each customer on how to manage their condition.

After collecting the necessary data, AllLife uses proprietary algorithms to deliver a cost-effective life insurance product. CEO and founder Ross Beerman told news website Business Insider in 2018: "The term now is robo-underwriting but it's using tech that pulls a vast amount of medical information and puts it through a decision tree process that allows us to automate most of the stuff that life insurance companies are doing manually."

Extending life spans, in addition to being a socially responsible use of information, also reduces the cost of insurance, funding further interventions. "We have a follow-on process," Beerman said. "We intervene in people's health. We tell people, don't forget to do this, you should really do this—we do that through text message, emails, sometimes calls. We intervene."

The results speak to the potential for data-driven enterprises to release trapped value across all four levels: enterprise, industry, customer, and societal. AllLife has improved the health and lowered the mortality rates of its clients, as measured by the improvement of a key blood count, by an average of 15 percent in their first six months as insureds.

ASSET SMART

The presumption that a company must own the assets that matter most to its strategy is no longer valid. Successful value releasers have learned to balance ownership with the ability to scale operations up and down quickly by relying instead on leased or rented IT and other assets, bulking up or shedding fast as market conditions change.

Rather than focus on asset ownership, these companies work closely with outside expert partners to ensure superior customer service and minimal risk. Without the capital burden of owning and maintaining every asset, they enjoy greater spending ability when the opportunity to buy truly valuable assets—including new technologies or even other companies—arises.

Take Apple, one of the most valuable companies in the world. It has thrived by pursuing an asset-smart strategy. The company owns very little of the physical infrastructure it relies on to make and distribute its products. One result: Apple needs almost no outside capital to operate on a day-to-day basis, avoiding the drag of interest payments and other lender constraints.

Being asset smart is not limited to heavy industry. It's also crucial for companies whose core assets are information, whether in the form of expertise, customer and market intelligence, or product design and marketing. These enterprises apply digital tools to aggregate and analyze data from multiple systems, or take information from written documents and translate it into reusable digital data, reducing bureaucracy and improving customer service.

Vehicle insurance companies, for example, can offer discounted rates and usage-based pricing for drivers who allow the company to collect actual operating data, using technology known as "electronic logging devices." With specific knowledge of how much and under what conditions a vehicle is being operated, insurers can create personalized premiums based on individual usage levels and driving habits.

Asset-smart businesses also employ technology that increases the utilization of the assets they still own. They use smart workflows to track the status of a wide variety of business processes in real time, including managing handoffs between different groups and providing statistical data to remove bottlenecks.

Rather than program for every possible exception, they build learning algorithms that generate new rules based on observed conditions, as when robots improve their own ability to spot defects by analyzing patterns in the items rejected by human quality-control engineers.

Being asset smart can also reduce the perennial headache of excess or obsolete inventory. Inventory handling costs alone can account for between 25 and 45 percent of a typical company's cost of goods sold. One global food and beverage company we worked with applied AI to large historical data sets to find previously unnoticed connections in consumer buying patterns. This led to better predictions of needs and reduced inventory levels. It also greatly enhanced the effectiveness of the supply chain planning team.

Perhaps the most obvious example today of asset-smart behavior is the development of robust cloud computing services. Cloud platforms allow enterprises large and small to offload all aspects of their IT infrastructure, storage, connectivity, data processing, and even applications development to providers that can offer world-class capabilities and competitive prices based on economies of scale.

Thanks to a computing architecture that splits storage and processing among a network of connected, general-purpose servers, cloud providers can easily and cheaply add or remove capacity on demand. This eliminates both the cost and risk for traditional IT departments, unlocking vast quantities of trapped value.

Accenture's own reinvention as a digital-first enterprise highlights the benefits of being asset smart. A three-year migration to the public cloud allowed our internal IT organization to deliver a more scalable, robust information infrastructure. Our IT systems are now over 90 percent cloud based. And optimization tools we developed allow us to drive discounts of up to 40 percent from the providers we contract with for these services, contributing tens of millions of dollars in ongoing savings.

Accenture's migration to the cloud generates benefits in the form of direct savings, but also from increased efficiencies in everything from storage costs to lower legal compliance fees, and the ability to quickly and cost-effectively utilize new technologies.

Or consider the case of start-up Digital Asset. The company uses asset and workflow management software, known as "smart contracts," to create efficiencies for its financial services customers, freeing up human and capital resources better utilized in innovation and other value-enhancing activities. (Accenture is an investor in Digital Asset.)

How? Trillions of dollars' worth of transactions are processed through financial institutions daily. For decades, however, record keeping has remained the separate and duplicated responsibility of each participating institution. Digital Asset offers an alternative in the form of blockchain, a distributed ledger technology that mutualizes this infrastructure. It replaces custom systems with an immutable, encrypted shared database that preserves transaction history across a network of servers.

Digital Asset's solution reduces the cost and time taken to reconcile disparate records in settlement and clearing processes, and potentially in virtually any other multiparty business workflow. Data can be shared securely, accurately, and in real time. Distributing the ledger also protects it from the risk of attack on a single source. And a combination of cryptographic techniques and physical segregation ensures the ledger is never altered or accessed without authorization.

Launched in 2014, Digital Asset is already serving global clients from offices in New York, London, Zurich, Budapest, Sydney, and Hong Kong. The Australian Securities Exchange is working to adopt the company's software, by 2021, as its official process for recording shareholders and clearing and settling equity transactions—the first major bourse to embrace to blockchain technology.

INCLUSIVE

Inclusive companies develop new services that better address customer aspirations, work closely with other network partners to develop a more efficient supply chain, and create platforms that enable consumers and suppliers to unlock trapped value.

Let's be clear: the rules of conducting business are changing. Traditional views of shareholder value are becoming more expansive. Investors now fully expect businesses to serve a wider range of constituencies, address the needs of unserved global customers, improve operational transparency, and engage the company's brand with an ever-widening group of inside and outside stakeholders.

In his annual letter to CEOs in 2018, for example, asset manager BlackRock's CEO Larry Fink wrote that his firm believes only companies that embody these environmental, societal, and gover-nance goals will be sustainable in the long term. CEOs are likely to listen to such advice—BlackRock is the world's largest asset manage-ment company, with over $7 trillion under management.

Value releasers practicing inclusiveness have reimagined their cor-porate cultures inside and out. They focus less on quarter-to-quarter sales and profits and look to the higher needs of an expanded ecosys-tem, knowing that doing the right thing will translate to even faster growth and higher profit. They provide more for their customers than just products and services, recognizing that value creation is yet another networked good. And they work to level the playing field to allow individuals and small firms to participate in technological prog-ress.

In China, for example, many of the country's largest courier compa-nies, based in the Tonglu area, joined a consortium created by e-com-merce giant Alibaba to improve the country's logistics infrastructure, a benefit not only to the couriers but also to Alibaba's merchant and consumer users.

The result has been increased business for both Alibaba and the couriers. In 2017, Chinese merchants shipped thirty-one billion pack-ages, over half of which were generated by orders from Alibaba. Nearly two-thirds of those were delivered by Tonglu companies.

Our research found that over half of the companies we identified as value releasers plan to build services that allow users to generate related revenue for themselves. Often this takes the form of interactive tools, such as those long employed by online markets. These include eBay and MercadoLibre, which host both buyers and sellers, providing the tools they need to safely and efficiently conduct transactions. This technique has more recently been employed to allow users to sell ev-erything from artisanal goods (Etsy) to ride sharing (Uber and DiDi) to travel experiences (Airbnb).

Now these same tools are being used to advance social values, letting people interact with you and perhaps even more with your extended network, in ways that help people make their lives more ful-filling. Consider Open Collective, which allows nonprofits of all sizes to collect and disburse money, providing complete transparency for how funds enter and exit accounts.

More than half of the companies we studied that have had at least some success releasing trapped value, plan to develop new services that better address customers' higher needs, be they autonomy, happiness, social connections, self-actualization, inspiration, or purpose.

At Accenture, we embrace this particular winning strategy in our Corporate Citizenship agenda, applying it internally, in our work with clients, and in the global community more broadly. In 2018, we committed more than $200 million over the next three years to equip people around the world with job skills for the digital age, using the same learning technologies we have been developing for our own employees and clients.

Our Skills to Succeed initiative has already trained more than two million people, leveraging digital innovation to help close employment gaps at scale. One of our partnerships in the United States works with the Institute for Veterans and Military Families to train veterans for a transition to the civilian workforce. We also provide consulting services to grow the Institute's capacity in employment training, housing, health care, and career services.

Another project, with Leonard Cheshire Disability in the UK, is increasing economic participation for persons with disabilities. The program has helped more than eight thousand people across Asia gain employment in several sectors, including IT and business process outsourcing. By the end of 2018, the program offered skills training to an additional thirteen thousand people in Bangladesh, India, Pakistan, the Philippines, South Africa, and Sri Lanka.

Releasing trapped value through expanded inclusion is the sole mission of some enterprises. GoFundMe and CaringBridge, for example, are social networks that simplify charitable fund-raising on behalf of individuals facing catastrophic medical needs, or for larger groups who have experienced natural or man-made disasters.

Another inclusive new form of business is microlending, which pools modest resources of a small group to make "microcredit" loans, typically less than $50,000, that help entrepreneurs start businesses. There are dozens of microlending sites disbursing hundreds of millions of dollars annually. (The inventor of the idea, Bangladeshi social entrepreneur Muhammad Yunus, was awarded the Nobel Peace Prize in 2006.)

Outside of finance, specialized social networking tools allow people to organize everything from casual meetups to the exchange of designer clothing. San Francisco–based Nextdoor, founded in 2010, has more than ten million members, who share community-level information in over a hundred thousand US neighborhoods, and another hundred thousand members across six other countries, including France and the UK.

Or consider efforts by Microsoft. The company has already deployed several inclusive technologies specifically aimed at users with disabilities. Microsoft Translator, for example, helps the deaf and hearing impaired by providing real-time captioning of conversations. Another application, called Helpicto, translates voice commands into images, which can improve the communication capabilities of children with autism. A third product, Seeing AI, "narrates the world around you" for people who are blind or vision impaired.

In 2018, Microsoft extended these efforts by initiating a $25 million "AI for Accessibility" program that will develop technologies to support speech-to-text transcription, visual recognition, and predictive text suggestions, all aimed at improving outcomes in employment, home, and social interactions. According to a statement from CEO Satya Nadella at the time of the project's launch, only one in ten people have access to such "assistive technologies."

The project includes seed grants to outside researchers and investors, accelerated incubation inside Microsoft for the most promising of these efforts, and adoption across the company's offerings of more assistive technologies. There will also be more tools for third-party partners to add similar features to their products.

TALENT RICH

Talent-rich companies develop senior leaders who can oversee innovation-led change, develop a highly adaptable workforce through job rotation and short-term or "gig" assignments, and harness smaller, cross-disciplinary teams for projects that target disruptive innovation.

A workforce advantage is at the heart of the success of every great company. The best and most successful companies, after all, are those with the best people. Indeed, most executives we have worked with count as their greatest achievement leaving their organizations healthier than when they took over, and feel that their company's health is best measured by the kinds of employees it hires and retains.

As Volvo began its pivot to a more premium car brand over the last decade, for example, the company quickly recognized a need for employees with very different skills. "Once, you needed mechanical engineers," Chief Human Resources Officer Björn Sällström said in a 2018 interview. "Today, there's a greater need for software engineers because cars are computers more than anything else."

Employees with IT skills, Sällström believed, were also more likely to bring with them an entrepreneurial mindset the company's culture badly needed. So Volvo has radically reconfigured its employee mix, notably by hiring from outside the automotive industry, including salespeople from Google, engineers from Nokia, and designers from the fashion industry.

In total, the company added three thousand new employees in engineering and research between 2011 and 2015. Key employees were given training and mentoring in innovation, and a "catalyst" group of thirty mostly younger workers were assigned to teach existing workers how to look for and eliminate outdated processes and other bureaucracy.

The result has been improved revenue and standing for the brand. Volvo's vehicles are getting rave reviews, and the company is well positioned for the automobile industry's next "new," the production of autonomous vehicles.

As the Volvo example suggests, the tools and techniques for optimizing talent today and in the future have changed radically in the last ten years. They will change even more dramatically as artificial intelligence becomes more fully deployed in the coming decade.

We are not among those who think AI will displace knowledge workers to a significant extent. We do, however, believe AI will substantially alter the nature of work, and in a positive way. Today, too many jobs are boring and repetitive, leaving workers unmotivated or worse. AI technologies offer an opportunity to redesign work away from the mundane and toward tasks that require human reasoning, empathy, and creativity.

Already, there is a wealth of trapped value accumulating at the enterprise level in companies that can't or don't get the most from their human capital. Employees want work that better fits their values and their preferred lifestyle. The people you hire could contribute much more if they were given the opportunity and training to expand their skills and apply them to new tasks and different roles.

That's true as well in the broader ecosystem in which you operate. Customers want to help you build better products, and suppliers want to be better partners, if for no better reason than their own self-interest. Regulators, civil society, and other external stakeholders want to participate as well, guiding you in directions they believe will benefit society as a whole. It's their raison d'être.

Historically, workers in many industries were pigeonholed early in their working lives into specific roles and career paths, with little opportunity to expand their skill base or to work in different parts of the company. Now, younger workers in particular are demanding more fluid assignments and the kind of continual training that nonstop technology-based disruption requires to stay relevant and valuable to employers.

The emergence of more fluid, or "liquid," approaches to human resource management, applied in everything from manufacturing to professional services, gives employees and outside stakeholders the tools they need to develop their skills and "sell" them back to the organization for particular projects or shorter-term assignments. It also forces a serious reconsideration of how education is developed and delivered, and in particular the growing need for lifelong learning.

This new approach to talent development and management draws insights from internet-based gig services developed over the last few years, especially ride sharing and other real-time platforms that match the supply and demand of particular skills. The successes as well as the limitations of these services have shown human resource executives how to promote efficient and effective liquid workforces inside their own organizations, releasing trapped value for both employers and employees.

Today, there are virtual labor exchanges to connect buyers and sellers of nearly any skill, and to solve any problem imaginable. You can easily identify and contract expertise for anything from gardening and home repair to learning a new language or musical instrument, or just getting help with ready-to-assemble furniture. Even complex software development projects can be bid out with tools like Gigster, a four-year-old company with a near billion-dollar valuation that bills itself as "the world's engineering department."

Based on lessons learned from these consumer-oriented services, the approach and technology of the gig economy is being applied to the internal and external workforces of many industries, blurring the line between employees and contractors.

Proprietary and open talent platforms, for example, connect networks of virtual problem-solvers with organizations looking for out-of-the-box thinking for particular design or production problems, dramatically extending the potential talent pool to a world of virtual collaborators with specialized skills.

Since 2000, one such platform, InnoCentive, has unlocked incalculable trapped value by lowering the costs for business- and technical-problem seekers and solvers to find each other.

Operating in over two hundred countries, the service supports a network of nearly half a million experts in every imaginable field, who have solved over two thousand posted challenges. Close to 80 percent of posted challenges lead to an award, paying a total $20 million so far.

Even internally, talent-rich companies are liberating employees to grow their skills over the course of their careers and find the best fit for their expanding talents. At Accenture, people move between roles, projects, tasks, and teams, collaborating, experimenting, and innovating in a culture that tolerates occasional failure for personal growth.

They also learn new skills every day, with digital technology as their trusted aide and guide. Accenture is planning to open ten new innovation hubs in cities around the United States between 2017 and 2020, and to create 15,000 highly skilled new jobs in the process. We also plan to invest $1.4 billion in training our own employees in new technologies.

Indeed, today's talent-rich companies don't fear the digitization of work—they embrace it. Rather than retire workers whose day-to-day tasks are replaced by more efficient digital alternatives, they teach them next-generation skills, retaining the best talent and unlocking even more trapped value.

As we'll see in a later chapter devoted to the workforce, communications and media giant AT&T has been reskilling thousands of workers whose expertise in analog technology is quickly becoming obsolete, giving them the digital skills they need to stay relevant, while narrowing AT&T's need to hire a replacement workforce that is both hard to find and expensive to recruit and enculturate.

To take full advantage of new opportunities in automation, the talent-rich companies in our research cultivate an interconnected relationship between humans and machines across the enterprise, which allows for task reassignment, reskilling, and on-the-job training to facilitate faster experimentation and innovation. In the automotive industry, for one, Mercedes continues to expand the use of robotics for repeatable manufacturing tasks, but has also expanded and enriched the role of human workers in personalizing features for individual customers.

NETWORK POWERED

Companies that are network powered use digital technologies to change onetime purchases into ongoing services, actively participate in external networks, and nurture broadly inclusive ecosystems to bring new innovations to customers sooner.

We are exiting the era of inanimate objects and entering the world of smart products and services. Billions of physical items already in existence will in the next decade become digital devices, connected and communicating not just with each other but also with the internet of things—the complete supply chain that builds, sells, and supports them.

Today's simple IoT applications, such as smart thermostats and programmable lighting, will expand to include component parts and even the raw materials from which products are made, keeping track of their whereabouts, working status, and use throughout the product lifecycle.

Products and services are blurring as smart products continue to sense, learn, and change in response to vast amounts of aggregated data. The insights they provide are unlocking a treasure trove of trapped value across all four levels, promising to substantially improve the efficiency of sourcing, manufacturing, distribution, retailing, and customer support.

Manufacturers in particular find themselves on the cusp of a new industrial revolution, driven by the continued convergence of the digital and physical worlds. Consider Caterpillar, which makes smart use of data generated from connected machines through its Cat Connect platform. Cat Connect relays key data on equipment performance to mine operators, who then analyze the data and make decisions on how to improve efficiency, boost productivity, and enhance job-site safety. Using Cat Connect, machines at the construction firm Strack Inc. can run for forty-eight hours straight, reducing fuel costs by 40 percent.

Network-powered companies build smarter manufacturing and supply chains, connecting processes and providers throughout production using IoT and AI technologies to cultivate a robust, creative ecosystem. They actively develop new products and services through collaboration, open innovation, and crowd engagement.

Increasingly, the value releasers in our study are combating disruption by building these ecosystems, forging deep links to partners who possess complementary skills and technologies that can be quickly deployed and scaled as opportunities arise. They're also expanding and focusing their activities in corporate venture capital, investing in start-ups alongside traditional venture capitalists. They actively participate as mentors and investors in internal start-up incubators, external accelerators, and other sources of innovation and early experimentation.

These are significant changes from even the recent past, when companies witnessing rising levels of uncertainty and volatility in their industries were encouraged to sit back and observe while others incurred the costs of experimentation, only then moving to outexecute them as "fast followers."

But in the digital age, early learners can earn a sizeable advantage. They experiment with new technologies, launch prototypes, and study the results, often dramatically reducing the time to develop new products. Early learners may already be working on subsequent versions while followers, even fast ones, are still trying to copy the first. Watching, waiting, and exploiting the innovations of others no longer works.

Remember as well that value gets trapped at the industry level when an infrastructure improvement, such as an open marketplace, would benefit everyone in the supply chain, but no single company has the incentive to develop it. Building flexible ecosystems solves that problem, sharing the value among the participants and the manager of the ecosystem itself, who may be an outsider, perhaps a technology platform company such as AWS, Microsoft, Google, or Alibaba.

The diffusion of trapped value across an industry is one of the obstacles holding back even more investment in the IoT. For those with the foresight to get in early, however, the payoff may be huge. The Bosch Group, the venerable German industrial giant, has been investing in the IoT since 2008, with an acquisition that became Bosch Software Innovations. BSI has designed, developed, and carried out over 250 IoT projects, piloting more than a hundred innovations in Bosch's own factories.

The strategy is bearing fruit. In 2017, the company sold nearly forty million web-enabled products, including sensors, devices, and other connected machines. By the end of this decade, the company reports, all of its electrical product classes will be connected to the internet.

And consider leading bedding manufacturer Sleep Number, which since 2017 has pivoted from a product company toward a network-powered IoT giant. Its revolutionary new offering, the 360 Smart Bed, includes embedded sensors that track heart rate, motion, and breathing. The company's patented SleepIQ technology interfaces with the sensors, reading hundreds of measurements per second. Every night, SleepIQ tracks hundreds of thousands of "sleep sessions," and analyzes over 8.5 billion biometric data points.

The 360 Smart Bed automatically adjusts firmness and support based on user movements, and can make recommendations on how to improve every aspect of a user's sleep behaviors, clearly an enormous source of trapped value for most humans.

Sleep data can also be combined with daytime activity tracking devices, including Fitbits and smart watches, all on a single smartphone app. Future applications will identify and warn of a heart attack and detect sleep apnea, which affects tens of millions of sleepers.

All this helps move the company deeper into an emerging wellness ecosystem. An ongoing collaboration between Sleep Number and the National Football League, for example, is building a database of the sleep habits of its high-performance athletes. Early users are convinced the system has helped them wake up more energized, with improved reaction time and focus.

Sleep Number hopes to use the data it's collecting from eighteen hundred players to help pinpoint the specific sleep needs of football players, and potentially that of different kinds of players: kickers, receivers, and quarterbacks, for example. The company is working with Pro Football Focus, which grades and ranks each player through analytics and statistics, looking for correlations between sleep and performance on the field.

Despite these early successes, however, few consumer-facing companies have yet to make any investments in the IoT. And while getting there first is no guarantee of long-term release of trapped value, it is clearly helping Sleep Number understand the potential and requirements for playing a central role in the emergence of an applied sleep science.

Partnerships like these are more than just onetime buyer-seller interactions. They are ongoing collaborations in which every participant leverages their own network assets and expertise, synchronizing and pacing investments together. Each innovation has a return well beyond the participants' balance sheets.

Consider German conglomerate Siemens, which has constructed an ecosystem around its cloud-based, open IoT operating system MindSphere, partnering with app developers, system integrators, technology partners, and infrastructure providers that include companies such as Accenture, Amazon, SAP, and Microsoft.

The MindSphere platform collects data from devices and other assets on the manufacturing shop floor, providing an open interface to consolidate operational and maintenance data from a wide range of connected equipment. Using analytic tools from Siemens and other app developers, participants are turning factories into digital-first assets that can be more fully automated and optimized.

PUTTING INNOVATION TO WORK

We started this chapter with an overview of efforts by Haier to unlock trapped value across all four levels: enterprise, industry, consumer, and society. Let's look further to see how using a combination of the winning strategies can multiply innovation and unlock even more trapped value. With Haier we can see the application of all seven. Let's look more closely at the company's integration and combination of technology propelled, hyper relevant, data driven, network powered, asset smart, and talent rich.

Haier began its pivot by becoming technology propelled, referring to itself not as an appliance company but a platform for software-enabled businesses. That claim goes beyond simple buzzwords. When demand for white goods declined as China's urban housing market slowed, the company made a strategic bet by providing retailing and logistics services to the burgeoning e-commerce sector in rural China.

A hosted platform for vendors called Shun Guang signed up a hundred thousand small businesses in just a few years. These retailers can now sell Haier products and other brands through the app, and order stock replenishment on demand. Customers can customize color and other options directly through the Haier website, with production routed to a smart factory.

Haier also practices hyper relevance by sensing and addressing changing customer needs, working directly with consumers to design and customize specific appliances.

In one example, the company learned from extensive WeChat discussions it hosts for parents about growing concerns with the impact of lengthy screen time on the developing eyes of young children. Working closely with the parents, Haier developed the iSee mini, a portable projector that wirelessly displays content on any surface, reducing reliance on digital devices. Based on early feedback, the company improved the brightness of early versions, and added built-in educational software.

Haier is data driven. It tracks detailed metrics about each of its microenterprises, including how much users are involved in new product development, and the percentage of profits that come from interactions with ecosystem partners. Every employee is focused on engaging with and responding to consumers, with pay linked to measured outcomes. When a product fails to meet target sales and interactions, incentive compensation is reduced.

Haier has become network powered by optimizing its manufacturing and supply chains, relying on its relationships to respond to fast-changing technologies and user demands. The Haier Open Partnership Ecosystem (HOPE), like InnoCentive, allows internal product teams and outside subscribers to bid out their most challenging engineering and design problems to a growing network of unaffiliated problem solvers.

HOPE now has over two million members. Every month, five hundred projects are registered, with more than two hundred innovation projects successfully incubated annually. Specialized ecosystems have emerged for air, food, body care, water, and health.

Haier is also asset smart. The company has acquired GE's appliance unit in the United States, Sanyo in Japan, and Fisher & Paykel in New Zealand to upgrade its global supply chain and customer reach. CEO Zhang Ruimin sees Haier's core as a platform upon which to collaborate with internal and external stakeholders equally.

The company's microenterprises, for example, contract for manufacturing, financial, technology, and human resources in an open environment. Each product finds its most efficient combination of internal and external suppliers, assemblers, and distribution channels, pushing Haier further from a traditional industrial giant and closer to a platform business.

Finally, Haier is talent rich, closing the gap between employees and customers by redeploying roughly sixty-four thousand employees into 180 microenterprises, each of which elects its own leader, secures its own resources, and accounts for (and shares in) its own profit and loss.

The microenterprises have the freedom, authority, and incentive to make decisions very quickly, and have launched dozens of innovative products in existing markets and in markets adjacent to Haier's traditional brands. Employees can also easily move from one microenterprise to another. And if the team feels it can do better outside the networked architecture of the company, it can spin off, leaving Haier as investor rather than employer.

In the cutthroat world of home-appliance manufacturing, a level of elasticity and paranoia is essential. As Zhang said when asked by the *Economist* how he balances entrepreneurship with corporate control:

"We don't need to balance! An unsteady and dynamic environment is the best way to keep everyone flexible."

As Haier and the other examples in this chapter make clear, releasing trapped value happens by design, not accident. Like expert skiers, the most successful and sustained value releasers keep turning—fluidly, regularly, and with great speed.

And while experts make it look easy, at some point they all mastered the art of choosing when and where to turn, planting their pole in the ground, and using momentum to rotate to the next pivot. Over time, the process becomes automatic. Experts just do it, without thinking about the mechanics of what they are doing.

The seven winning strategies are the ski poles of the wise pivot, your stakes in the ground and your centers of gravity. They determine the type of trapped value you'll target, where to find it, and which combination you'll need to release it.

But just as with learning to ski, releasing trapped value requires no small amount of courage, daring, and falling. Disruptive innovations built with the latest emerging technologies are adding to the inventory of trapped value in every industry, generating both opportunity and risk. Few companies are able to convert that potential into reality. Fewer still can do it more than once.

Over the last five years, in fact, the return on innovation spending overall has actually declined, and declined dramatically. Most large companies, it seems, are unable to apply innovation fast enough to drive growth while avoiding obsolescence—victims of the wrong turns.

There is, however, reason for optimism. Some companies—our trapped value releasers—have bucked this trend, translating their innovation investments into accelerated growth. In the past five years, these companies have outgrown their peers on every key measure, and expect to continue on that trajectory for the foreseeable future.

They pursue innovation with commitment and discipline, essential virtues in overcoming the wrong turns. They have embraced the search and rescue of trapped value as a core tenet of their corporate culture, starting at the top. More than that, they have found ways to achieve not just one successful application of the winning strategies, but to innovate as a matter of course.

Competitive advantage, after all, is defined as sustainable above-average performance. Anyone can get lucky once. To make innovation your core product requires much more.

The second part of this book puts it all together: the search for trapped value, overcoming the wrong turns, and mastering the winning strategies. The next step will be to embed those skills throughout your organization, embracing an approach to strategy and execution that applies creative energies not just yesterday, today, or tomorrow, but to all three. At the same time.

So the first thing you'll need to do is invent a time machine. We'll show you how.

part two
THE WISE PIVOT

chapter 4

THE WISE PIVOT

Discovering Value and Creating Growth
in the Old, the Now, and the New

THE PREVIOUS CHAPTERS explored how companies—young and old, big and small, public and private—successfully targeted and released trapped value by avoiding the seven wrong turns and focusing instead on the seven winning strategies.

But the technology revolution is far from over. As both big bang and compressive disruption continue remaking industries in unpredictable ways, releasing even large quantities of trapped value isn't a onetime event. The companies we identified as trapped value releasers were those that consistently outperformed their peers both in current and future value creation. They simultaneously improved current earnings and future earning potential not just once, but year after year, over and over again.

The need for a dramatically different approach to strategy and execution is obvious. Yet, even as CEOs across industries see with clarity the need to change, most of them struggle to translate vision into action. Fewer still have the tools to steer their organizations decisively and sustainably.

Why? For one thing, most companies remain overly focused on their core business, unable to recognize a future coming up faster all the time, not unlike the car you see in your side-view mirror that is, as the warning puts it, closer than it appears.

Others neglect their core in a chaotic me-too dash to the new, leaving themselves unable to muster the investment capacity they need, or the infrastructure required, to support future pivots.

A truly wise pivot is one that is repeatable. That means managing core assets not as discrete resources with diminishing value from creation through to retirement, but as a dynamic investment portfolio, continually rebalanced across the three different lifecycle stages we refer to as the old, the now, and the new.

The "old" are products and services that have reached the peak of their growth and either have, or are soon likely, to stall. The "now" are offerings in the middle of their development, growing rapidly but already shifting from a focus on innovation to one based on efficiency and eventual commoditization. The "new," finally, are emerging parts of your businesses just beginning their journey, whose speed and trajectory are largely unknown.

To pivot wisely means embracing a constantly evolving strategy, one that integrates all three stages as you manage your portfolio from one set of assets to the next, growing and reshaping your old core into a new one built with new technologies.

Here's how we made that real at Accenture, discovering in the process the tools and techniques of the wise pivot.

ACCENTURE STARTS ITS PIVOT

Accenture faced a series of existential threats in the first decade of the millennium. Our core consulting and technology businesses were being squeezed on several sides.

From the bottom, good-quality providers in India were offering global customers low-cost outsourcing for application development and maintenance, data centers, and other technology services.

From the top, hardware and software giants were leveraging proprietary products and their long-standing customer relationships to become massive services companies. They hastened the transition by taking advantage of the speed, customization, and cost benefits of new software development and cloud technologies, to move toward offering lower-priced substitutes for Accenture's professional services. This disruption threatened Accenture's strategic relationships with senior executives across the Global Fortune 500.

Pressure also came from Wall Street. Some investors worried that a rapid migration to the cloud by more and more businesses would seriously impact the business of installing and modifying packaged software, a service Accenture had been successful in for decades. Accenture's differentiation in the consulting and advanced technology industries was no longer as clear to investors and industry analysts.

By 2013, Accenture had successfully responded to the initial threat of outsourcing companies based in India. We built our Advanced Technology Centers, combining the lower costs of offshore operations with deep client relationships based on trust and experience, one of our competitive advantages. These centers allow us to offer our clients competitively priced solutions, with the added benefit, mostly missing from our competitors' offerings, of onshore, hands-on industry and technology experts.

We now have over fifty of these software and operations factories, including in growth markets such as India and China, where we can leverage industry and software development expertise to compete against the outsourcers.

We also pivoted much of our traditional consulting practice away from back-office systems to applications that engaged directly with our clients' customers, in the process expanding our services business for mobile applications development and cloud operations.

To speed development work, we automated much of the error-prone and time-consuming process of testing new software, enhanced our software engineering tools, and extended partnerships with leading packaged software providers, including SAP, Oracle, Salesforce, and Microsoft. Reducing the need for human testers using our Touchless Testing platform demonstrably improved the speed with which new installations of these products could be debugged, in some cases by 50 percent.

At the same time that our traditional consulting markets faced increased competition, happily, the internet revolution was creating enormous new opportunities for us in digital services. Just a partial list includes advertising, social media, advanced customer interactions, and the integration of robotics, artificial intelligence, and other new technologies into the supply chains of the industries we served.

These technologies created new industries and new ecosystems of businesses that helped incumbent enterprises become digital first. Within those ecosystems, demand was growing fast for expertise in social media, mobile computing, data analytics, and cloud computing.

So as part of our move to becoming digital-first consultants, we launched new practice areas in business analytics, cybersecurity, applied AI, blockchain, virtual reality, and other emerging disruptors. To support the emerging internet of things ecosystem, we created a business unit called Industry X.o, which leverages experts in product innovation and connected device technologies with new digital tools our clients use to build their own smart products.

The problem was that these new service areas didn't quite line up with our brand or business model, which slowed their growth and limited their impact on Accenture's performance overall. As we struggled to incorporate them, we found ourselves more at risk of what we described earlier as compressive disruption. All the signs were there—growth and profits were being squeezed by new competitors, while the risk of substitution over time was growing, slowly but surely.

After a couple of bumpy quarterly earnings reports in 2014, senior management got both a reality check and a wake-up call.

We needed a new plan. As early as 2013, then-Accenture CEO Pierre Nanterme laid out what he named the "Ambition 2020" framework. It called for Accenture to become the world's leading professional services player at the intersection of business and technology. This was quite a step, since for the entire history of Accenture we had always been a much smaller competitor in an industry dominated by tech giants like IBM.

Ambition 2020 posed a serious challenge to the organization. Omar Abbosh, in particular, remembers being surprised when he first heard the details at the global management committee meeting where it was introduced. What was so shocking was how ambitious and all-encompassing it was across so many areas—not just for our services or geographic footprint, but for our brand, our financial architecture, our ways of working, our investments in software and technology, our ecosystem, and our philanthropic activity.

For Omar, the challenge became personal when at the end of 2014 he was appointed Accenture's chief strategy officer, tasked with making Ambition 2020 a reality.

"When I first sat down with my new team in early 2015," he says, "I posed three questions: How will Accenture become embedded in the fabric of the technology sector? How will we become a bigger force in global business in general? What conditions need to be true for us to double our market capitalization, from $50 billion to $100 billion?"

His new strategy came from studying the lifecycles of different technology markets, ranging from mainframe computers to the World Wide Web to the internet of things and AI. Omar quickly realized that the real source of disruption for incumbent businesses like ours wasn't so much new entrants to the market as it was the innovation and the new technologies powering them—the ones we described in chapter 1.

In the past, successful companies like Accenture focused on building products and services whose underlying technologies were at the mature end of their lifecycle, when markets were large and stable.

But that approach wasn't going to work in a world of constant technology-driven disruption, plenty of which was already coming at us in all our core markets. After all, as we noted earlier, digital technologies continue to experience declining prices for core components, including sensors, cameras, memory, and microprocessors, translating to innovative combinations that quickly become better and cheaper.

In response, consumers increasingly embrace the new en masse. So what was once a long lag between early adoption and mainstream use is becoming shorter all the time. As users demand offerings that take full advantage of the features and functions the new technologies make possible, a window of opportunity can open suddenly: the trapped value gap.

That opening attracts the most valuable innovation and the most disruptive innovators at the beginning of new markets, just as supportive ecosystems are forming. The trapped value gap grows suddenly and often closes almost as quickly. If you aren't there at the beginning, increasingly there's little chance of becoming a significant player in those ecosystems later, let alone profiting from them.

That meant we had to swallow hard and change one of our most strongly held beliefs: that Accenture's key success factor was to wait for new technologies to become widely adopted and relatively low risk before developing services to support their implementation. When, in other words, our traditional consulting and technology clients were ready to adopt them. Our approach had been to make our move then, scaling up our ability to provide advice and support, a strategy management experts call "fast following."

Given the accelerating pace of change, following fast wasn't going to be fast enough. We would need to enter new markets as soon as business opportunities appeared, even if it wasn't entirely clear how big those markets might become, and who all the supply chain participants—buyers, suppliers, competitors, and other stakeholders—would be.

There was vigorous debate in the management committee about so momentous a change. In the final analysis, we had to acknowledge that the risks of obsolescence and substitution of our core offerings were far worse than the cultural shift we would need to navigate to overcome those risks.

In a world of rapidly improving technologies, with disruptive innovations appearing faster and moving ever-more quickly from experimentation to full market acceptance, the time had come to completely rethink our strategies for each of our core businesses. We needed to view our portfolio of offerings in a very different way, one that was compatible with the speed of technology and accompanying business change—adapted, in other words, to a world of continuous disruption.

THE OLD, THE NOW, AND THE NEW

As hard as it was, accepting the continuous nature of digital disruption led us to the most important insight undergirding the wise pivot: for the foreseeable future, we were going to need to make major investments in innovation. Investments that required not just continued income from today's offerings but new growth—more revenue, more profits, and new customers.

That meant we could not, and must not, abandon our business in the old or the now and devote all our resources to getting ready for the new. We had to generate more profit out of today's core, using some of the very technologies disrupting it.

Rather than cutting investment in older products and services to feed a fast move to the future, in other words, we needed to do just the opposite. We needed to renew and restart investment in older businesses whose growth had slowed, even knowing that in their current form, their days were numbered.

At the same time, we had to accelerate and expand investment in newer, still-growing businesses, generating the kind of profits we were used to seeing in mature markets.

Finally, we needed to take and apply that renewed and expanded growth, and the extra revenue it produced, to reach economies of scale in emerging businesses as quickly as possible.

By carefully planning these turns, we found we could accelerate growth in all three lifecycle stages at the same time, creating an engine for repeated and sustainable pivots, squeezing out essential, if diminishing, trapped value from the old and the now to apply as fuel for getting to one fast-approaching new after another.

As we developed the framework for what became the wise pivot, we revisited much of a generation of earlier management thinking, and in particular a long shelf of books that advised businesses on how to think about strategy and competition in tomorrow's markets.

Though helpful, the conventional wisdom proved incomplete. In their 1994 book *Competing for the Future*, for example, business school professors Gary Hamel and the late C. K. Prahalad advised companies to jump-start entry into new markets by focusing on a "core competence," which they defined as "a harmonized combination of multiple resources and skills that distinguish a firm in the marketplace."

A business's core competence, they explained, provided the momentum needed for success in future markets, engagement with future customers, and differentiation from future competitors. That, according to the authors, is how businesses achieve competitive advantage in tomorrow's markets and industries.

Preparing today for tomorrow's markets is still as important as it ever was. But what many leaders following the advice of Hamel and Prahalad, and others, lost sight of was what made them successful in the first place: today's products and services. Even more important were the deep relationships with customers, suppliers, and other stakeholders, as well as industry and technology expertise, and corporate values and culture.

These assets and resources form the core of your business. Yet in the rush to get to the new, businesses were leaving them behind, abandoned and mistreated, undermining any hope of using them as the foundation for differentiation in the future.

It's not enough simply to identify abstract competencies and project them into new markets. In a world of new technologies that rapidly create markets and enable competitors new and old, it's just as important to retain and refine your focus on the concrete realities of today's offerings, today's markets, and today's technologies.

For us, that insight led to the sobering reality that increasingly powerful waves of innovative technology would continue to disrupt our businesses, and would do so at an accelerating pace.

In the short term, for example, neither our skills nor our culture lined up well with the kind of new digital services clients were beginning to demand. In the longer term, Accenture's expert professionals were at risk of being displaced by software and new communications networks that could substitute for what they were doing.

Looking deeper still into the future, we lacked the kind of R&D capacity needed to identify and embrace the next generation of disruptive technologies and the opportunities they would generate. Yet we now needed to do so consistently faster than competitors old and new.

We couldn't fuel the changes needed to juggle these three different time frames by continuing to grow in the traditional way: by building or acquiring new businesses while exiting those that were old and rapidly maturing. Instead, we would need to pivot simultaneously inside the different stages in the lifecycle of our offerings: the old, the now, and the new.

To explain the concept of the wise pivot, we graphed the three lifecycle stages along what mathematicians call the "S-curve." Business academics have long argued that S-curves map the typical rise and eventual decline of revenues and profits from once novel products and services. They show that as the price and performance of new products and services improve through continued technology innovation and economies of scale, users will embrace them slowly at first (the so-called early adopters) and then more rapidly (the majority). Figure 4.1 shows the expected S-curves of the old, the now, and the new, noting where in the lifecycle you'd typically find business offerings in each stage.

As figure 4.1 suggests, businesses are constantly moving through all three stages at the same time. As markets become saturated, the next wave of disruption has already begun. New enabling technologies are

Figure 4.1 Three Stages of the S-curve

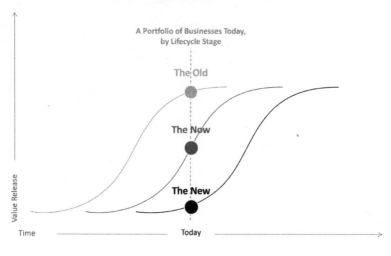

Value Release over Time

introduced, tested, and then mature. Offerings built around them generate the next S-curve, and so on.

The growing trapped value gap, however, offered us opportunities to improve the performance of each lifecycle stage beyond the assumed S-curve. By investing more strategically, in fact, we found that we could dramatically alter the shapes of the respective curves of our old, now, and new, releasing trapped value in all three at once.

Employing new technologies to unleash innovation improved revenues and profits across all three S-curves. The opportunities for accelerated growth were, naturally, greater the earlier we applied more investment. But offerings at every point on their respective curves had growth potential—potential that competitors focused entirely on the future weren't seeing.

Figure 4.2 reflects the new S-curve shapes we achieved at each stage. The growth in older consulting services, such as systems integration and outsourcing, which had been slowing, was restarted. Revenue growth in newer services, including digital marketing and our other digital-first offerings, was accelerated.

Most dramatic of all, supercharged investment in the new allowed us to quickly develop expertise in emerging technologies, jump-starting

Figure 4.2 Releasing Trapped Value in the Old, the Now, and the New

Value Release over Time

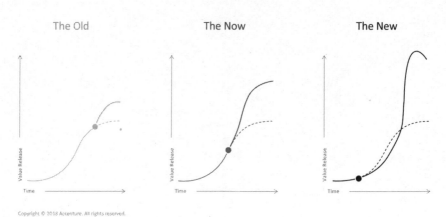

the introduction of unique offerings using AI, cybersecurity, cloud services, virtual reality, and other new technologies, along with broader industry disruptors including the IoT. We were able to reach new customers and achieve economies of scale much more rapidly.

Stretching the shape of all three S-curves wasn't easy. It required significant alterations to both the structure and operation of our organization. We had to radically reengineer old businesses through technology-led innovation, and ramp up investment in today's most profitable offerings to grow them faster. We also sped up the launch of new businesses, both organically and through a greatly expanded acquisition program that targeted emerging disruptors.

Adopting the kind of continuous strategy the wise pivot requires also demanded a major reset in investment thinking. In the conventional model, managers are traditionally taught to treat investments throughout the lifecycle of products and services in a linear fashion from birth to death. Investment is focused on the front end, building new capabilities and launching new products and services through research and development.

Once a business is up and running, however, the focus shifts to squeezing out the most profit possible, streamlining processes in a search for incremental improvements and measurable gains in market share.

As once unique offerings became commodities offered by others at or near cost, managers were taught to exit, selling off, if possible, mature assets, including factories and distribution networks, while downsizing employees whose careers were defined by old products and the technologies that drove them.

That approach doesn't work in a world of accelerating, technology-driven disruption. For one thing, as we learned, even businesses nearing the end of profitability have the potential for a rich second life if given the right fuel. Likewise, increasing investment in new technologies can leapfrog today's successful product over those of competitors, gaining not just market share but new customers.

And in the fast-approaching new, investments in traditional, proprietary R&D may not assure your place in future markets and future products. Instead, you'll need to secure a starting position in emerging industry ecosystems, not just by launching successful new products, but by doing so with the ability and capacity to rapidly scale production and delivery of them when mainstream customers are ready to make the leap—a leap that arrives more quickly all the time.

ACCENTURE EXECUTES ITS PIVOT

Making your own wise pivot will require, as it did for us, substantial changes in the allocation of resources within and across the three life-cycle stages of the old, now, and new. In essence, that's the difference between a simple pivot from one product, or one set of customers, to the next, and a wise pivot in all three lifecycle stages at once. It is the difference between what popular management thinking refers to as "business transformation" and a wise pivot in the old, the now, and the new, again and again.

Easy to say, hard to do. For us, executing this strategy meant overcoming some pretty massive obstacles. Our brand and market positioning, for example, were all about delivery of complex business change, typically underpinned by large information systems and their customization for specific industries and clients. The emphasis was on dependable outcomes and predictable delivery.

Now we needed to change that positioning, becoming more edgy and innovation oriented, forcing our business out of the back office and into new territory, such as the design and implementation of new consumer services and user experiences.

A second obstacle was that the skills we needed to deliver this new set of offerings were scarce, typically residing in small entrepreneurial companies and start-ups. The Silicon Valley mind-set of those companies, and the employees who worked there, were not an obvious fit with Accenture's culture at the time. Frankly, like many large companies, we had a poor track record when it came to buying and integrating small companies.

Third, our investment, budgeting, and resource allocation processes were fully optimized around the efficient operation of our then core. The reality of compressive disruption, however, required a shift from maintaining the existing core to renewed investment. This was a critical insight for us, one that would require overhaul of much of our business model and processes.

The scope of our pivot to the future was set, as always, by the needs of our clients. Omar and his team took as a starting point the strategies businesses would need to drive success in a digital era, such as the ability to increase brand relevance. These approaches were later organized as the seven winning strategies.

He also needed to increase the level of discretion in the investment budgets themselves, dealing with what we affectionately referred to as "permafrost": investment profiles locked in during previous years.

As clients began adopting the winning strategies to fuel their own pivots, we asked ourselves a simple question: What kinds of industry and technology specialization would we need to offer to help them succeed?

In some sense, that's a question Accenture's leaders have continually asked. As a professional services firm, our differentiation has always been our ability to guide managers undertaking large-scale investments in new innovations. Our core skill is and has been managing the intersection of new technologies and practical business applications that can employ them, delivering the kind of competitive advantage and measurable value creation that justified our clients' investments.

Now we needed to enhance those capabilities, pivoting from the mature technologies we knew best to the next generation of disruptors we saw approaching fast—in effect, building our own new core.

But which new technologies should we focus on? Here Accenture's leadership team looked to the trapped value gaps that challenged clients in the industries we served. Given our assessment of their biggest opportunities, we zeroed in on several we believed could quickly generate new businesses capable of supporting the kind of rapid scaling needed to make them profitable. These included interactive services (including AI), mobile services, data analytics, cloud migration, and cybersecurity.

From there, the next step was to build those new businesses quickly and efficiently, through a combination of home-grown innovation, large-scale reskilling of our employees, acquisitions of leading companies already delivering solutions, strategic investments in start-ups with promising offerings we could leverage, and partnerships with leading providers of the new technologies we targeted.

Truly reinventing Accenture proved to be a challenge not just of insight and smart strategy. It required bold actions and real change—the kind of change that only comes from significant reallocation of resources driven from the top.

What changes in emphasis and approach would be required to achieve Ambition 2020? What resources and assets would need to be reconsidered, reallocated, and restarted? What levers would we need to pull?

There are, of course, an unlimited number of ways companies can allocate their resources. Our own experience led us to organize around three key areas: innovation, finance, and people. Our reinvention required us to look carefully at how we were investing in each of them. We have made numerous adjustments, some big and some small, throughout the course of our ongoing wise pivot.

Here are some of the real changes we've already made:

THE INNOVATION PIVOT— To break the mold of being a fast follower, we had to go beyond just creating new services. We needed to create a new business architecture, as well as a completely different approach to investing.

Accenture's scope of businesses was quite broad, ranging from strategy consulting to process outsourcing, so our new business architecture was designed to reflect the fact that our people operated in distinct markets with different customers and different competitors.

This meant setting different cost structures for Accenture Strategy, for example, as compared to Accenture Interactive. It meant different career paths and performance measures, and accepting different work styles. The folks developing new customer-experience technologies at our design agencies couldn't really be hired, trained, or evaluated using the same tools and criteria as those working on military-intelligence cybersecurity missions.

As you can imagine, creating brand new business entities such as Accenture Interactive and Accenture Security, initially composed of pieces extracted from existing business units, was not all smooth sailing. As in any company, senior leaders were mindful of their own domains and responsibilities, leading to some predictable friction.

What made our pivot possible, however, was the management committee's strong alignment. A clear vision of where the strategy was intended to take us made it easier for committee members to accept, and even accelerate, the changes in organization and control required for success.

Finally, resolving questions of business architecture demanded clarity on the scope of the business. For example, what would be our position on owning proprietary software products? We had to hammer out disagreements about the continued value of some of our existing software product investments, particularly about the synergies they did or didn't have with our service businesses.

One concrete result of that debate was the creation of a joint venture with private equity investment group Apax Partners, where we relocated Duck Creek Technologies, a previously acquired developer of software for the insurance industry. The joint venture allowed us to continue advancing the frontier for industry automation, but without all the challenges for Accenture that sole ownership entails.

But the biggest change to our approach to innovation was yet to come.

We understood that we could never reinvent our core, let alone scale its next incarnation, without establishing and committing resources to innovation. To best realize the potential of a global organization and capture trapped value across all three lifecycle stages, we deployed and refined what we call our "innovation architecture." This is a collection of facilities around the world, each populated by people whose job it is to focus innovation for our clients at different stages of market maturity; that is, at different points on the S-curves of specific technologies.

That architecture, detailed in figure 4.3, was built principally to help co-create client solutions. But it also serves as our own innovation engine. Its breadth, we believe, is unique.

At The Dock, for example, our Dublin-based innovation hub, four hundred industry specialists, designers, and IoT, AI, and analytics experts work with clients, university researchers, and start-ups to incubate, prototype, and pilot new technologies in a dynamic environment. The focus is on testing the application of these technologies to different industries, developing relationships with providers and early users, and sharing best practices.

One example of work at The Dock involves ID2020, a global alliance deploying biometric and blockchain technology to help approximately one-sixth of the world's population—over a billion people—who cannot fully participate in cultural, political, economic, and social life because they lack even the most basic documentation of their identity.

The ID2020 system will capture fingerprints, iris scans, voiceprints, and other individual data sources and store them on a secure, distributed database. After that, every life event—health-care visit, job, education, marriage, and child birth—will be recorded and added to the individual's record. This will make it possible to verify citizenship, employment, and entitlement to vote, travel, and other government benefits.

One measure of the benefits our innovation architecture provides has been substantial growth in intellectual property. Our patent portfolio, for example, has greatly expanded in areas such as artificial intelligence, cybersecurity, drones, virtual agents, and the internet of things. Since 2012, we've filed hundreds of applications for emerging technologies, including quantum computing, smart robotics, blockchain, extended reality, and AI. As of 2019, we had over seven thousand patents and patent applications worldwide, over four thousand of them for inventions in the new.

Figure 4.3 Accenture's Innovation Architecture

ACCENTURE RESEARCH

280+
Research experts in 23 countries

Thought Leadership

Tech Vision, annual report of the top 5 technology trends

AI is the Future of Growth

Creating Artificial Data for Data Science

The Smart Way to Open your Innovation Process

What Every CEO should know about Blockchain

ACCENTURE VENTURES

10
Countries running Open Innovation

175
Strategic Partnerships

24
Equity investments

5000+
Startups on our radar

Working with incubators including ParTech, 1871, and RocketSpace

ACCENTURE LABS

7
Lab locations, including: Bengaluru, Beijing, Dublin, Israel, DC, Silicon Valley, and Sophia Antipolis

5
R&D locations. Focus areas include AI, Cybersecurity, and Extended Reality

7000+
Pending and issued patents

ACCENTURE STUDIOS

30+
Digital and Liquid Studio locations

23
Liquid Studios opened

ACCENTURE INNOVATION CENTERS

1
Flagship innovation center, The Dock

100+
Innovation Centers located worldwide across technologies and industries

40+
Industries

ACCENTURE DELIVERY CENTERS

50+
Delivery Centers around the world

120+
Client countries served

While your architecture may not need to be as elaborate as ours, we believe that formalizing both the approach and the institutions responsible for coordinating and disseminating innovation across your organization is critical.

In any case, it's no longer enough simply to exile a small group of employees to a separate location and give them the job of figuring out how to make something out of oncoming disruptive technologies: the solution proposed for the so-called innovator's dilemma. That may have worked when disruptions were relatively few and far between. Now disruptive thinking must be ubiquitous and constant, as much a part of today's business and planning as tomorrow's.

THE FINANCIAL PIVOT—By 2015, our insights about the changing shape of the three S-curves made it clear that we needed to splice innovation expertise into our corporate DNA. The process of investing in each next set of services needed to be continual. A rotation to the new would not be a onetime event.

As strategists, we recognized that not only did our allocation of resources need to change, but also the ways in which we made them. This meant agreeing on the biggest innovation priorities for the business and then committing to fund them. Given that we hadn't yet developed major new sources of revenue, the only option was to raid the existing budgets of our biggest business units, looking in particular for spending that no longer lined up with our new priorities.

This did not increase Omar's popularity. But because all management committee members and their teams had taken part in developing the strategy, people at least understood why we had to do it. So we sold off assets that were no longer strategic, including real estate, and found ways to improve the utilization of our consultants' time.

We then took the hard-earned savings and refocused our investments across the old, the now, and the new. This included, in the short term, creating automated software development tools our consultants take with them in client work. At the other end of the spectrum, it included building out the new part of our portfolio, by helping to establish and work closely with start-up accelerators. One example is the FinTech Innovation Lab, which has raised over $1 billion to support entrepreneurs working to reimagine financial services using digital technology.

We also launched our own minority investing organization, Accenture Ventures, where our leaders take strategic stakes in emerging technology businesses already in the growth stage of development. Accenture Ventures, unlike the corporate venture capital funds of some companies, evaluates all its investments for their alignment to specific growth initiatives. A named sponsor inside Accenture then works closely with the portfolio company to shape its offerings to Accenture client needs.

One critical change came in the way we made these investments. We separated decisions about how much our company should allocate for investments overall from decisions about where Accenture needed to invest each year in order to properly execute our pivot. The former remained the responsibility of the chief financial officer, while Omar as the chief strategy officer took charge of the latter.

This assignment of responsibilities has an attractively simple logic, but it is not easy for most companies to achieve in practice. It worked for us because Pierre Nanterme, our then-CEO, believed strongly in the need to align investments with the strategy, and because CFO David Rowland and Omar had developed a strong partnership that made the division of responsibilities easy to manage.

We also needed to do better at completing acquisitions, both in terms of the speed with which we evaluated and closed deals and in bringing the acquired company's employees on board quickly, with as little stress as possible. This meant Omar had to work closely with other officers, including those in finance, operations, legal, and human resources, to create new processes for originating and closing deals, and then integrating the acquired companies quickly.

Historically, Accenture had been overly conservative about its acquisitions, demanding strong proof up front of an immediate and strong financial benefit before deals were approved. The result was that we had limited experience in acquiring and integrating other companies, which in turn led to some bad experiences the few times we actually did it.

For example, we found that once a deal closed, more than a dozen corporate functions, including human resources, operations, and IT, would immediately swoop in, overwhelming the founders and employees of the acquired company with well-meaning orientations, trainings, and compliance processes, distracting them from the market. That approach had to change.

Fortunately for Omar, he had spent many years as a strategy consultant helping clients with their own mergers and acquisitions. This background, coupled with the similar experience of other Accenture executives scattered across the company, and strong support from the marketing, legal, human resources, and corporate development functions, gave Omar the team he needed to take on Accenture's rigid approach.

In the end, that translated to three key improvements: dramatically increasing our speed in finding, reviewing, and closing acquisition deals; simplifying how the employees of acquired companies were brought on board; and establishing long-term accountability for sponsoring executives of each acquisition to make sure the results they promised to the capital committee were actually delivered.

In 2017, the growing momentum of our initial pivot encouraged us to step up the pace of acquisitions, deploying approximately $1.7 billion across thirty-seven transactions—nearly twice our investment in fiscal 2016—with the majority being acquisitions we deemed part of the new core.

These included SinnerSchrader, a digital agency in Germany, and Paris-based OCTO Technology, a leading digital consulting firm. For our fast-growing cloud business, we acquired DayNine, one of the largest providers of customized installations of enterprise software from Workday, which provides a single system for finance, human resources, and planning. In security, we acquired Arismore, a French company specializing in digital identity and access management, and iDefense, a cyber threat intelligence business.

We also strengthened our capabilities in the latest IT architectures, including the agile development methodology, with the acquisitions of SolutionsIQ in the United States and Concrete Solutions in Brazil. We continued to invest in deepening industry expertise, acquiring Kurt Salmon in retail, Invest Tech in capital markets, and Seabury Group in aviation.

THE PEOPLE PIVOT— The leadership team was fully on board with the need to get ahead of both big bang and compressive disruption heading our way. But what about the wider organization, now some 450,000 employees? To succeed with our wise pivot, we clearly needed new talent strategies.

First, we needed to help our Accenture managing directors, who run the day-to-day business of serving clients, understand what the new strategy demanded of them personally.

We started by surveying our top leaders on the characteristics they believed essential for success in the future. When the synthesis of this was presented to a receptive management committee, one thing everyone agreed on was that being a digital-first organization required continual reskilling.

Pivoting to the new would mean retraining and redeploying each and every one of our employees for a sometimes vaguely defined future, even as we asked them to dig in deeper to achieve revenue, quality, and market share gains in the present.

Management's responsibility, we agreed, was to make sure our people would have the skills they needed to serve current and future clients, able to compete head-on with competitors old and new. And to do all of that in a coordinated effort across a global footprint. So since 2015 we've invested approximately a billion dollars in employee education every year.

In addition to classroom learning at five global learning centers, the resource at the heart of our reskilling imperative is Accenture Connected Learning (ACL), a digital-learning environment that connects users directly to knowledge as well as to experts they can learn from.

ACL reaches more than 370,000 employees around the world. We offer tens of thousands of courses that have made it possible to redeploy over 220,000 technology professionals as experts in new technologies, including AI, cloud services, mobile applications, and security, all in less than three years.

Fortunately, Accenture is blessed to have more than 75 percent of its employees from the millennial generation, a cohort with a hunger to learn and to improve its own employability.

New learning content, in fact, is increasingly generated and distributed by our employees themselves, using crowdsourced collaboration spaces we call "learning boards." A typical learning board might include links to a dozen or so different sources, including YouTube videos, white papers, TED talks, articles, and self-assessment tests. Topics range from A (acute respiratory distress syndrome, relevant to our health-care practice) to Z (Zuora, a cloud software company).

For us, success in the wise pivot also requires an extremely diverse mix of people. All our leaders know that in addition to its being the right thing to do, inclusion is a business imperative.

But sometimes altering perceptions at the field level is hard. Why? Research in human resources shows that leaders hire and promote in their own image, and that people tend to follow role models they can relate to. What's more, we all suffer from unconscious biases. And across cultures, people have different expectations for their careers at different points in their lives. All these factors make moving the lever on diversity difficult.

Here, Accenture has experienced tremendous gains in recent years, thanks to the singular and uncompromising leadership of our then-CEO, Pierre Nanterme, who made inclusion and diversity a priority. By 2018, we had increased the number of women in our workforce to 42 percent. Women now comprise more than 45 percent of our new hires, putting us well on the way to our goal of gender balance by 2025.

Outside of Accenture, we're also working with Girls Who Code, a nonprofit organization working to increase the number of women in computer science. The goal is to help break up the "boy's club" of the digital economy. Our people host summer immersion programs and year-round Girls Who Code clubs across the United States, offering skills training and exposure to real-world mentorship opportunities in technology fields.

Achieving our goals in hiring, retraining, and diversity required a complete overhaul of our human resources function. Rankings and annual performance reviews have been largely eliminated, replaced with more direct day-to-day feedback. Employees with the same job title, such as "analyst," but with very different responsibilities, are now evaluated based on the work they really do rather than their title.

To combine the value of our acquisitions with our existing expertise, we also broadened the range of career paths available, successfully advancing the CEOs of some of our acquired companies into leadership roles elsewhere in Accenture.

Finally, we needed to retire what had been a core tenet of Accenture's corporate culture: that despite our size and geographic reach,

Accenture could still have a single set of processes, methodologies, and a culture that applied to everyone everywhere—our "one firm" model of operation.

While the one-firm model had served us well in the past, our continued expansion made it unsustainable. We have retained a single set of core values, of course, such as creating value for clients and respect for the individual, and hold all our people to the very high standards of our code of business ethics. Still, we recognize that delivering strategy advice to an investment bank in New York is not the same as running part of the bank's payment process in Bengaluru. We needed to have, and be comfortable with a truly diverse culture, a "culture of cultures." (We'll say more about that in a later chapter.)

One practical implication of a culture of cultures is that employees from differing backgrounds prefer and are better served by different work spaces. Our office layouts are no longer identical. Different functions and different geographies call for different designs.

This imperative really hit home for Omar when he became intimately involved in shaping Accenture's flagship innovation center, The Dock. The Dock features configurable work spaces, where industry experts, researchers, clients, and visiting university academics comingle, working on projects or just experimenting with a wealth of new technology products. He quickly saw firsthand how the look and feel of the working environment could have a profound effect not only on culture, but also on the ability to innovate.

PIVOTING TO THE FUTURE

It became clear to us early on that we were onto something big, not just in our own pivot, but in the new strategies and tactics we were creating to achieve it.

Very quickly, our enhanced investments in the old yielded improvements in core revenue. In addition to the cost savings that came from an unsentimental review of how we did business, investments in the new were driving fast growth, too. We were yielding results not just in our financials but, often surprisingly, in the reinvention of our core culture and long-standing assumptions about the kind of firm we were and would be.

We've now fully developed the skills to make strategic and often rapid-fire acquisitions of smaller and more nimble businesses while keeping the entrepreneurial, largely millennial talent of the acquired companies intact.

We devote a third of our investments to today's business, recognizing that it not only continues to provide crucial revenue but also is itself a profitable target for technology-based improvements.

The majority of our $1–1.7 billion in annual acquisitions since 2014, however, has been focused on investments in tomorrow's markets. We've acquired nearly a hundred companies, whose expertise includes everything from creating unique digital experiences to mobile programming interfaces. In 2018, notably, we added Mackevision, which developed special effects for *Game of Thrones*, giving our clients access to state-of-the-art 3D visualization, augmented and virtual reality, and animation.

Thirty of our other acquisitions came together to form Accenture Interactive, a business that marries digital marketing with our long-established expertise in creating compelling customer experiences. Accenture Interactive, which generated $6.5 billion in annual revenue in 2017, has become, for each of the last three years, the largest provider of digital marketing services in the world.

We now build solutions for clients that allow them not just to serve their customers, but to truly engage and collaborate with them. These include projects for customer-focused leaders like Disney and Carnival. For Disney, we helped develop the wearable MagicBands that park guests use to reserve ride times and restaurants, pay and arrange in-room delivery for anything in the park, and even open their hotel room doors.

On the investor relations front, Wall Street analysts were fully engaged in our pivot to the future. We gave regular reassurance that our new investments would not slow growth in the old business. That is, at least not until our new core emerged as both a substantial source of income and the engine driving accelerated innovation and even more sustainable future profits.

An existential threat—and the wise pivot approach it inspired us to develop—proved to be the greatest opportunity in Accenture's nearly sixty-year history. Investors approved. Between late 2014 and 2018, our market capitalization doubled, reflecting the creation of $50 billion in new value.

We are far from finished with our own reinvention, nor will we be any time soon. In the wise pivot, each rotation is followed by the next and the next, demanding a dynamic strategy that surfs regular waves of disruption. Markets driven by continuous technology-driven change demand a continuous response. As our research shows, increasingly that means every market, every industry, every geography—including yours.

>

We hope the story of Accenture's wise pivot illustrates the opportunities and risks in your own journey to find and release trapped value. In the next chapters, we'll highlight case studies of other value releasers who embraced their own pivots to grow across all three lifecycle stages, the subject we turn to next.

chapter 5

THE OLD, THE NOW, AND THE NEW

Restarting Growth, Accelerating Profits, and Scaling to Win

THE ONGOING TECHNOLOGY revolution has made it demonstrably clear that no market will go undisrupted for long. If you ever had the luxury to patiently develop and implement a strategic plan that assumed competitors and new entrants would stand still, that time has long passed.

Now, regardless of the age of your business or the maturity of your industry, disruptors big and small are visible on the horizon. And as any hiker can tell you, it's dangerous to confuse a clear view with actual distance.

The wise pivot mitigates the risk of uncertainty by developing strategies for all three stages of the business lifecycle: the old, the now, and the new. A winning portfolio requires balanced and integrated investment in all of them.

Now that you've seen the wise pivot in action, it's time to get tactical. Managing each of the three different lifecycle stages of your offerings will require you to throw out conventional wisdom and replace it with new pivot wisdom. You'll need to renew and restart mature businesses in the old, accelerate growth in your most important offerings in the now, and scale the growth of your new businesses to deliver profitability in the new. We'll show you how the companies we've worked with and studied developed the discipline to manage repeated and constant pivots, multiplying their impact through balance and focus.

FROM TUPELO, MISSISSIPPI, TO HOGWARTS SCHOOL OF WITCHCRAFT AND WIZARDRY

Let's begin by looking at technology and entertainment giant Comcast, and how the company embraced the wise pivot to create a winning portfolio.

Comcast's unique culture has helped its leaders make the kind of balanced wagers in the old, the now, and the new that are essential for successful pivots. From its humble beginnings as a local cable company in Tupelo, Mississippi, Comcast has become, over its fifty-year history, one of the most influential companies in the world—a powerhouse in television, movies, sports, wired and wireless broadband internet access, theme parks, and home security—with more to come.

The greatest challenge for Comcast, however, is the dizzying pace of technology change with which its managers must contend. In entertainment and communications, the trapped value gap keeps getting bigger, creating opportunity and risk in equal measure.

Yet, from the messy analog world of the 1970s and 1980s and its local cable television franchise wars, Comcast and its subsidiaries, including NBCUniversal, and now European pay-TV giant Sky, stand as a great example of an enterprise that successfully pivots around one unmovable fulcrum: the determination to become digital first, and do so as quickly as possible.

That's no small achievement. As with Accenture's own maturing core, Comcast's business faced multiple challenges during its wise pivot, including diminishing customer enthusiasm for traditional pay-TV bundles, the rising threat of Netflix and other internet-based streaming competitors, a generational shift to mobile displays and self-produced video content, historic changes in communications technology and its multilayered regulation, and the 2007–2008 financial crisis. To name just a few.

Still, CEO Brian Roberts (who succeeded his father, Ralph, the company's founder, in 2004) has managed to repeatedly re-create the company, yielding at each turn an enterprise that is bigger, stronger, and better equipped for an uncertain technological future.

That success was by no means a foregone conclusion. Indeed, some Wall Street analysts responded to Comcast's bold moves with skepticism. When the company scooped up NBCUniversal's broadcast, cable TV, movie studio, and theme-park assets from GE for nearly $40 billion in 2011, the deal raised eyebrows, with one of those analysts calling it a "strategic plan of yesterday."

What did a regulated communications company know about television, movies, or theme parks? How could it expect to rescue a floundering NBCUniversal, whose film division at the time ranked fifth in market share out of the six major studios, while the NBC broadcast network ranked last?

The Universal Studios Florida theme park, meanwhile, which opened in 1990, had struggled under multiple owners and the economic downturn of the late 2000s. Though attendance had begun to improve by the time the deal was completed, both the Universal Florida and Hollywood parks needed massive investment. And the parks, NBCUniversal CEO Steve Burke told investors in late 2011, were "probably the last thing on our list."

Comcast's leadership team was determined to find and release trapped value it was sure had long lain dormant in NBCUniversal's aging but still valuable intellectual property, doggedly applying many of the seven winning strategies in the process. An old culture of self-sufficiency was replaced with incentives for collaboration. In what the company calls its "Symphony" approach, every part of the business is now involved in the launch of new films, TV shows, and theme park attractions.

Comcast also invested heavily in new technologies and new content. It spent nearly $4 billion to acquire DreamWorks Animation, giving it access to the most advanced digital filmmaking expertise. Accelerated expansion of the parks, including the addition of popular new Harry Potter attractions, accounted for much of the company's $1.6 billion in capital spending in 2017, a 10 percent increase from the previous year.

The turnaround is nearly complete. In 2018, Universal ranked second out of the major studios in market share, behind only Disney, with franchise properties including *Jurassic Park* and *Despicable Me* improving Universal's share of US movie theater box office to 15 percent of the total. NBC television narrowly edged out CBS in total viewers for the first time since 2002, thanks to a string of hits including *The Voice*, *This Is Us*, and *The Good Place*.

Parks revenue grew 150 percent between 2011 and 2016, contributing more profit than the film unit and broadcast TV. Overall, revenue for NBCUniversal rose from $23 billion in 2012 to $33 billion in 2017.

In a span of about five years, Comcast took old-media entertainment assets and turned them into the scalable building blocks for a digital entertainment titan that can compete head-on with its global competitors.

Even as the company has breathed new life into NBCUniversal, however, Comcast's original pay-TV business faces daunting challenges. Older viewers are beginning to cut the cord. More ominous still, younger consumers are postponing signing up at all for traditional cable service.

Instead, millennials are cobbling together à la carte solutions from a growing number of internet-based streaming services such as Netflix, Amazon Video, Hulu (which Comcast partly owns but does not manage), Sling TV, and DirecTV Now. Their offerings include original produced and amateur content, "skinny bundles" of limited channels, and even individual networks such as HBO Go and CBS All Access. Even more disruptive streaming services from powerful content, technology, and distribution competitors including Disney, Apple, and Walmart are in development.

Comcast is contending simultaneously with the rise of all these new entrants. Additionally, there is the wild card of amateur video produced on the cheap by the consumers themselves, available on platforms such as YouTube, Snapchat, and Twitch, the latter featuring expert video gamers paid by viewers to watch them play. YouTube alone accounts for over a billion hours of viewing a month, more than traditional TV. Snapchat boasts ten billion video views per day by an audience that is 70 percent millennials. There, user-produced "stories" simply disappear after twenty-four hours.

Rather than exit the content distribution business under a barrage of big bang and compressive disruption, however, Comcast steadfastly focuses on releasing residual trapped value in pay-TV. By becoming technology propelled, data driven, and hyper relevant, Comcast was able to seamlessly pivot from analog to all-digital distribution between 2009 and 2013, for example, giving itself the pole position to offer future innovations in ultrahigh-definition, 3D, customized advertising and augmented reality video.

More recently, Comcast invested billions in its X1 software platform, which includes user-friendly and voice-activated programming interfaces for navigation of its own and third-party content, such as Netflix and YouTube. X1 likewise supports bingeable, on-demand viewing and includes a cloud-based digital video recorder (DVR) that allows users to access recordings from any device.

X1 has migrated from stand-alone hardware to software. The service runs not only on Comcast equipment but also on streaming services including Roku and Samsung's smart TVs, eliminating the need for a separate cable box.

Even as Comcast continues to innovate around its traditional pay-TV properties, the shift is on to rely more on revenue from internet access, providing a high-speed, reliable, multidevice service for consumers to access content from wherever they prefer. This includes a digital dashboard with parental controls, called xFi, which simplifies management of home Wi-Fi and IoT devices.

To support that pivot, the company has invested billions more in upgrading its core infrastructure, embedding fiber-optic cable deep into its network, and adopting the latest compression and channel-binding protocols from CableLabs, a research asset run as an industry consortium. By the end of 2018, Comcast was able to offer gigabit-speed internet to nearly every consumer and business customer across its US footprint.

Its pioneering Internet Essentials program, which offers access to low-income households for $9.95 a month, has signed up over six million new households since its launch in 2011. Acknowledging the shift in emphasis, in 2010 the company rebranded its bundled distribution assets—pay-TV, internet, and telephone—as "Xfinity."

Yet even the relatively newer businesses of phone and internet access face current and future technology disruption, as the trapped value gap in communications continues to widen. Telephone service, which Comcast disrupted in 2005 with the launch of internet-based digital voice technology over its cable infrastructure, is migrating from fixed home service to the high-speed mobile devices consumers adopted in record time.

The mobile threat, in fact, looms across Comcast's core businesses. Even ever-faster home internet may soon be challenged by mobile, with next-generation 5G networks promising speeds and reliability that could compete with fiber-optics. In response, the company cleverly flipped its lack of a cellular network from a competitive liability (relative to AT&T and Verizon) into an advantage, leveraging millions of in-home Wi-Fi access points into a nationwide network all its video and internet customers can use.

Looking further out, finally, Comcast is also investing heavily to scale in the new. The company's patent portfolio includes innovations in home automation and the internet of things. In particular, Comcast's acquisition of iControl Networks in 2017 brought with it patents relating to home security and home automation.

Like many of the value releasers in our research, Comcast also relies on corporate venture capital as a platform for early investment and access to innovations near the beginning of their lifecycle, when opportunities for releasing trapped value are their most potent.

Given the operating scale of Comcast's largest business units, the company can in turn offer robust collaborations with the companies in which it invests. To optimize its nearly $1.5 billion annual spend on employee health care, for example, Comcast was the first company to adopt services offered by portfolio company Accolade, which offers AI-driven advice to help employees navigate and maximize their health benefits.

Still, Comcast Ventures' investing philosophy is primarily focused on financial returns, on the assumption that realized value is a leading indicator of strategic value. Some early investments, including in electronic signature start-up DocuSign and grooming supplier Dollar Shave Club, completed successful public offerings or have been acquired. The fund has invested in everything from ride-sharing giant Lyft, to home design platform Houzz, group communication and collaboration software developer Slack, neighborhood social network Nextdoor, and news services including Vox and Cheddar.

FROM CONVENTIONAL WISDOM TO PIVOT WISDOM

For Comcast, as with every company in our study, there are of course no guarantees of success. Both big bang and compressive disruption are rampant in the company's core markets now and well into the future. But Comcast's balanced portfolio of investment in innovation, assets, and human capital across the three lifecycle stages has given the company its best hope for thriving in both the sudden and stealth decline of markets.

How did they do it? As with Accenture's own wise pivot, Comcast first had to avoid the wrong turns described earlier: management practices like innovating to Wall Street expectations or treating regulators as key customers. In the face of perpetual disruption, for Comcast such onetime business gospel was dangerously counterproductive.

The seven wrong turns, however, don't cover the full range of old thinking you'll have to shake off. Successfully building a portfolio of assets requires abandoning even more conventional wisdom of management.

Figure 5.1 The New Wisdom of Future Growth

Lifecycle Stage	Conventional Wisdom	Pivot Wisdom	Pivot Wisdom Logic
The Old	Exit Mature Businesses	Innovate to Create Investment Capacity	Companies can find new, higher levels of profitability in old businesses by applying technology
The Now	Milk the Cash Cow	Shoot for the Stars	Companies can no longer out-innovate the pace of technology change, so aggressive investment in growth markets is essential
The New	Get to the New	Scale to Win	Companies face more opportunities and more uncertainty, requiring deliberate innovation, experimentation, and ability to scale

Figure 5.1 introduces three new wisdoms and the old thinking they replace, one for each of the lifecycle stages in your portfolio. They

reflect radical shifts in both planning and execution. The new wisdoms follow the logic of the winning strategies, which are aimed at closing rather than falling further behind the trapped value gap.

In brief, you must improve your core capabilities, squeezing the last bits of profit from mature technologies (the old). You must also accelerate growth in offerings that might appear to others to be approaching their peak (the now). Finally, you must simultaneously embrace new technologies to create innovative products and services, preparing for rapid customer adoption (the new).

Together, following the pivot wisdoms will lead you to create a new core, ready to begin the process all over again.

As we learned firsthand, these new wisdoms represent a radical change in traditional strategy and execution. Yet, our research shows that most business leaders, even those who accept the reality of imminent and continued disruption, continue to apply linear approaches to managing their businesses. So be prepared. Our alternatives to the conventional wisdom may seem counterintuitive to managers trained in the business paradigms of an earlier era. Adopting them may cause substantial culture shock throughout your organization, and among key stakeholders too.

We'll look at each of the three new pivot wisdoms in detail in the rest of this chapter. For now, though, let's return to Comcast to see how each has been applied so far in the company's ongoing pivots:

THE OLD—Don't exit mature businesses prematurely. Instead, reinvest with new technologies to release trapped value that others overlook, and use the resulting profits as investment capacity for faster growth elsewhere.

At one time, commoditized products, services, and businesses were inevitably slated for exit, either by closing them down or selling them off. But thanks to the fast-growing trapped value gap, even businesses close to the end of their lifecycle can often experience a second life through careful application of innovation.

Investors and industry analysts believed that GE had gotten all there was to be had from the aging technology and intellectual property assets of NBCUniversal. Comcast saw something different: trapped value that could be released with new investment and integration with its distribution infrastructure. By unearthing the company's diamonds in the rough and applying a little polish, Comcast gave them a second life. NBCUniversal now drives revenue growth for its parent through content and product licensing, improved box office, and newly vibrant theme parks.

At the same time, Comcast doubled down on set-top box technology even as other pay-TV providers rushed to technical architectures that eliminated cable boxes and the costs of distributing and maintaining millions of them. The X1 platform unlocked trapped value for consumers with a dramatically improved interface, voice control, and cloud-based DVR services that removed the need for more expensive and feature-poor stand-alone solutions from TiVo and others.

By keeping its own hardware and software at the forefront, Comcast is now positioned to participate in personalized advertising and, as with new entrants including Amazon and Netflix, apply analytics to determine what new programming consumers want, how they want to watch it, and on which device.

THE NOW—Don't just milk your cash cows expecting that their productive lives can't be improved or degraded. Instead, recognize that new technologies create opportunities to extend their lifespan and expand the revenues and profits they produce.

Rather than starve a core business in the middle of its lifecycle, value releasers look for opportunities to stretch the S-curve and accelerate revenue growth and profits.

That's certainly how Comcast approaches investment in today's offerings. Seeing serious and unavoidable technology threats to the core technologies of its pay-TV business coming from the top, bottom, and sides, Comcast nonetheless continued to invest capital and innovation resources, infusing today's core with new technologies that improve their competitiveness.

While younger audiences may be reluctant to subscribe to the traditional bundle of channels, for example, baby boomers still value continued improvements in video quality, expanding channel options, and improved user interfaces. To attract millennials, Comcast has integrated its network with the streaming services those consumers are rapidly adopting, offering an alternative to à la carte solutions that are still expensive and relatively inconvenient.

Anticipating next-generation wireless technologies that may some-day offer strong competition for home internet access in speed, reliability, and mobility, Comcast has accelerated infrastructure investments, rebuilding its wired network for gigabit-speed internet well ahead of market demand. Through Internet Essentials, it has also dramatically closed the digital divide within its geographic footprint, bringing un-derrepresented viewpoints to the online conversation, and introducing the company's products and services to new customers.

Even if 5G technology achieves its ambitious goals, wireless net-works are increasingly dependent on high-speed internet backbones for wholesale transit, or what is known as "backhaul." So if consum-ers do wind up shifting from wired to mobile internet access at some point in the future, business customers, including the mobile provid-ers themselves, will still need Comcast's added capacity. The compa-ny's accelerated investment in a maturing core will likely pay off, no matter what.

THE NEW—Rather than adopting a me-too strategy for emerging markets and the technologies driving them, experiment aggressively across a wide range of future options, creating a balanced portfolio that maximizes opportunities to scale rapidly, when and if a shark fin appears.

Conventional wisdom says the time to move to the new is when customers start to embrace disruptive technologies. At that point, if nothing else, incumbents feel they have to offer something—any-thing—that resembles the business plan of the disruptors.

By the time a new market is serving real customers, however, it is likely too late for incumbents to jump in. If you haven't developed a portfolio of options to apply in the new, a me-too approach won't get you new customers or revenue. More likely, it will only accelerate a tailspin of revenue and asset decline in the old and the now.

As noted, Comcast has invested heavily in its corporate venture cap-ital portfolio, targeting early-stage investments in start-ups, many with technologies complementary to the company's diverse businesses and products. These include stakes in next-generation video, interactive sports applications, collaboration tools for business customers, and community-building digital services.

The company's home-grown innovation includes patents for home security and smart homes. These are natural extensions to Comcast's rich data channel to and from its customers' homes, improving the company's ability to pursue a hyper-relevant strategy of extreme customization.

For mobile-first users, especially the next generation of customers, Comcast leveraged millions of Wi-Fi access points in the homes and offices of current customers, creating the largest noncellular wireless network in the world. By bundling integrated cellular service through a marketing agreement with Verizon, moreover, Xfinity Mobile offers nationwide mobile service, effectively building a new wireless network at a fraction of the cost of its competitors.

>

The rest of this chapter explores more examples from our work and research of organizations applying the new wisdoms. It highlights how they apply across industries, to companies large and small, old and new, all singularly focused on a mission to search and release even more profit at the upper limits of the trapped value gap.

THE OLD: INNOVATE TO FUEL FUTURE GROWTH

Why leave so soon?

In analyzing the stories of hundreds of global businesses, we saw a consistent pattern: companies unsentimentally and quickly disengage from their older businesses and longtime customers as they enter new, more promising ones. Who can blame them? Strategy experts have long obsessed over the importance of an early exit; indeed, abandonment of mature markets is at the heart of many leading strategy textbooks.

There's also a personal, even psychological, aspect to the phenomenon. The natural desire of company leaders to leave their enterprises in better shape than they found them may drive premature exit of products and markets that are approaching but haven't yet reached their end. CEOs considering their legacy may prefer, in other words, to focus on the new. That's especially true when a once-successful product is suddenly replaced, thanks to a growing trapped value gap, by better and cheaper alternatives.

The problem is that even better and cheaper offerings don't always scale as quickly as might be imagined. For one thing, longtime customers may not be ready to give up on products they have come to rely on, and which they've integrated into daily life. You may have to depend on healthy revenues from the mature business and the goodwill of legacy customers far longer than you think.

Case in point: Netflix's leaders rightly predicted in 2011 that the growing ubiquity of high-speed home internet access would soon mean the end of their once-disruptive DVD mailing business. So CEO Reed Hastings decided to split the company in two, leaving the old business largely to fend for itself while the company's best employees and most of the money went to building a first-of-its-kind streaming alternative. The old business, renamed Qwikster, would have required a separate subscription, effectively a 60 percent price hike for the two together.

Hastings had the right idea, but he was too quick to announce the death of the company's old core. Loyal customers who still saw value in the convenience and cheaper cost of the mailing service felt betrayed and alienated. Investors revolted. Before Qwikster had even launched, the company's stock lost 60 percent of its value, along with 800,000 subscribers, the first such decline in years.

Netflix quickly reversed course, making clear it hadn't stop improving the old service. "There is a difference between moving quickly, which Netflix has done very well for years, and moving too fast, which is what we did in this case," Hastings acknowledged in a statement.

The cancellation of Qwikster proved to be a stitch in time. For one thing, resuscitating the DVD service gave the company ample time to work out unexpected technical and licensing bugs that slowed the planned implementation of the streaming service. As it turns out, the DVD business is still going strong. In 2017, the mailing service had 3.4 million customers—many in rural areas with less reliable broadband service—and annual revenues of roughly $450 million. To paraphrase Mark Twain, reports of the death of DVDs had been greatly exaggerated.

That revenue not only fueled investment in the steaming business but also helped Netflix with its next multibillion-dollar pivot, this time to producing original content. Netflix's streaming service, at the same time, now has 125 million subscribers, validating the company's early investment in a scalable new technology.

Like Netflix, the value releasers in our research learned, sometimes the hard way, to avoid premature abandonment of the old. Even when products or services become commoditized or begin to implode, smart leaders buck conventional wisdom and devote financial and technical resources to extend their life span, applying technologies previously neither mature enough nor cost-effective.

Consider the example of adult beverage giant Anheuser-Busch In-Bev, which in recent years has seen mass-produced beer sales slide as a new generation of consumers embrace the advent of technology-enabled microbrewing, or "craft beer."

The story is a familiar one of a long-stable industry experiencing compressive disruption as new entrants discover significant trapped value previously unknown or unreachable.

Despite working with much smaller batch sizes, artisanal craft brewers are taking full advantage of falling technology costs to innovate, using everything from the latest factory automation tools to learning algorithms that refine their formulas, and the IoT to track production and distribution. Sensors measure and report key variables, including flow rate, pressure, temperature, weight, and time. Some craft brewers are even using predictive analytics to determine when to sample during fermentation, improving product consistency and reducing the number of nonconforming batches.

In 1988, at the peak of its popularity, more than one in every four beers sold in the United States bore the iconic red-and-white Anheuser-Busch–owned Budweiser label. But over the last quarter century, the "king of beers" found itself being deposed, in danger of losing not only its crown jewels but the rest of its kingdom along with them.

Around the world, "macro" beers have seen eroding popularity in the face of declining cost advantages over craft brews. In the United States alone, more than four hundred microbreweries opened in 2012, an increase of 17 percent from the year before. The total now exceeds six thousand. Craft beer consumption continues to grow in many markets around the world, even as overall beer consumption declines.

Following conventional wisdom, AB InBev would have likely beaten a hasty path for the exit. But the company wasn't willing to accept defeat. Instead, it doubled down on its core products, markets, and branding. It rejected conventional wisdom that would have meant downsizing, plant closures, and divestitures of the most underperforming legacy products.

Management focused instead on releasing trapped value in underserved markets and renewed cost cutting. AB InBev is expanding in countries where gross domestic product is increasing and the middle class is growing, a key demographic for efficient mass-market beer production and consumption. In Africa, for example, Budweiser uses local crops to sell local brands at appealing price points and healthy margins.

On the cost-cutting front, the company's key innovation was to embrace zero-based budgeting (ZBB), something we at Accenture have relied on for years as a cornerstone of our own pivot. The concept, first described in a 1970 *Harvard Business Review* article by Texas Instruments accountant Peter A. Pyhrr, is intuitively simple. Rather than using last year's budget as a starting point and then adjusting up or down, a process that invariably leads to political in-fighting and counterproductive efforts to game the system, the new fiscal year instead begins with all accounts at zero.

Expenses must then be justified for each new budget period based on their fit with an overall strategy, demonstrated either by showing an item's contribution to projected profitability, revenue growth, or other corporate initiatives, such as sustainability.

With ZBB, you quickly and transparently remove costs that cannot be justified. Basing resource allocation on what's needed now rather than on last year's goals frees up capital that can then be used in ways that will have the most impact on building innovation and fueling growth. At Accenture, ZBB is an annual closed-loop cost management process, not just a onetime exercise. It helps us create a culture of cost consciousness, so that spending is always rationalized and aligned to the business strategy.

Over the last few years, we've worked with AB InBev to turn what we learned from our own experience with ZBB into fuel for the company's pivot to the new. InBev first adopted the technique in 2004, applying it to holdings in North America, Europe, and Asia over the next few years. ZBB played a leading role in squeezing out as much as $1.4 billion in costs as part of InBev's merger with US-based peer Anheuser-Busch in 2008, which created AB InBev.

Using the cost savings from more realistic budgeting, the company invested heavily in scaling new product businesses by leveraging the marketing and distribution advantages of the old to beat the new entrants at their own game. AB InBev has become a serial acquirer, adding popular craft labels such as Goose Island, Elysian, 10 Barrel Brewing, Golden Road, and Blue Point to its roster. In all, the company has spent hundreds of millions of dollars to buy twenty-one companies. While most of these purchases were focused on microbrews, the company has also expanded into adjacent beverage categories, including start-ups focused on soft drinks, ciders, and nonalcoholic beverages.

As each acquisition is completed, the ZBB philosophy is applied to shed duplicative costs better served by centralized corporate functions. Anything not directly related to the acquired company's product or market, such a travel and expenses, administration costs, or facilities, is deemed "nonworking money" and zeroed out at the start of each budget cycle.

The savings are invested back into the business as "working money," useable for any expense that adds direct value for the product or customer, such as media buying, promotions, or point-of-sale acquisitions. The operating improvements have been tangible. In France, for instance, AB InBev's premium Leffe brand has vaulted to the second most popular brand in the country.

"We look at [ZBB] as an investment," explained Tony Milikin, chief procurement officer at Anheuser-Busch InBev, in a video for Accenture Strategy. "If a company is consuming ten thousand calories a day, and it only needs two thousand calories a day, the company's going to get fat, lazy, and out of shape."

Following the new wisdom of innovating to fuel future growth, AB InBev expects to realize an added $3.2 billion in cost savings from its 2016 $100 billion merger with SABMiller, up from an earlier target of $2.3 billion. That's a serious fitness routine.

THE NOW: SHOOT FOR THE STARS

The first of our new pivot wisdoms looks at ways to release hidden value in aging products that competitors might already treat as liabilities, searching for an exit. The second looks at the now part of your portfolio: products and services selling well today, but whose underlying technology, while still on a growth trajectory, may soon approach the flattening out of its S-curve.

But that assumes the shape of the curve can't be altered, an assumption regularly upended by new entrants who destabilize mature markets using new technology. But when incumbents try to respond, they're frequently met with poor customer reaction. Even though incumbents often apply the same digital components and target the same sources of trapped value as the start-ups, they invariably find themselves outmaneuvered at each pivot.

There's nothing particularly proprietary in the technology used in an e-commerce website, for example, yet traditional retailers, as we saw in chapter 1, largely foundered in efforts to beat Amazon at its own game. Cloud-supported video and music-streaming, apps, and mobile networks, likewise, are by now completely unremarkable, yet online offerings from incumbent music- and video-content producers had little impact on the rapid consumer adoption of new entrants such as Spotify and Amazon Prime Video.

And while Comcast and other content and distribution leaders are making inroads in streaming media, there's little question they are chasing Netflix and others, even in the creation of original content. Yet that is the incumbents' core skill, one honed by decades of Hollywood evolution and technology advances.

So why are so few incumbents winning in the new?

Our research suggests the answer has to do with how companies manage the now. Rather than leveraging today's core assets to accelerate and scale their entry into new markets, too many incumbents treat those assets like cash cows, milking them for revenue and little else.

Value releasers, on the other hand, embrace a different metaphor. Rather than look at their most profitable products, services, and technologies as an aging set of assets with a fixed value and life span, they see today's core as a living business that can grow even faster by applying the optimal fuel for continued innovation and investment. Rather than accept the shape of the traditional S-curve, they redraw it, turning cows into stars that shine even brighter, expanding at a faster pace and steeper trajectory than before.

"Cash cows," as the name implies, are products and businesses that can be left to operate largely independently, relied on for dependable profits with little to no reinvestment or innovation. Examples include everything from popular brands of toothpaste, cereals, and sodas to life insurance and tax services. Generating predictable revenue, cash cows can help finance new systems, plants, and acquisitions, and can take up the slack for weaker or still-growing businesses during times of economic downturn.

So it's perhaps not surprising that today's executives were taught to milk their cash cows, deriving as much revenue from them today as possible, with little regard for their long-term health.

The expression comes from Boston Consulting Group's product portfolio matrix, first published in 1970, which recommends different strategies for four distinct categories of offerings: dogs (products with low growth and low market share); question marks (products in high-growth markets but with low market share); stars (products in high-growth markets with high market share); and cash cows (products in low-growth markets but with high market share).

The simple rule applied to the last category, according to its authors, is to "milk these products as much as possible without killing the cow." In other words, focus on efficiencies and deny the business additional innovation investment, beyond the incremental, that might lower profitability.

But an expanding trapped value gap upends the logic of the growth-share matrix. The relentless capacity of digital and other technologies to simultaneously become better, cheaper, and smaller undermines traditional assumptions about both the upside potential and competitiveness of even mature products.

With the right infusion of new technology, few products should be considered "low growth." What's more, the propensity of new entrants to target growing trapped value means high market share today.

You can't take the cash cows for granted, in other words, nor should you assume they can't be rejuvenated or cloned into new, healthier calves. It's not just that you may have an opportunity to get more out of them at a faster clip. Rather, in the world of the wise pivot, doing so has become a strategic and competitive imperative.

Just step into nearly any New York City taxicab and you'll see what we mean. In most cities around the world, private transportation companies long operated under a strict regulatory regime that limited, sometimes severely, the number of for-hire vehicles that could be on the road, and what they could charge.

Limited supply and commodity pricing long ago killed any incentive for transportation companies or individual drivers to invest in innovation that differentiates their service. Over the years, the general quality of vehicles, drivers, and user experience more or less sank to the least common denominator. Vehicles are operated in barely roadworthy condition, and customer service, including availability, comfort, cleanliness, safety, and courtesy, sank even lower. The only nods to new technology since the 1940s have been credit card readers and flat-screen monitors blaring short loops of local news and repeated ads.

That sad reality equated to decades of bottled-up customer frustration. Still, enormous regulatory and capital investment barriers meant there was little risk of a new entrant translating that frustration into the sudden release of fast-growing trapped value.

That is, until the mobile revolution put GPS tracking, digital maps, messaging services, and online payment tools into the hands of billions of consumers. As deployment and rapid improvement of mobile devices and applications surged, the capital and regulatory advantages of incumbent transportation companies disappeared overnight. Uber, Lyft, and other ride-hailing services simply combined the ubiquity of GPS-enabled cell phones with scalable cloud computing services to offer alternative transit, at once better and cheaper than the regulated alternative.

As transportation network companies matched up riders with non-professional drivers and private vehicles, traditional providers were sent reeling. In New York alone, the collective value of each of the city's 13,587 taxicab medallions plummeted between 2013 and 2017 from a record $1.3 million to as little as $150,000, a release and transfer of trapped value shared by the new services, their drivers, and a growing number of grateful consumers.

The cash cow is yielding curdled milk. And so far, it seems, incumbents haven't found a way to reverse the trend.

Milking the cash cow, as the taxi business suggests, is hard to resist when entry barriers are high and consumers have little leverage in expressing the need for, let alone securing, improvements that would release vast amounts of trapped value.

But resist it you must, especially when the cash cow lives in an open field. In the most competitive markets—including consumer packaged goods, fashion, and electronics—today's competitive advantages, even those that translate to market dominance, can rarely be counted on to last, or at least not as long as you might imagine. Today's hottest food trends, clothing brands, and smartphone models are just one disruption away from obsolescence.

Even in saturated markets, in other words, sustaining a powerful competitive advantage may still prove elusive, especially when trapped value and the technology to release it are simmering just below the surface, growing in volume and heat.

That's the moral of the story for a long succession of early internet companies, each of which, for a bright shining moment, not only led the pack in offering the leading web browser but also enjoyed seemingly unstoppable momentum.

With new algorithms, interfaces, devices, and business models emerging quickly in the frenzy of Silicon Valley's venture capital–fueled ecosystem, Netscape was toppled by Internet Explorer, which lost out to Firefox, which fell to Chrome and Safari as users moved from laptops to phones and tablets. In 2017, Chrome controlled almost 50 percent of the browser market, while Explorer retained only 15 percent of the more than 90 percent share it once held.

The same phenomenon stalked companies offering internet search where, again, potent kings of the castle were dashed to the ground in lopsided battles. For years, winners continued to rise and fall rapidly, including AltaVista, Excite, Lycos, AOL, MSN Search, Ask Jeeves, and of course Yahoo.

That is until late 1998, when yet another search engine was launched from yet another Palo Alto, California, garage. Google Search, with its unique algorithmic approach, was soon followed by Google AdWords, a novel auction-based platform for selling related advertising.

That combination proved fateful. Google rose quickly to become the dominant provider of internet search and advertising by the end of 2002, tracking with a dramatic rise in the number of internet users, the spread of high-speed access, and, with the launch of the iPhone in 2007, the even faster spread of mobile devices.

Today, Google's dominance is unprecedented. It controls as much as 90 percent of the global search market and is the number one internet advertising platform in the world, commanding, together with Facebook, a combined 63 percent of the United States' $83 billion digital advertising market as of 2018.

That market continues to grow quickly, even as internet user adoption approaches total saturation in the developed world. In 2017 alone, the company's advertising revenue grew nearly 25 percent, a 7 percent acceleration from 2016. At the end of 2018, Google was reporting over $110 billion in annual revenue, commanding a market value of over $750 billion.

Talk about a cash cow! Yet Google, learning from the painful collapses of its defunct rivals, has never taken its market position or advantages for granted. Even as parent company Alphabet pivots at lightning speed toward new, scalable products and what the company calls its "big bet" investments in everything from self-driving cars to home automation (more on that in a moment), the search products team continues to innovate the core products as if every day might prove their last chance to delight users who request the company's assistance with 3.5 billion searches each day.

Though costs aren't broken out by product, it's abundantly clear that Google has never for a moment stopped shooting for the stars, competing more against itself than any real or imagined new entrant. R&D expenses alone have grown from $226 million in 2004 to over $16 billion today.

You don't have to dig too deeply to see that much of that money is being spent to accelerate growth in the now. Core algorithms are constantly updated to improve results, tested by a network of ten thousand paid raters. In 2017, Google ran 31,584 side-by-side experiments, resulting in 2,453 separate changes to its core search product.

Beyond pure text-based search and advertising, the company has pioneered a wide range of innovations and new technologies, consistent with a clearly stated mission "to organize the world's information and make it universally accessible and useful."

Just in the last ten years, a few of the major innovations the company has added to its core offerings include everything from autocompletion to automated language translations, directions and traffic, versions optimized for a wide range of mobile devices, and voice- and image-based searching.

The value of that kind of continuous innovation in the now certainly contributes to Google's bottom line, scaring off potential competitors foolish enough to think they can outmaneuver, as so many did to the company's predecessors, the current market leader.

Perhaps as much as any other company, Google's strategy embodies the insights we gleaned from our own experience and research. Google doesn't just attack the trapped value gap, it works to make it bigger, almost as if the company is challenging itself and its competitors to see who can stretch the furthest to close it.

THE NEW: SCALE TO WIN

Applying our new way of thinking for managing the old and the now will help you create a portfolio that generates revenue and the competitive freedom to focus on an increasingly uncertain future: the new. Improving your core and growing it at the same time protects market share, and generates revenue growth that can be reinvested in higher-risk technologies and innovations with the potential to help you complete a wise pivot.

It might seem that making that case for future investments would be the easy part of creating a portfolio. As we explained earlier, the technologies growing the trapped value gap don't distinguish among industries. There is an increasing likelihood of big bang or compressive disruption, whether your company creates software, commercial aircraft, or commodity chemicals.

Indeed, those industries left largely alone in the first wave of digital disruption are the ones now most at risk from the kind of creative destruction that is least expected, both in its ferocity and the speed of its impact. Just ask any cab driver, music producer, camera maker, newspaper publisher, travel agent, or retail store owner.

Still, old habits die hard, and sometimes the most difficult challenge in a wise pivot is making the case not just for future-oriented investments, but more specifically for investments that can and will be quickly scaled into new businesses. Managers in mature industries, after all, are evaluated based on their ability to maintain the status quo, to make incremental improvements, and to keep the revolutionaries away from the barricades.

Adopting a disruption mind-set takes time, beginning with the sometimes painful acknowledgment that change, even positive change, is traumatic. Accenture might have been quite happy to continue improving our core consulting, technology, and outsourcing businesses, growing at a decidedly manageable pace. When new entrants wielding new technologies threatened, however, the decision to pivot, though difficult, became unavoidable.

Having made it, we found ways to revitalize older services, to grow newer ones that many thought would have a shortened life, and most of all to leverage our core assets into entirely new businesses we honestly never expected to be in when we started the process.

So we know from our own reinvention, and those of our clients and the companies in our study, that pivoting to the new, let alone winning there, is hard. We also know it can and must be done.

Critical to your success will be starting out on the right foot. What distinguished the value releasers in our study was how well they scoped their pivot to the new, right from the outset.

As we learned in our own experience, the key is to start with an honest assessment of your competitive advantages, core values, and brand differentiators. With this shared understanding as your fulcrum, you next look to the new technologies aimed at your business, industry, and customers, focusing on the ones most likely to expand risks and opportunities in the trapped value gap. Then ask which of these approaching disruptors offers you the best chance of building products and services that can scale quickly to become profitable new businesses. And how, through a portfolio of investments that might include market experimentation, organic growth, reskilling, start-up investing, and acquisitions, you can test and validate your pivot.

With plan in hand, equally important in your successful pivot to the new is the ability to execute rapidly. Those who invested early, widely, and wisely in new technologies disrupting their industries were able to launch new products and services even when the future arrived, as it often does, sooner than expected.

You'll need whatever edge you can get. That's because, thanks to near-perfect market information for consumers from social networks and other digital tools, and ever-increasing speed to market for networked and platform businesses, fewer companies can achieve a first-mover advantage. But maybe it's enough just to get to *the right place at the right time with the right level of product availability* and do so sooner than competitors, securing instead what we call a "major mover advantage."

Markets prone to major mover advantages, whether for the latest smartphone game, binge-worthy TV show, or must-have flat-panel display, are short-lived, and winning in one is no guarantee of winning in the next. But it clearly helps. When the US airline industry was definitively deregulated in 1978, for example, it created waves of disruptive shocks still being felt today. Venerable carriers including Braniff, Eastern, and TWA imploded in the face of new competitors and new kinds of competition, replaced by start-up market leaders such as low-fare pioneer People Express.

People Express, in turn, gave way to even more innovative airlines, which released even more trapped value with affordable fares, more convenient schedules, and strong operational discipline.

The remaining incumbent carriers lumbered along, entering and sometimes surviving bankruptcy in the face of new competition, fuel price spikes, and unpredictable global economic and political shocks. Along the way, most tried to imitate the innovations of the newcomers, but without addressing the underlying structural and cultural problems that made them uncompetitive.

Early in the 2000s, for example, some incumbent carriers launched low-cost, no-frills alternatives to their own traditional premium air travel services and its attendant complications in fares, classes of service, and yield structures.

The problem was that the new subsidiaries were only a nod to innovation, launched with little enthusiasm and fatally compromised from the beginning. For one thing, they used the same unionized employees, equipment, and other infrastructure as the legacy operation they were in theory competing against. The subsidiaries inherited all the operational and cost disadvantages the incumbents were trying to overcome, with none of the potential for going the discount carriers one better.

The incumbents' pivot to the new was both too late and designed to fail. There was no way their no-frills brands could scale; indeed, the more successful they were, the more money they were certain to lose. Most were quickly retired.

Compare that experience to Toyota's successful pivot to hybrid vehicles. Despite the uncertainty of the technology and the cultural shift among consumers it relied on, the Japanese automaker put aside its historically conservative approach to product innovation and started investing seriously in battery technologies in the early 1990s, even as US competitors were dismissing the idea as a certain money loser.

Toyota spent more than $1 billion in developing its first hybrid vehicle, the Prius, rushing it to market in 1997 and cutting margins to ensure it achieved scale quickly. By 2001, Toyota's hybrid line was profitable. In less than a decade, Toyota was earning about $3,100 for every hybrid it sold, similar to margins on traditional internal combustion vehicles.

As of 2017, Toyota had sold 4.3 million hybrid vehicles and was the only company in the world to make a profit from the technology. Counting plug-in hybrids, Toyota accounts for nearly two out of three electrified cars ever sold, with plans to offer fully electric versions of all its models by 2025.

Toyota's competitors, meanwhile, are now playing catch-up. As recently as 2004, then GM vice chairman Bob Lutz was still referring to hybrids as "an interesting curiosity." But when gas prices rose sharply the next year, Lutz admitted GM had missed its best opportunity to scale in the new. "The manifest success of the Prius," he said in an interview, "caused a rethink on everybody's part."

Scaling to win is also proving a powerful strategy for some incumbents in the energy business, one of several regulated industries experiencing significant disruption. The rise of renewable energy sources, including consumer-owned wind, solar, and fuel cell technologies, is depressing prices for traditional power throughout the developed economies. It is also forcing the reconfiguration of a complex energy grid that long assumed power distribution moved electricity from producers to users in one direction only.

The power business is changing, releasing trapped value for consumers and society as a whole in the form of more sustainable practices. In response, many power companies, long seen as a conservative investment delivering reliable returns, are breaking themselves into pieces, merging to delay the inevitable, or exiting the sector altogether. Others are leveraging their still-viable core businesses into fuel for new ventures, looking to scale up rapidly in emerging fields such as energy management and electric vehicle infrastructure.

Enel, Italy's largest energy company, is finding ways to turn the shift to renewable energy from a source of competition to a source of new profit. As part of its wise pivot, Enel is selling off or retiring assets the company no longer believes to be strategic, investing over $5 billion of the proceeds and savings across all three lifecycle stages.

In the old, for example, Enel is leveraging its real estate, rights of way, and distribution infrastructure by deploying fiber-optic cable throughout its network, with plans to launch a wholesale internet-access business it calls Open Fiber.

Enel is also investing in a more technology-propelled version of the company's traditional energy business, the now of its businesses. The company has already digitized its relationship with two-thirds of customers, installing smart meters throughout Italy and beginning in its other European markets, making billing and other operations more efficient. More importantly, a two-way data connection with Enel's sixty-five million users can track energy contributed back to the grid from customer-owned generating capacity, including solar panels and batteries. Enel is creating, in effect, a smart grid.

The data pipeline will also play a starring role in the new, as Enel invests in smart home and smart building energy management applications, where every energy-using device is connected to the IoT. This gives users more control while providing Enel with up-to-the-minute usage information, especially valuable for managing the energy needs of plug-in vehicles. Enel is investing heavily here too, installing charging infrastructure throughout Italy.

To prepare for its simultaneous pivots, Enel first migrated all its data-processing activity to the AWS cloud. The company retired the equivalent of ten thousand server computers and was planning to close its last data center in 2018. Its move to the cloud has already yielded significant cost savings in the now, including in power and storage costs. It has also greatly improved the speed with which new data-processing capacity can be added or removed, going from three to four weeks in Enel's own data centers to only two days for AWS.

With its customers connected and its IT virtualized, Enel was ready to accelerate its pivot to the new. This included the acquisition of several energy-management start-ups, which were combined into a new business unit called Enel X. Enel X will operate all of Enel's new businesses, including smart home solutions, fiber-optic lighting, signaling and security, smart city services, electric mobility, and stand-alone "off grid" distribution solutions such as solar-powered systems with battery storage.

One of the companies Enel acquired is EnerNOC, the biggest provider in the United States of "demand response" solutions, which give institutional energy consumers lower rates for agreeing to reduce usage during peak times. EnerNOC negotiates with consumers on behalf of producers, provides software to hospitals, factories, and office buildings that identifies ways they can improve energy cost management without disruption to regular operations.

Information collected and analyzed from these smart grids releases tremendous trapped value that can be shared among industry participants and their customers, whether through dynamic pricing, better integration of nonrenewable and renewable energy sources, reduced power theft, and improved design for everything from power plants to the devices that rely on them. Enel plans to deploy EnerNOC's software in the company's non-US markets as well.

These initiatives show how Enel embraced many of the seven winning strategies, becoming, for example, technology propelled, data driven, and network powered. According to Enel CEO Francesco Starace: "Today we are more efficient and more sustainable and, therefore, in a position to derive value from that evolution and to seize every opportunity created from the radical change that is involving the entire energy sector."

INTEGRATING THE OLD, THE NOW, AND THE NEW: THE PORTFOLIO PIVOT

As Enel's pivot highlights, our three new wisdoms must be applied not just individually, but in a coordinated strategy, creating a single portfolio balanced across the lifecycle stages. It does little good to free up capital and grow revenue in the old without plans to invest those funds wisely in scaling the new. Likewise, continuing to shoot for the stars without the necessary capital at hand could mean taking on too much debt, one of the seven wrong turns that can derail a wise pivot.

Beyond the creation of an overall strategic vision for each rotation in your wise pivot, our new wisdoms require both balance and focus. To better understand each of these, let's look at some good examples of value releasers that have mastered both.

BALANCE—A balanced portfolio must divide investment rationally and intelligently across the three lifecycle stages. While the majority of investment and innovation decisions may remain with the managers directly responsible for them, a common governance structure, perhaps the executive team or an investment committee of your board, should review the portfolio regularly to ensure the relative allocation of resources among the stages remains appropriate, or when necessary that it be reset.

Consider again Alphabet, the parent company of tech giant Google. As we noted earlier, Google exemplifies the pivot wisdom of investing heavily in its core search and advertising products despite a lack of serious competition. At the same time, Google is constantly scanning the trapped value gap, searching for its next new, fueling future initiatives with profits from today's core.

In the now, Alphabet is diversifying its revenue sources. Its other businesses, like cloud computing, hardware (smart speakers and phones, and IoT products such as Nest smart thermostats), apps in the Google Play store, and subscriptions to YouTube Red make up more of Google's total revenue over time, growing to over 10 percent by 2017. Google believes, however, that these innovations remain far from their full potential.

In the new, Alphabet's most speculative investments are collectively known as "other bets," comprising nearly every division of Alphabet other than Google. The company invests roughly 7 percent of annual operating revenue in these initiatives, including the Waymo autonomous vehicle unit and tech lab X, which oversees initiatives, such as broadband delivered by high-altitude balloons and a drone delivery effort called Project Wing.

Other bets also include Access, the new name for Google Fiber, which deployed ultra-high-speed home internet access in a handful of cities before scaling back future deployments. The company's multi-billion-dollar investments in start-ups outside the company are also housed in "other bets." Its corporate venture capital arm, known as GV, manages a portfolio built around emerging technologies in the life sciences, agriculture, robotics, and other fields.

In Alphabet's balanced portfolio, each other-bet business is managed with a goal of financial independence. Each has its own CEO, budget, and revenue target established by Alphabet's executive team, with a defined path to profitability. Across all three lifecycle stages, more importantly, every investment is tightly related to the company's core product and its long-standing mission to collect and organize the world's information sources and make them available to consumers worldwide.

Naturally, some of the other bets don't pay off, leading to expensive failures. But Alphabet has a process in place to minimize both the risk and the losses. Senior management evaluates every investment regularly, accelerating or decelerating them based on actual performance of the technology and business model involved. Google Cloud and the acquired driving directions application Waze, for example, proved to be hits, and were scaled rapidly. On the other hand, after less than successful market launches, Google Fiber, Google Glass, and the also-ran social networking platform Google+ were scaled back, returned to the lab, and canceled, respectively.

Keeping innovation balanced across all three horizons, as we learned in Accenture's pivot, is a challenge. Our own budgeting shares many of the same attributes, and challenges, of Alphabet. Spending was once doled out largely based on current and future projected revenue, for example, a process that has been radically reinvented. We now establish explicit strategic priorities and allocate our substantial, but not unlimited, innovation funding to the initiatives that best align with those priorities.

Both Accenture and Alphabet employ a top-down and bottom-up approach to innovation. That means management sets the rules but gives employees considerable freedom to suggest and develop new initiatives. When Google was still in its start-up phase, employees were even encouraged to spend a day each week working on their own projects, an investment that paid off with scalable new products. Gmail and AdSense, staples of Google's core for over a decade, began as employee projects.

Each bet Alphabet makes, however, must feed the core and help it evolve to scalable products in the new. Alphabet is organized and religiously focused around information collection, analysis, and curation; in effect, in finding and releasing trapped value from increasingly complex sources of information by applying all seven winning strategies. That philosophy makes the company less about the products and services it offers at any given time, and more a fine-tuned engine of innovation.

While it's likely your own pivoting objectives and appetite for investment risk are more modest than Alphabet's, the company's balanced approach to structuring, investing, and evaluating its portfolio is one every company can learn from.

FOCUS—A balanced portfolio of innovations, investments, and human capital is a necessary condition for a successful wise pivot. It is not, however, sufficient to ensure your journey from an old core to a new, scalable one. Investing without a plan is like throwing darts while blindfolded. You might hit the target, but if so it's only by happy accident. No portfolio is complete without a vision for the future you hope to reach, and a strategy for getting there.

In short, you need focus. That focus includes an unsentimental evaluation of your current business and the core technologies you employ to serve customers. While our first pivot wisdom warns against simply exiting an old business approaching obsolescence, that's not to suggest there's never a good time to call it a day. If you follow the approach of the wise pivot, you maximize the chances that when the time comes—that almost-certain moment when your industry is re-created by either a big bang or compressive disruption—you'll already be operating a new core. Not just with an experiment, but with a real business.

Accenture's focus has been achieved largely through a set of strategic visioning exercises. As noted in chapter 4, our Ambition 2020 initiative had all the typical elements of strategy, including ambitious stretch goals for growth. More importantly, it visualized the digital future we ultimately realized as part of our wise pivot. Following the pivot wisdoms, you can time your shifts between the S-curves just right.

Let's take another example. As we noted in the introduction, Royal Philips proved that knowing both when and how to pivot is possible even if you haven't done so for over a century—a century during which you dominated your old markets.

In 2006, Royal Philips embarked on a bold strategy to retire its incandescent lighting business, a highly profitable product line it had helped to invent in the nineteenth century. This was no small shift in strategy. It was a dramatic reinvention that took genuine insight, courage, and the wisdom to know that devastating disruption was imminent and inevitable.

The emerging technology in this case was light emitting diodes, or LEDs. Since the 1960s, LED technology was on an exponential development path of better and cheaper improvements, a parallel to the digital revolution. LEDs even had their own version of Moore's law, known as Haitz's law, which predicted the unit cost of light provided by LEDs would fall by a factor of ten every ten years.

Coincidentally, the amount of light generated per LED increases by a factor of twenty at a given wavelength. What's more, LEDs are programmable, allowing for real-time changes to color and intensity as part of the emerging internet of things.

Haitz's law convinced Philips that at some point LEDs would be more cost-effective than incandescents, a technology that had changed little since World War I. There are also environmental benefits to LEDs. Incandescents are highly inefficient, giving off more heat than light and wasting most of the energy they consume. And their manufacture involves dangerous pollutants, which raises the costs and risks of their disposal.

For consumers, the poor performance of early LEDs was likely to be overcome by the sustainability potential of the new technology, a release of trapped value at the societal level. In Europe alone, consumers replace two billion bulbs a year. LEDs will save over $9 billion in energy costs alone, and eliminate twenty million tons of greenhouse gases.

That made a compelling case for imminent disruption. It might take LEDs a decade or two longer than Haitz's law predicted, but Philips recognized that in the foreseeable future, sooner rather than later, LEDs would surpass incandescents in every dimension that mattered to consumers. The cash cow would stop producing.

That seems easy to understand now, more than a decade later, when most governments (in part at the urging of Philips) have mandated the retirement of incandescent products, and the benefits of smart lighting, including Philip's own LED product line, Hue, are becoming clearer. But as late as 2009, Philips Lighting accounted for 30 percent of the company's total revenue of over $26 billion. Most of that came from the sale of incandescent bulbs, which contributed $396 million in profits.

Consequently, Philips set off considerable shock waves when it declared in 2006 that it was eliminating incandescent technology, and then challenged its competitors to do the same. The company kept its focus throughout a difficult transition. Core manufacturing and distribution assets were sold off, even as the company innovated in LED production and applications. Philips acquired several smaller companies in an emerging LED ecosystem, including, in 2007, a leading US maker of next-generation lighting fixtures for $4.3 billion.

After growing the LED business to nearly $7 billion, Philips accelerated its exit from the old core, spinning its new lighting businesses into Philips Lighting in 2016. It has since cut its interest in the company to less than 30 percent. (Philips Lighting is now known as Signify.)

An important part of Philips' pivot was the parallel expansion of a new core in the health-care industry. By 2017, three-quarters of the company's revenue came from diagnosis and treatment equipment, and a smaller IoT-based connected care and health informatics business. Most of Philips' earnings now come from high-end medical equipment, including MRI scanners.

Philips' new focus required a carefully timed divestiture from lighting, the old core. The company's foresight and early adoption of a balanced portfolio strategy, however, allowed it to execute its pivot largely on its own terms, forcing other incandescent bulb manufacturers to adapt to Philips' preferred timetable.

The company is already unleashing the power of its formidable innovation culture in newer markets. In 2014, for example, we worked with Philips to develop breakthrough technology that gives patients with ALS (amyotrophic lateral sclerosis) greater autonomy. ALS, affecting more than 400,000 people, impairs brain and spinal cord nerves, gradually diminishing a patient's voluntary muscle actions.

In the prototype, a wearable display and the Emotiv Insight Brainware, which scans EEG brainwaves, were connected to a tablet device. Users could then issue brainwave commands to control Philips products, including the Philips Lifeline medical alert service, Philips smart TVs, and Hue personal wireless lighting.

The tablet also allows control of these products using eye movements and voice commands for patients who still have that ability. In both cases, patients could communicate preconfigured messages, request medical assistance, and control TVs and lights.

Accenture's Technology Labs in San Jose, California, collaborated with the Philips Digital Accelerator Lab in the Netherlands to create the software that interacts with the Emotiv Insight Brainware and the wearable display. Fjord, our design consultancy, built the display's user interface.

As that example highlights, the search for trapped value can often lead you in radical directions, answering the challenge of a future that can neither be postponed nor predicted.

>

Pivoting is inevitable. The question is whether you'll do it wisely, with a portfolio of assets and investments balanced among the three lifecycle stages, or whether you'll simply spin out of control, appearing to be doing something but making little if any actual progress.

To get successfully to the new, and get there every time, is the essence of the wise pivot. As we know firsthand, getting it right takes patience, determination, and resolve.

Along the way, you'll both rely on and reinvent three core assets: your ability to innovate, your financial discipline, and the human capital of your employees and stakeholders. Together, they comprise the essence of your company's history, culture, and potential. The next three chapters look at these resources in detail, as we see how Accenture, our clients, and the companies in our study have learned to pivot around each.

chapter 6

THE INNOVATION PIVOT
Concentration, Control, and Aspiration

THIS AND THE FOLLOWING two chapters explore in detail how to build and maintain the portfolio of assets and resources you need as you begin your pivot from an old core to a new one. This chapter explores the part of your business dedicated to innovation itself—your research and development, incubation and other experimentation, and corporate venturing and acquisitions.

Managing your innovation pivot, as with the finance and people pivots to follow, requires you to review and adjust three key sets of decisions. Think of these settings as the levers of control that determine the shape, speed, and trajectory of your strategy: the pivot points around which your portfolio turns. (See figure 6.1.)

Your approach to innovation, for example, will be either more or less centralized, senior management will exert some level of oversight over how innovation gets done, and your investment model will define an acceptable level of risk. In each case, you'll start by looking at where the lever is currently set, then ask whether it's time for a small or even a large adjustment. That decision will be based, among other factors, on the level of disruption your industry faces and the opportunities new technologies offer to release trapped value.

Regardless of what you decide, however, as part of your wise pivot, the processes for setting and adjusting these levers must be formalized. For some organizations, rules may already be in place, with both well-established timetables and management processes to revisit each of the nine levers.

But for many companies, as we found in our study, current settings may only be implicit and may not have been reviewed or changed for

Figure 6.1 Nine Levers of a Wise Pivot

INNOVATION	FINANCE	PEOPLE
Concentration Centralized vs. Decentralized	**Fixed Assets** Own vs. Pay-As-You-Go	**Leadership** Operators vs. Entrepreneurs
Control Directed vs. Autonomous	**Working Capital** Ready Made vs. Made to Order	**Work** Human vs. Machine
Aspiration Incremental vs. Disruptive	**Human Capital** Reskill vs. Redirect	**Culture** One Culture vs. Culture of Cultures

years or even decades. In mature industries, where offerings and prices are largely commoditized or regulated, every competitor may have the same or very similar strategies and, therefore, nearly identical settings for the strategic levers.

As even the most mature industries are reconfigured by either big bang or compressive disruption, however, achieving a wise pivot will require adjustment of at least some of the levers, and a more frequent review of how well current settings serve the portfolio. That won't always be easy, but this is where real change occurs, and, for the value releasers in our study, where real future growth is created.

When and how will you make your own modifications? Before answering that question, let's look at how one leading food and beverage company approached the innovation pivot in markets that began to change suddenly after decades of relative stability. And how the company's leaders embraced the opportunities in the new with an eye toward improving not only their own corporate health but also that of millions of consumers.

PIVOTING TO VALHALLA

PepsiCo is a global giant in the food and beverage industry, with twenty of its numerous brands each generating more than $1 billion in annual retail sales. Consumers purchase one billion of its products every day of the year.

But after over a hundred years of continued growth and frequent expansion through acquisitions, in 2010 then CEO Indra Nooyi began to see ominous signs of future disruption taking shape.

A move to healthier lifestyles, stimulated in part by an anti-obesity campaign led by US First Lady Michelle Obama, was putting pressure on the sale of PepsiCo's core soda and convenience snack products. Nooyi, who embraced the campaign, recognized the shift in tastes was no mere fad. PepsiCo, she decided, would need to change with the times, and change dramatically.

The easy part was introducing new products that responded to new demand, which PepsiCo did with gusto. Over the next few years, the company launched healthier versions of many of its existing products, and accelerated the acquisition of emerging health-conscious companies, including vegetable snack maker Bare Foods Co., probiotic beverage producer KeVita, and SodaStream, an Israeli company that produces home carbonation systems.

But for the long term, Nooyi needed much more. That's where the company's wise pivot really began.

PepsiCo's R&D, centered in the aptly named Valhalla, New York, had long been focused on incremental improvements in ingredients, production, and packaging. Research and development resources and investments were distributed broadly across the company. Most brands did their own innovation, with engineers and researchers operating largely independently.

There were valuable efforts to strengthen and extend the company's long-standing core products, but not the stuff of disruptive change. PepsiCo's innovation strategy left few resources available to develop Nooyi's new core, one based on healthier products and rapid response to fast-changing food trends, ingredients, and packaging and delivery technologies.

So Nooyi set about to change not just PepsiCo's approach to innovation, but the company's culture more broadly. From the top, every product was reclassified into three basic categories focused on impact rather than brand: "fun for you" (convenience snacks, including Lays potato chips, Doritos, Fritos, Cheetos; and Pepsi and Mountain Dew), "better for you" (the diet or low-fat versions of those same snacks and sodas), and "good for you" (health-conscious brands, such as Quaker Oats).

As part of a broad restructuring, Nooyi expanded the roles of her new chief scientist and chief designer, tasking them with the creation of more everyday nutrition products (including water, unsweetened tea, and nutrients such as grains, fruits, vegetables, or protein) as well as a new guilt-free line of drinks with fewer than seventy calories per twelve ounces, and food with lower levels of sodium and saturated fat.

That was just the start, but an important one. "I knew this journey was going to be long, arduous, and it was going to be filled with pitfalls," Nooyi later acknowledged in an interview with the *Freakonomics* podcast, "because it's not just the desire to change the portfolio. We had to line up the entire company's innovation, marketing, execution, and budgets to go where this marketplace was going, and then we had to change the culture of this company."

As PepsiCo's scientists and designers shifted gears, Nooyi's set out to win over two other important constituencies: employees and shareholders. While both groups could see the same trends Nooyi saw, successfully pivoting an organization with the size and momentum of PepsiCo around a new approach to innovation required regular and explicit reinforcement from the CEO.

Nooyi needed, as she described it, to "paint the future in a personal way" for employees. If their own eating and drinking habits were changing, how could they not imagine the rest of world was changing as well? Once workers realized they themselves were part of a bigger social trend, the innovation culture of PepsiCo started to shift.

Then there was Wall Street. Nooyi had to bring the company's analysts along carefully, giving them regular reassurance that increased investments in new-product R&D would not slow growth in the old businesses they were expert at measuring and analyzing.

That is, at least until a new core emerged as both a substantial source of income and the engine driving accelerated innovation and even more sustainable profits going forward.

PepsiCo's pivot expanded. R&D spending tripled, financed by a targeted $1 billion in annual cost cuts from current operations through automation and plant closures, some of which required innovation and investment of their own.

The company's innovation assets and resources became more centralized and coordinated across product lines. In 2018, PepsiCo opened The Hive, an internal technology incubator focused on developing and accelerating start-ups and emerging brands. The Hive nurtures smaller brands, like Maker Oats and Stubborn Soda, that might not otherwise get attention within the larger organization. It will also house experiments with new brands based on fast-changing consumer interests in new ingredients, such as seaweed or coconut water.

These activities have also been more tightly integrated with start-up investments by PepsiCo Ventures Group, the company's corporate venture capital fund. The fund's strategy is to look for companies that have already demonstrated accelerating market acceptance, and whose emerging brand aligns with PepsiCo's "performance with purpose" mission.

To speed the company's shift to the new, PepsiCo's chief scientist, himself an endocrinologist by training, began recruiting innovation talent from the life sciences, biotech, energy, pharmaceutical, automotive, and beauty care industries, bringing new disciplines and new ways of thinking into the mix.

To further push PepsiCo's technology frontier beyond the organization's borders, the company in late 2018 launched an external accelerator called Nutrition Greenhouse, which will award ten start-ups $20,000 each and match them with a mentor from PepsiCo. At the end of a six-month program aimed at speeding up development for the new businesses, the most promising company will be awarded an additional $100,000 to expand its partnership with PepsiCo.

Finally, Nooyi set new expectations for both the risks and rewards of future innovation. Nooyi encouraged all employees to approach innovation from a deep understanding of consumer wants and desires, identifying unmet or latent needs before consumers ever realize those needs are not being met. PepsiCo now needs to predict and provoke, inspire change, and imagine rather than simply create.

That aspiration radically changed the balance in Valhalla. "We had more development in PepsiCo than we had research," as Nooyi put it bluntly. "We could do flavor extensions of our products. Occasionally we could buy and build on a new product, but we were not very good at meaningful innovation, or meaningful package transformation, or meaningful ingredient development that could in fact apply to multiple products."

THE INNOVATION PIVOT

PepsiCo's disruption challenge was severe. Consumers worldwide had identified vast quantities of trapped value at the societal level: the potential to live longer, healthier lives. Could PepsiCo help release it? Nooyi was determined to try.

Nooyi's bold reshaping of PepsiCo employed many of the seven winning strategies. Her rebalancing of the innovation portfolio from development to research, for example, moved the company to being technology propelled and network powered. By embracing an emerging global health consciousness, PepsiCo's brand moved from one associated with fast foods to one that was hyper relevant and inclusive. Raising the profile of innovation and hiring from new disciplines made PepsiCo more talent rich.

Was PepsiCo's pivot a success? So far, the signs are good. From 2010 to 2017, even as its revenue from carbonated beverages fell, PepsiCo improved overall sales by more than $5 billion, doubled market capitalization, and largely held the line on market share.

In Nooyi's last year as CEO, the company continued to outperform traditional rivals, driving 18 percent of the total sales growth in retail food and beverage industrywide, even though PepsiCo accounts for less than 10 percent of industry sales. (Rivals experienced declines.) More impressive, the company's newest products captured nearly 20 percent of emerging food and beverage categories, more than the next four producers combined.

After twelve years at the helm, in 2018 Nooyi stepped down as PepsiCo's CEO. Though her achievements were impressive to say the least, the company is already working toward its next pivot under new CEO Ramon Laguarta, as consumer attitudes about nutrition continue to evolve.

PepsiCo's reinvention underscores much of what we learned in Accenture's wise pivot and from the companies in our research. Achieving a balanced allocation of core assets and resources is the heart of successful strategy execution, an imperative multiplied across the three lifecycle stages.

First and foremost is how you approach innovation itself. Whether from the sudden threat of big bang disruption or the slower-moving attack of compressive disruption, a wise pivot demands constant innovation in each of them: the old, the now, and the new.

Our research found that few leaders are responding quickly enough to the risks of disruption. But their failure isn't due to a lack of available funding. A recent Accenture Research survey of 840 C-level executives found that nearly every company reported increased investment in innovation over the past five years. Many are now doubling down, with nearly three-quarters of respondents saying they plan to increase innovation spending by more than 25 percent between 2017 and 2022.

Where does the money go? Corporate venture capital, in particular, is a source of both success and frustration. In the late 1990s, many companies launched funds in Silicon Valley that invested in start-ups unrelated to their business or its goals. With the dot-com crash in 2000, many of these efforts quickly and quietly closed down. Corporate venture capital has now returned, with nearly a thousand companies investing billions alongside traditional venture capitalists in 2016. Corporate venture capital investors are involved in nearly a third of all venture deals in the United States, and even more in Asia.

What's different is that today's corporate venture funds are more closely tied to the strategic goals in the new of their funders. Emerging best practices include ensuring each investment is tied to a specific corporate sponsor, which acts as a target customer for the venture's products, and which is responsible for testing and ultimately integrating offerings when they become mature.

According to research firm CB Insights, corporate venture capital has also become more standardized. Funds now have dedicated budgets, for example, with most corporate venture capital efforts completing more than five deals a year.

Still, few companies seem to be getting the kind of return on their investment they need. Our research found that over half the companies that said they had substantially increased innovation investments in the previous five years nonetheless underperformed industry peers in growing their profits or market capitalization.

Just spending more money isn't enough to release trapped value effectively. Getting innovation right is getting harder, as more money than ever chases the next big idea. Being too bold with innovation investments might create a major breakthrough, but it can also lead to a major washout.

Our analysis shows that much of the problem stems from companies spending predominantly on incremental innovation, which is how most of the underperforming companies told us they directed their investments, rather than on disruptive innovation.

Being cautious, of course, can improve your chances of success. But what good is success if it doesn't move the needle on business performance, especially as competitors, old and new, are targeting larger pools of trapped value accumulating right under your nose?

How can you reset your investment strategy to improve innovation outcomes as part of a wise pivot? We'll look at three levers—concentration, control, and aspiration—you'll need to consider in answering that question.

- **CENTRALIZATION.** Centralizing innovation improves integration, but may interfere with your ability to act on the best ideas of employees and outside stakeholders. This approach can also be countercultural for companies whose operating model gives autonomy to its business units.

- **CONTROL.** Giving R&D staff and corporate venture fund managers freer rein to pursue the projects they think are most promising respects their expertise, but it may mean dead-end projects go on way too long, diverting precious resources from more promising efforts.

- **ASPIRATION.** While experiments with emerging technologies at the upper bounds of the trapped value gap maximize the potential to create a big bang disruption, no company, not even technology leaders, can bet solely on moon shots. Some innovation bets, especially those aimed at growing the core, need to be more circumscribed in scope and reasonably certain of success.

Let's be clear about one thing. There is no perfect setting for any of the levers that applies to every enterprise. Depending on the nature of trapped value in your industry, your innovation portfolio will require greater or lesser scrutiny, autonomy, and risk. Your answer will be based on the kinds of value you target, the new technologies you apply, and the winning strategies you embrace.

Do you need to grow offerings for the new, either organically in a corporate incubator or externally by participating in so-called start-up accelerators? Do you need a formal program of corporate venture capital? How much of the CEO's time should be devoted to managing the innovation pivot? Just how radical a change to your innovation strategy is needed to survive the next wave of disruption? These are the questions we'll review, in the context of our own pivot and those of the companies we studied.

THE CONCENTRATION LEVER: HOW CENTRALIZED SHOULD INNOVATION BE?

The value releasers in our study learned the sometimes painful lesson that innovation performs just as poorly under a dictatorship as it does in anarchy.

Too much control translates to incremental product improvements, with researchers strongly discouraged from taking risks. Yet leaving every division, product team, or individual developer to their own priorities—a failure to leverage the combined expertise of the entire organization—leaves to chance alignment with an overall innovation strategy.

It's also harder for individual business units to hire scarce talent in key areas, including data science, machine learning, and other new technology disciplines. The best designers and developers, to be honest, may well prefer to work at Alphabet or another high-profile technology company rather than for you.

For your own wise pivot, the question is where along the concentration spectrum your organization works best, able to deliver growth today and in the future. PepsiCo's wise pivot includes elements of both centralization (Valhalla) and decentralization (Nutrition Greenhouse). Some efforts are very clearly directed from the top and others left entirely to outside innovators experimenting on their own, with PepsiCo providing mentorship but not direct supervision.

Based on the experience of the companies in our study, being overly distributed may help boost margins in the short term, but risks your missing out on bigger growth opportunities in the future.

Consider, at one extreme, Illinois Tool Works, the Fortune 500 industrial parts and tools manufacturer once described as "the most decentralized company in the world." The company's approach to innovation is demand pulled. Product developers elicit insights from key customers, then focus on designing and patenting new products and components that address specific challenges or opportunities.

This keeps R&D costs low and innovation output high relative to peers in the manufacturing industry, and the results have been impressive. Illinois Tool Works is often among the top one hundred patent recipients in the United States every year, ranking fourteenth in 2017.

"We are not a traditional innovator in the sense that we don't aspire to invest in or create science," CEO E. Scott Santi told investors. "We're not what I would describe as an R&D-centered company. What we do instead and what we're really good at is taking and combining known technology to create clever and robust solutions for our biggest customers and our most challenging business segments."

Relying entirely on today's market for innovation direction, however, leaves Illinois Tool Works betting its future, and its ability to pivot, solely on the known needs of current customers. But what if today's buyers are too risk averse, lack imagination, or are themselves more vulnerable to disruption than they realize?

Illinois Tool Works faces considerable risk of compressive disruption. Today's customers may become less profitable over time, or worse, simply fade away as new competitors in industrial manufacturing, relying on more forward-thinking suppliers, overtake them.

There are dangers too in overly centralizing innovation, especially when it is physically and culturally cut off from the rest of the company. Think tanks and research parks provide work environments that maximize creativity for your most innovative employees, but without regular interaction with company leaders, let alone actual customers and day-to-day managers, researchers can become detached from reality, working on the wrong problems.

Worse, they may be developing products for a future the rest of the business doesn't believe in. The most infamous example is Xerox's Palo Alto Research Center (PARC), the Silicon Valley incubator whose brilliant computer scientists and engineers invented many of the revolutionary features of modern desktop computers during the lab's 1970s heyday, including graphical user interfaces, networked computers, and laser printing.

As PARC researcher Alan Kay famously said: "The best way to predict the future is to invent it." And certainly PARC's vision of the future of office automation turned out to be eerily accurate. But while PARC developers enjoyed the freedom to work without corporate direction or constraints, they lacked the most basic communications channels back to the business or to its strategic direction. As a result, none of PARC's breakthrough innovations were ever successfully capitalized on by Xerox.

Instead, the considerable trapped value PARC spotted and targeted was left to others to release. A young Steve Jobs and Steve Wozniak famously visited in 1979, amazed by the inventions they saw lying around, none of which Xerox seemed serious about commercializing. Recognizing the revolutionary change ready to explode, Jobs and Wozniak embraced the PARC ideas and used them to redesign their own line of personal computers at the fledgling Apple, changing the course of history.

Xerox PARC had the solution to closing an enormous trapped value gap, but without broader involvement from the company as a whole, that achievement was wasted. As John Seely Brown, onetime director of PARC, acknowledged: "Not everything we start ends up fitting with our businesses later on. Many of the ideas we work on here involve a paradigm shift in order to deliver value." Or, as Jobs colorfully put it: "They grabbed defeat from the greatest victory in the computer industry."

If nothing else, PARC is the archetypal failure that today's innovation managers are determined to avoid. The largely privately held New York Times Company, for example, recently executed an innovation pivot to bring its own R&D efforts closer to the now than the new, recognizing that without more innovation in the short term, they may not have the capacity to play a leading role in the future.

Like all news organizations, the company faces an existential crisis in its core business. Consumers have not only abandoned printed newspapers in favor of digital alternatives; they are also eagerly embracing new sources of information, much of it coming not from professional journalists but from less expensive if less reliable sources, including social media. The advertising revenue that has long subsidized mainstream news collection and reporting is following the consumers online, a second hit to revenue.

In response, over the last two decades the New York Times Company has struggled mightily to rebalance its R&D, playing catch-up to industry disruption that came more quickly than anticipated, and which continues to stymie incumbents trying to chart their course, speed, and trajectory amid shifting and often contradictory consumer preferences.

A few years ago, the company's R&D group operated under a broad mandate to think three to five years out and not worry about connecting their work back to today's newspaper. Using Microsoft's Kinect voice- and motion-detection technology, the group prototyped something straight out of the movie *Minority Report* that it termed a "magic mirror." Fixed to a wall, the magic mirror could execute a user's voice commands to surf the web, send e-mails, and of course browse through the *Times'* full slate of articles and video content.

As impressive as this demonstration may be, the company has perhaps waffled more than it has pivoted between embracing a digital-first strategy and retreating to the relative security of being one of the only, and most prestigious, national print sources left. As a 2014 internal report titled "Innovation" put it: "In the coming years, the *New York Times* needs to accelerate its transition from a newspaper that also produces a rich and impressive digital report to a digital publication that also produces a rich and impressive newspaper."

In 2017, the New York Times Company pivoted again, recasting the R&D unit to be more tightly integrated with the newsroom. Now renamed Story[X], this five-person team has a new mandate: do less dreaming and more building. Story[X] serves three of the company's functions—editorial, product, and advertising—with an emphasis on editorial.

R&D is no longer an innovation hub, but a widely distributed team charged with accelerating innovation already happening across the organization. That largely translates to technology the *Times* and its advertisers can use in the near future, including augmented reality, messaging apps, and integration with smart speakers and connected vehicles. For now, the real focus is on enhanced video offerings, including experiments with virtual reality to make news stories more immediate for consumers.

"There's a value to doing that R&D, but what didn't really happen in practice with any sort of regularity was connecting it back to what the rest of the company was doing," said Marc Lavallee, who has worked at the New York Times Company since 2011 and is now leading Story[X]. "I wanted to flip the model and say, instead of developing this first, then see if there's an application, start with the need of the newsroom and advertisers and move out from there, instead of crash-landing with something no one was asking for."

As these examples show, there are trade-offs between centralized and decentralized innovation; trade-offs that must be regularly reevaluated as part of your wise pivot. That's certainly a lesson we learned during our own reinvention. To survive, let alone thrive, we realized we would have to out-innovate the fastest Silicon Valley companies in disrupting our own core business, and do so before others did it to us.

Key to pivoting faster for us was a decision to make big changes in how we managed our innovation portfolio. At the time, our innovation assets were siloed, a sprawling collection of activities, energetic but uncoordinated. To harness these raw forces, we needed to exert leadership from the top, or what we call "managed innovation."

The result is the innovation architecture described in chapter 4. It integrates innovation activities across all three lifecycle stages, from pure research to real-time improvements in daily client work. Utilizing the capabilities of Accenture Research, Accenture Ventures, Accenture Labs, and Accenture Studios, we can now quickly develop and scale new ideas for our businesses and our clients. The goal is always to invest appropriately for the relevant stage of maturity, spending more intensely the closer an idea gets to commercialization.

The new structure is driven and nurtured from the top down, with Omar as its chief architect. Former Accenture CEO Pierre Nanterme was the communicator of our innovation strategy across the old, the now, and the new, both internally and externally.

At the same time, bottom-up innovation was, and continues to be, necessary. In 2017, as noted, we opened The Dock in Dublin, our multidisciplinary research and incubation hub, where, as Nanterme put it: "The entire innovation architecture comes to life." At The Dock, staff, clients, and visiting academics collaborate to create and rapidly prototype innovative solutions for Accenture and its clients.

At a recent two-day design and programming "hackathon" we hosted there, fourteen global teams—made up of entrepreneurs, enterprise technology teams, universities, and more—pitched blockchain-based solutions aimed at releasing trapped value at the societal level.

We were blown away by the quality of the ideas presented after just thirty-six hours of coding. The prototypes addressed everything from a homeless crisis in Ireland to climate change, to tracking ethically sourced halal meat, to tools to give users more control of their data, and many more issues.

The Dock really does prove that top leadership doesn't have a monopoly on the best ideas. Reflecting on our experience so far, Omar notes that he would never have conceived on his own how teams could use computer vision to manage quality defects at the end of a car component manufacturing line; how they could apply AI to manage the highly complex process of pharmaceutical labeling; or use natural language search to help collect and organize the evidence needed to process insurance claims.

In addition to The Dock, we now have more than one hundred subsidiary innovation centers around the world, bringing our efforts closer to local markets and their unique sources of trapped value. In

2017 alone, we opened sixteen "Liquid Studios" that accelerate advanced software development, along with eight delivery centers, and new innovation hubs in Bengaluru, India, and Houston, Texas, bringing together multiple elements of the innovation architecture.

The Liquid Studios, as the name suggests, use rapid application development principles and tools, combining them with fast-evolving technologies such as the IoT and wearables. The focus is on turning ideas into experiments, or what is sometimes called "pretotyping."

Along the way, our investment in innovation has increased each year, growing by $100 million to over $700 million between 2015 and 2017.

A similar desire to stay several steps ahead of disruptive forces shaped our work with Schneider Electric, which is leading the digital transformation of energy management and automation across key markets, including industry, power, buildings, data centers, and infrastructure.

Working side by side with Schneider Electric, we co-created its Digital Services Factory in 2016 to rapidly build and scale new offerings in areas such as predictive maintenance, asset monitoring, and energy optimization, with the goal of putting the customer at the center of the innovation process. Schneider Electric's plan is to deliver an IoT platform that supports emerging industry standards, with an open development platform and an extensive ecosystem of partners.

Crossing different businesses, the IoT will embed sensors, communications, and computing power in equipment throughout the manufacturing and distribution supply chain, allowing real-time collection and analysis of data at every stage in the product lifecycle. As more machinery gets connected, manufacturers like Schneider Electric know they will be expected to embed the latest digital capabilities in their products, becoming both network powered and hyper relevant.

As our research shows, industrial manufacturers recognize digital technologies are vital for their future. Yet their level of digital adoption and innovation has been slow, risking lost market share and profits to start-ups and other digital disruptors. In fact, two-thirds of industrial companies Accenture surveyed said they are feeling the impact of digital disruption, yet half of them are not yet investing in IoT solutions as part of their business strategy.

Schneider Electric wants to be different. To compete in the digital economy alongside new entrants and other disruptors, the company is transforming its customers' experience and seizing new market opportunities. It actively empowers digital change agents throughout the company to foster innovation to create synergies between new and legacy businesses while also developing new digital services.

That's where the Digital Service Factory comes in, as a successful engagement model that can push forward Schneider's convergence of its traditional corporate and new digital DNA. Schneider Electric and Accenture staff generate and incubate new ideas for digital service offerings, such as predictive maintenance services or asset-monitoring suites. Following a secure product lifecycle development process, the Digital Service Factory brings these offerings to market in less than eight months, as opposed to three years in the pre-digital days. This agility and responsiveness translate into rapid-fire digital innovation in connected products and services, control at the edge of the network, and analytics, apps, and services.

Overall, Schneider is aiming to cut its time from product ideation to market delivery by 80 percent. That translates to rapid-fire innovation in connected products and services, controlling all the new devices at the edge of the network, analytics, and apps.

Together, these stories underscore the importance of managing the location of innovation more deliberately. But we're not suggesting a fifty-fifty breakdown, or any other magic ratio of centralization versus decentralization. The right balance will vary depending on market conditions, industry, and your company's culture.

In contemplating your own balance, however, consider the findings of our 2018 wise pivot survey of 1,440 C-level executives from companies with revenues exceeding $500 million across eleven industries and twelve countries. The research looked at how large companies respond to disruptive change, both in reimagining their legacy business and expanding into the scalable new.

The survey covered four key topics: portfolio change approach, innovation approach, investment approach, and new leadership mindsets. The responses revealed some valuable insights. When compared with industry peers, for example, the value releasers in this study— those that reported at least 75 percent of their current revenues came from business activities, investments, and ventures less than five years old—were more deliberate about structuring their organizations to innovate by design and get the most out of their innovation efforts.

By concentrating innovation capabilities under a strong leadership team, with dedicated investment and defined innovation roles and responsibilities, they embed innovation into, as with Schneider Electric, the corporate DNA. Three-quarters of the value releasers have already adopted centralized innovation strategies, with innovation resources combined into a single dedicated function with its own leadership and budget. By contrast, only one-third of the other companies we asked have done the same.

That's an important shift. At least some form of centralized strategy allows companies to spot promising innovations and prototype them early. In a world of accelerating disruption across industries, some centralization may prove essential to identifying quickly ideas with the highest potential and turn them into commercial reality ahead of competitors.

THE CONTROL LEVER: HOW MUCH AUTONOMY SHOULD INNOVATORS GET?

Establishing a healthy balance between centralization and decentralization is a vital first step in a successful innovation pivot. Having done so, the next challenge is to consider control in relation to autonomy. How much direction should management provide in hopes of keeping innovation focused, without squashing creativity and the potential for inspiration and serendipity?

At the extremes, too much or too little control yields less than optimal results. Leaders can be highly directive, instructing their employees, especially their scientists, engineers, and researchers, on what to innovate and for what purpose. That approach maximizes the strategic alignment of the innovation portfolio, but unless your CEO has a crystal ball into the future, it will almost certainly undervalue the creativity and domain expertise of developers.

An alternative might be to let a thousand flowers bloom, encouraging and incentivizing innovation throughout the organization. In

that model, all employees and even outside stakeholders become inventors. Senior management's job is simply to choose from among
the most promising experiments and nurture them into new products
and services.

That approach isn't likely to work either. Innovating without direction or alignment is no more likely to lead to useful new product or
service offerings at any of the three lifecycle stages than picking ideas
out of a hat. Employees might have good instincts, but without mentorship and direction, even good ideas may not reach their potential,
and may prove a distraction from the day-to-day business of serving
customers.

To quote once again from Alan Kay: "Most ideas are bad." We regularly hear from CEOs about their struggle not to originate ideas, but
to evaluate what could be dozens of proof-of-concept proposals coming in from across their organizations.

How then do you adjust the lever to achieve just the right level
of innovation directedness without constraining it? And how do you
know when it's time to shift the balance as part of an ongoing wise
pivot?

Consider the experience of 3M, the global science company whose
name has long been synonymous with innovation. 3M has garnered the
country's highest award for innovation, the National Medal of Technology and Innovation, and consistently ranks in *Fortune* magazine's annual survey of "America's Most Admired Companies." With products
based on nearly fifty different technology platforms, 3M boasts over
$30 billion in annual sales and nearly a hundred thousand employees.

More to the point, throughout the company's more than hundred-
year history, its engineers and designers have routinely turned out scalable innovations by following a rigorous methodology. They measure,
monitor, and control their focus, aiming to find the right balance between performance and innovation.

Still, even great innovators may need to tweak the formula from
time to time, especially when core technology changes are accelerating. So at the start of the information revolution two decades ago, 3M
pivoted closer to the top of the trapped value gap. Management introduced a new core metric known as the "Freshness Index," which cal-
culated the percentage of revenue that came from products less than

four years old. The goal was to derive 25 percent of revenue from new product introductions within five years.

In response to the threat of big bang and compressive disruption, many of the value releasers in our study—including tech giants such as Google, Amazon, and Tencent as well as companies like global industrial leader Bosch and Starbucks—are adjusting the lever toward more, not less, investment in the new technologies, looking for their own "moon shots." Though that may not prove to be your answer, these companies are executing wise pivots at least in part by taking a long view of what they mean by "new," scanning the horizon for emerging technologies with the potential to utterly rewrite the rules of their industries.

Such efforts, staffed by the most creative and least bureaucracy tolerant employees and outside partners, invariably require freedom of movement. But they can't just be launched into space and forgotten, with hopes they'll return someday with the future, fully developed and comfortably in tow. Even moon shots need to be aligned with the rest of the innovation portfolio, benefiting from the guidance and discipline of corporate managers in matters of human capital, budgeting, and project management, to name a few.

That control, however, must be applied carefully, even lovingly. That's the model followed by retail giant Walmart in the 2017 launch of its new Silicon Valley–based incubator, known as Store No 8. (The name is a nod to Walmart founder Sam Walton, who used the real store no. 8 in Arkansas as a place to experiment with retail innovations.)

Store No. 8's charter is to get ahead of the curve on retail innovation and disruption before someone else beats them to it. (By "someone else," read Amazon, which is leveraging its dominance in virtual retailing into the physical world, acquiring organic retailer Whole Foods Market and opening experimental physical stores that use sensors and cameras to automate checkout, among other radical changes.)

Walmart is using Store No. 8 to incubate some of the company's highest-risk bets. Recent efforts include tests of potential applications using many of the new technologies we frequently mention, such as robotics, virtual and augmented reality, machine learning, and artificial intelligence.

These experiments include a subscription-based personal shopping service, called Jetblack, that will give shoppers recommendations and allow purchases via text messages. Another reported effort, Project Kepler, reimagines the in-store experience using technologies such as computer vision.

Store No. 8 is an important component of Walmart's broader innovation portfolio, which the company continues to expand and rebalance regularly. Walmart Labs, for example, addresses the "now" stage of the company's pivot, developing improvements in customer experience technology that can be implemented within six to twelve months. With over two thousand employees in Silicon Valley, Walmart Labs recently piloted a new service connecting independent drivers to customer delivery requests as they come in.

Store No. 8's charter is to look for innovations at least three years ahead. While Walmart has set up its incubator as a company within a company, start-ups launched from it will nonetheless be wholly owned by Walmart. And rather than use the typical venture capitalist models for evaluating the potential and progress of its portfolio companies, Walmart measures Store No. 8's efforts using what it calls "operational and strategic returns"; that is, how its innovations could generate value for a specific future retail experience.

With the launch of Store No. 8, Walmart acknowledged both the need for more visionary thinking and the difficulty of integrating it into a company famously focused on operational efficiency in today's customer-focused retail ecosystem. Its creation followed the 2016 acquisition of online retailing innovator Jet.com for $3 billion, widely seen as a catch-up effort to make Walmart an e-commerce powerhouse and, not incidentally, to infuse digital culture into the company's analog corporate fabric. The scale of e-commerce and other digital acquisitions before and since the Jet.com buy continues to turn heads both inside and outside the company.

Store No. 8, not coincidentally, is run by Jet.com founder Marc Lore, who manages all US e-commerce operations. So beyond Jet.com's immediate value as a source of online revenue, Walmart's ability to leverage Lore's skills and expertise has generated dividends across the company's efforts in the old and the now, as well as the new.

Lore, for example, spearheaded expanded inventory on the company's website, and the implementation of free two-day shipping on orders of $35 or more. As a result, Walmart's e-commerce sales are taking off. In 2018 alone, the company was on track to increase digital revenue by 40 percent.

Store No. 8, Lore said at a 2017 retail technology conference, "will be ring-fenced by the rest of the organization and backed by the largest retailer in the world." It will have the financial resources of a giant corporation, but the freedom of a start-up—precisely what an organization of Walmart's size and industry dynamics will need to complete its pivot to the new.

Store No. 8 also plans to facilitate collaborations with outside start-ups, venture capitalists, and academics to develop even more disruptive innovations. So far, it has a wide-open mandate to do so.

As with all our value releasers, however, the courage to devote strategic resources to chasing the trapped value gap came from the very top. "It came down to the senior leadership team taking the view of being where retail is going over the next twenty years and which areas we need to lead in so we can disrupt rather than have others disrupt us," Lori Flees, Walmart's senior vice president of corporate strategy, said in an interview.

The real key to Walmart's pivot was the Walton family's support. They still own 50 percent of the company, and decided around 2016 that Walmart required significant change to thrive for the next hundred years. They backed a decision to reduce earnings in the short term, in order to lower prices for consumers and to support increased investments in digital innovation. While those investments have yet to pay off in current earnings, they are recognized by investors in the future value component of the company's stock price.

Not every public company has the strong support of its shareholders to take a long-term view. That kind of foresight is especially impressive here, given that Walmart was and remains the biggest company in the world by revenue. Then again, Walmart began as a disruptor, having the same impact on retail twenty years ago that Amazon is having today. Now they're disrupting themselves to stay relevant.

In the home appliance industry, one venerable incumbent is taking an even more radical approach in its pivot to the new, borrowing heavily from the philosophy of the "maker community," where individuals get together to tinker with the latest technology-enhanced hardware and software gadgets just to see what they come up with.

Since its acquisition by Haier in 2016, GE Appliances (GEA) has been working to adopt its Chinese parent company's unique innovation model, which we described in chapter 3.

Historically an admitted also-ran when it came to major innovations in white goods, GEA now prioritizes the search for trapped value at the customer level, launching new products responsive to changing demographics and a growing demand by consumers for more customizable products. In the ten years before being acquired by Haier, GEA's revenue dropped more than 10 percent, but in 2017 it increased by 6 percent. Even more impressive, profits that year increased by more than 20 percent, its first-ever double-digit growth rate.

To reflect Haier's mantra of "zero distance to the customer," GEA renewed its commitment to FirstBuild, an experiment in open innovation GEA launched in 2014.

In the open innovation model, companies reverse the historically secretive R&D process, collaborating transparently with problem solvers from across domains, innovating in broad daylight and in full view of competitors.

Located on a college campus close to GEA's Louisville, Kentucky, headquarters, FirstBuild is a microfactory for appliance innovation, open to anyone who simply signs up. FirstBuild has over twenty-three thousand registered users (about double the number of GEA employees), giving GEA access to off-the-wall but potentially valuable ideas that can be tested and even produced at the speed of a Silicon Valley start-up.

The facility is truly open—no nondisclosure agreements, no proprietary technology. "What we're doing at FirstBuild couldn't be more different," GEA president Kevin Nolan said recently. "It's completely open. Anyone can come in anytime. If you're a competitor, if you're just someone that wants to see what we're doing, anyone can come in."

The facility is stocked with 3D printers, laser cutters, circuit board fabrication equipment, and other high- and low-tech tools to maximize experimentation. Materials and equipment are available free of charge for appliance-related projects. Developers who can't come to

Louisville can submit ideas online and work with FirstBuild's team to develop them. With several products already launched, FirstBuild may become fully self-funded by 2018.

All ideas, whether proposed in person or online, are voted on by FirstBuild members. The community then does everything from product concept through design, engineering, manufacturing, and initial sales, for perhaps as many as a thousand units. Inventors earn a small cash prize for winning concepts, along with royalties of up to .5 percent.

And to keep FirstBuild as lean as possible, inventors fund production not through GEA, but using crowdfunding platforms including Indiegogo and Kickstarter. The Opal Nugget Ice Maker, which produces cubes that are easy to chew, is based on an idea submitted on the FirstBuild website in 2015. After proving the concept, the development team raised nearly $3 million through crowdfunding, generating seven thousand pre-orders, which were filled in 2016. (A smartphone-controlled version is now available for $499.)

Where there's demand beyond the trial run, GEA may elect to produce the product at scale, but the community can also take their innovations to GEA competitors, a trade-off of control that GEA believes it can manage, thanks to a growing capacity to be first to market.

Reflecting on FirstBuild's success, Nolan credits physical separation, community-validated ideas, agility, short turnarounds, and the use of hackathons (rather than product-planning meetings) to source new projects. "We're all about experimenting," Nolan says of First-Build. "We don't have a plan, which sounds odd from GE."

Odd indeed. In pivoting to the new, however, that's often what's required to fend off disruptors who can experiment at will and scale with ease.

With Store No. 8, Walmart dramatically shifted the balance in its allocation of innovation resources, betting big on the new even as it enhanced its ability to respond to disruptions in the old and the now. With FirstBuild, GEA has adopted a radically open approach, in part to make up for lost time and in part to force itself to develop the capacity to be first to market when an innovation proves scalable.

As these examples suggest, the wise pivot invariably changes the character of senior leadership, requiring C-level executives to learn invaluable start-up skills that can direct innovation without choking it. Ironically, for senior executives, it can require more discipline to unleash controlled chaos.

One way to manage the delicate balance between too much and too little control, as we found in our own pivot, is to be very clear about metrics. We keep them simple and perfectly aligned with our strategy, changing them quickly when priorities change. Effective metrics, understood and supported by multiple levels of leadership, give us a level of directness we need to realize our strategy, but also the flexibility our innovation leaders need to hit their targets.

THE ASPIRATION LEVER: HOW MUCH OF THE TRAPPED VALUE GAP SHOULD INNOVATORS AIM TO CLOSE?

Walmart's pivot to the new underscores the third lever that must be considered in the design and management of your innovation portfolio. While the first two levers determine where innovation takes place and how much autonomy developers are given, the final lever determines how much of the trapped value gap your efforts should aim to close: your aspiration lever.

In effect, the aspiration lever determines how you allocate resources within the three lifecycle stages. How much of your innovation should be incremental, and how much disruptive? And how will you allocate resources within each stage, based on your level of aspiration?

Answering those questions requires sober analysis of the trapped value across the four levels: your enterprise, your industry, your customers, and society at large. The answers may differ based on the lifecycle stage.

Within each business, if your industry is still relatively stable, you may find more of your portfolio is focused on incremental improvements to existing products, services, and operating models that bring in new technologies rather than investing directly in future disruptors.

On the other hand, if disruption looms close, you may have little chance of surviving without bold thinking—new partnerships, venture investments, and real-world experiments with the technologies new entrants and competitors have already deployed, and which your customers are adopting with enthusiasm.

In either case, it's not enough to simply swing for the fences and hope for the best. Doing so leaves no plan B when technology doesn't evolve as expected or, more likely, customer acceptance and adoption prove hard to predict. What's more, taking any one of the seven wrong turns can lead you into a blind alley, like so many start-ups that launched with a bang but just as suddenly disappeared from view have demonstrated.

As with all aspects of the wise pivot, there's no single best setting for the aspiration lever. How you allocate innovation resources targeting the trapped value gap will depend on many factors, and will, as with the other elements of a balanced pivot, change over time as market conditions change.

As we just saw, for example, Walmart had a long history of retail innovation, the source of the company's formidable competitive advantage over incumbent competitors large and small. But Walmart's strategy had long been focused on the old and the now. It improved the efficiency of its physical supply chain, for example, by building robust digital connections to suppliers and using point-of-sale technologies such as bar code scanners and RFID (radio-frequency identification) tags to optimize inventory, pricing, and promotions.

That approach, copied by many of the company's traditional competitors, may have once been enough. The advent of e-commerce in the late 1990s, after all, initially posed little threat to Walmart's business model or its innovation portfolio. As recently as 2018, e-commerce sales represented less than 10 percent of total retail, hardly a big bang disruption. And millions of consumers in developed economies have yet to make a single online purchase.

What Walmart realized, perhaps only a little late, was that it was experiencing instead compressive disruption. Revenue growth masked declining profit growth as online retailers picked off the most attractive product categories for virtual sale, and a new breed of cost-focused retailers drove down prices generally. The real challenge was further obscured by the fact that weaker retailers were exiting the business, propping up, if only temporarily, the market share and revenue of the survivors. It only looked like they were winning.

The company's bold acquisitions of Jet.com and FlipKart, along with the launch of the Store No. 8 incubator, represent a significant movement of the aspiration lever toward closing the trapped value gap. Walmart is now making billion-dollar bets not just on increasing its strength in traditional markets but in emerging digital retailing technologies, too.

As with all pivoting, however, going too far or too soon in either direction can make a difficult competitive situation worse. Consider, on the one hand, Tesla, which has clearly captured the imagination of high-end car buyers eager for a more environmentally conscious electric vehicle that doesn't sacrifice design or performance.

The company was able to pre-sell an impressive number of its first mainstream vehicle, the Model 3. But when it came time to manufacture them, Tesla found it had been too bold in its radical push to close a trapped value gap, not just for battery and motor technology but also for robotics, high-voltage cables, displays, and fuses, among other components.

The strategy, at least so far, has not proven to be scalable. Tesla experienced what CEO Elon Musk himself acknowledged to be a "production hell," leading to output far below promised deliveries or market expectations. In the first months of full production for the Model 3, the company made only 260 vehicles, not the 1,500 it had planned.

At the other end of the spectrum, consider big petrochemical companies, which outsourced much of their R&D to oil field service providers in the 1990s and 2000s as a cost-saving measure. The resulting lack of visibility into new exploration and production technologies meant most of them missed the shale gas revolution in North America, requiring them to purchase assets at peak prices just to catch up.

What's more, the increasing urgency to reduce carbon emissions—trapped value at the societal level—means oil companies may be carrying billions of barrels of reserves on their books that will never be produced. In response, many producers have redirected innovation resources to their core business, hoping to drive up efficiency. Yet, despite the fact that reliance on today's fuels has an ever-clearer end date, few of these companies have found new, scalable energy sources they can invest in instead.

At Accenture, our approach to managing the aspiration trade-off has been to diversify. By innovating big enough and regularly enough, we never have to rely on the success of one large innovation investment to secure the fortunes of the company.

Which is to say that we don't allow ourselves to get too hungry before we start hunting again. Similarly, our research shows that companies less dependent on big bets can pivot more successfully and consistently. Leaders who need fast, large-scale hits, on the other hand, make more wrong turns, including rash decisions, often reflected in poorly chosen large-scale acquisitions. You need to control your appetite.

Hunting before you're hungry, to push the metaphor perhaps a little far, may require you to cannibalize products still selling in the now in order to get ahead of competitors in the new. In the brutally competitive video console market, for example, pioneering manufacturer Nintendo consistently releases its next-generation product before slowing sales of the previous generation requires it.

Nintendo anticipates, usually correctly, that users eyeing a growing trapped value gap, fed by fast-improving computing technology, will soon enough make the jump, if not to one of its own products, then to one from its competitors. Figure 6.2 maps the result: a series of disciplined yet dramatic pivots from one core product to the next, most of which Nintendo executed with considerable success.

Note how each new platform, whether the Wii in 2006 or the Switch in 2017, was introduced as sales of the previous generation product were clearly winding down, but well before they ended. It's likely, in fact, that introduction of the next-generation system sped up the retirement of its predecessor. But that is often a necessary trade-off in markets prone to big bang disruption.

Stretching, as Nintendo does, to close the trapped value gap ahead of market demand is at the heart of what makes many leading tech companies so exciting to watch and risky to invest in. Netflix famously introduced its internet-based streaming service, for example, when its DVD mail-order business was still profitable, and competitors were few. Tencent likewise created the WeChat social media platform even though its QQ instant-messaging service was still popular.

In both cases, the risk paid off handsomely. Netflix's streaming revenues in 2017 were over $8 billion, around a fourfold increase over what the DVD business earned at its peak. WeChat, likewise, has over a billion monthly active users.

We've embraced a similar philosophy at Accenture. We acquired and built skills in digital marketing and in creating new customer experiences for our interactive and digital businesses, while our IT systems implementation and integration practice was still performing well.

Figure 6.2 Evolution of Big Bang Disruption at Nintendo

Nintendo Console Sales: Accelerating Sales, Accelerating Declines

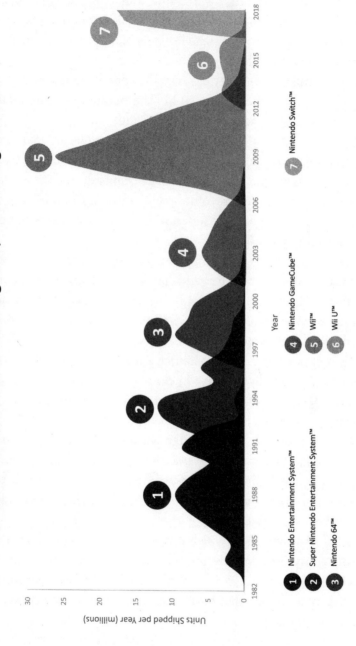

The acquisition of Fjord, Karmarama, and many other companies has contributed to making us the largest provider of digital marketing services in the world, with revenue of $6.5 billion in 2017, and 35 percent year-over-year growth.

Like Nintendo and Netflix, we also appreciate the need to sometimes pivot even when doing so has the potential to cannibalize mature businesses and accelerate their decline.

Our "Cloud First" strategy is a good example. In 2014, we made the decision to migrate all our IT systems to the cloud, and to develop quickly the skills and scale to help our clients do the same. Based on our research, we knew a revolution in computing architecture was underway. Cloud computing's superior operational and economic advantages are simply irresistible.

Having committed to the substantial investment we made in our own migration, we next forged alliances with leading cloud platform companies, as well as "software as a service" application providers. We also acquired several firms, such as Cloud Sherpas, that were leaders in cloud advisory and technology services.

By 2015, we were ready to launch Cloud First, committing to train a thousand of our own people in cloud technology. This included five hundred developers for the Accenture AWS Business Group, certified experts in Amazon's cloud platform.

We made this pivot even though we knew cloud computing would, if successful, put at risk some traditional systems development work, then still a significant source of our revenue. That gamble paid off handsomely. We are now the leading global provider of cloud migration and consulting services.

Our early pivot also helped us develop deep relationships throughout the ecosystem. We are the leading partner, for example, of SAP, Oracle, Microsoft, Salesforce, Workday, Amazon Web Services, Google, and many others that have made the cloud revolution succeed at such an amazing pace.

Still, that kind of moon-shot investment at the top of the trapped value gap carries substantial risk, unavoidable in hypercompetitive, technology-propelled markets like ours and others, including electronics, food and beverage, and fashion, to name a few. Returns can be dramatic or zero, but rarely anything in between.

Tilting your innovation portfolio too far toward the heavens often means depriving other less dramatic investments of funding and management attention. To hedge some of that risk, many industries have historically used joint ventures and consortia to spread the costs and benefits of big innovation, effectively hunting in packs.

Innovation at every point on the S-curve of the new increasingly comes from companies working together, sharing risk and reward. This has long been the model in producing products as different as Hollywood blockbuster movies, oil field drilling, and insurance for large-scale infrastructure projects.

In the era of technology-driven disruption, it's an approach being adopted more broadly. Consider the development of autonomous electric vehicles, a revolution in the automotive industry that shifted in only a few years from an "if" to a "when." The technology for safe and affordable self-driving cars is well on the way to becoming cost-effective for mainstream consumers.

The next leap, however, will be to establish standards for vehicle-to-vehicle communications, and for integration of self-driving cars and trucks with roads, lights, and other parts of the transit infrastructure. For reasons of both cost and coordination, no company can develop or deploy that kind of innovation alone, making partnerships essential.

Daimler AG, one of the industry's longtime technology giants, understands that imperative. The company is determined to play a leading role in shaping the future of many of the key technologies driving the new in transportation, including connectivity, autonomous driving, asset sharing among consumers, and electric drive systems.

Beyond its own investments, Daimler is also leading the development of a comprehensive ecosystem to accelerate self-driving innovation. To speed up creation of a mass market for long-range electric vehicles, for example, it has invested in IONITY, a joint venture with other automakers focused on deploying a cost-effective charging infrastructure for electric vehicles.

Daimler is likewise collaborating with longtime components supplier Bosch to pilot self-driving taxis. Daimler will provide the vehicles, while Bosch will equip them with sensors, actuators, and control units. In 2017, the company also entered into an agreement to build self-driving cars for ride-hailing leader Uber.

As that example suggests, artfully adjusting the aspiration lever requires development of the kind of organizational muscle essential to collaborating with a much wider range of partners than you may be used to. In our study, value releasers regularly work within an ecosystem of stakeholders experimenting with the same new technologies, often with different but complementary goals.

A third way to manage the trade-off between incremental and disruptive innovation is to take your most successful products in the old and the now and leverage them into the new, preferably in someone else's industry, where incumbents may be caught relatively off guard.

To return to our hunting metaphor, history shows that, from the slingshot to the rifle, the right technology can make small hunters extremely dangerous even to the largest game. Amazon, for example, focused its earliest e-commerce efforts on incumbent book retailers that, owing to large-scale decentralization, were less able to respond with technology innovations of their own.

Haier, as noted earlier, likewise grew in large part by acquiring weaker competitors that felt comfortable for too long being also-rans protected by local advantages; advantages that proved easy to overcome with the right technology.

To pull off a big kill necessarily requires that you have a technology advantage to leverage, and the courage to enter unfamiliar territory in hopes of bagging new customers.

Consider chip maker NVIDIA, which has managed to pivot multiple times around the fulcrum of its graphics processing unit (GPU), the GeForce series, first launched in 1999.

The GeForce was initially marketed as a high-end chip for processing images in video games, where it became the industry leader. But NVIDIA saw beyond that success, recognizing the chip's processing speed made it valuable for other applications. In 2006, for example, the company used its GPU expertise to develop a parallel computing architecture that allowed scientists to run extremely complex models on thousands of GPUs at the same time.

NVIDIA has since developed solutions for specific industries, including autonomous vehicles and data centers, with chips that can rapidly process vast amounts of data. With that early lead, NVIDIA's parallel processing GPUs have become the chip of choice for emerging artificial intelligence applications, beating out deep-pocketed competitors like Intel that remained focused on serial-processing products.

Underpinning NVIDIA's success is its commitment to adapt GPU technology for future applications. R&D spending for AI alone increased by nearly 10 percent annually between 2012 and 2016, reaching $1.3 billion, or nearly 30 percent of the company's total revenue. That's a much higher investment ratio than those of NVIDIA's peers, highlighting the impact very different strategies can have on the aspiration lever. Other semiconductor manufacturers have instead cut back dramatically on R&D spending, hoping to protect revenue in the now.

NVIDIA has also nurtured a vibrant GPU ecosystem, training developers, funding start-ups, and forming partnerships to create even more solutions that incorporate GPU products. That inclusive strategy turns customers into advocates, making them the best unpaid salesforce imaginable.

While NVIDIA CEO Jensen Huang admitted to *Fortune* magazine that he couldn't anticipate how self-driving cars would evolve or when AI would become mainstream, he has always maintained confidence in the superiority of graphical computing for these applications. Huang invests close to the edge of the trapped value gap, and is determined to capitalize on opportunities released by major shifts in the needs of current and future customers, whenever it happens. "I've been talking about the same story for fifteen years," Huang quipped. "I've barely had to change my slides."

>

As NVIDIA's pivots make clear, sustainable performance in the face of constant disruption is as much a matter of money as it is of innovation. No matter how you decide to adjust the levers of your innovation pivot, successful execution will require an equally rigorous management of capital. Money is the principal fuel that keeps innovation revving across all three lifecycle stages.

In the next chapter, we'll see how the most successful pivots manage not only to keep their foot on the gas, but also how they leverage financial resources to optimize shifts from one core to the next.

chapter 7

THE FINANCIAL PIVOT

Fixed Assets, Working Capital, and Human Capital

MAKING THE INNOVATION PIVOT will have a profound impact on the finances of your business, especially your most important hard and soft capital resources: fixed assets, working capital, and human capital. So we now turn to the financial pivot.

Whether your strategy requires big or small changes in asset management depends on the size and the shape of the trapped value gap you face. Even within an integrated ecosystem, the particular expertise, culture, and mission of any given player may suggest different settings for these levers at different times.

One thing is clear, however. No company can successfully execute the wise pivot without substantial financial investment in the new. The specific contours of that investment, as with the innovation pivot, are a function of the kind of disruption facing the industry. But, generally speaking, the bigger the trapped value gap and the faster it's growing, the greater the need to adjust the levers of your financial pivot. Perhaps in the exact opposite direction of your competitors.

That, in any case, is the moral of the story of Uniqlo, Japan's casual wear giant, and how the company used digital technology to pivot from a model of selling what it produced to producing only what it can sell.

FROM "MADE FOR ALL" TO "MADE FOR YOU"

Uniqlo's story begins in 1972, when twenty-three-year-old Tadashi Yanai went to work at his father's chain of roadside tailor shops in Japan.

Twelve years later, he took over the company and promptly opened a new kind of store, the Unique Clothing Warehouse. Uniqlo was born.

Yanai has become the richest person in Japan, having built his father's company, now known as Fast Retailing, into a formidable alternative to a wildly successful global "fast fashion" retail market dominated by brands such as Zara and H&M. (In fast fashion, retailers take the latest runway looks and translate them quickly into relatively inexpensive ready-to-wear goods, accelerating the once seasonal nature of fashion into day-to-day trends.)

How did he do it? Inspired by travels to Europe and the United States, where he studied large casual apparel chains like Benetton and Gap, Yanai saw limitless potential in a largely undeveloped casual wear market in Japan and Asia. He quickly changed the family business from selling suits to less formal clothing, buying fashion goods in bulk at low cost.

Then in the 1990s, borrowing from the strategy of Western chains, Yanai chose to vertically integrate his supply chain, taking control of the entire process from design through production and retailing. In 1998, when shoppers started to view Uniqlo as a discount retailer selling cheap apparel to people who lived in the suburbs, Yanai opened a three-story store in the hip Harajuku district of central Tokyo. It was an expensive move, but consumers soon began to associate Uniqlo with high-quality, fashionable yet affordable clothing.

The combination of Western-style retailing, vertical integration, and premium branding worked. By 1998, Yanai had successfully opened more than three hundred Uniqlo stores across Japan and started a move into China and Taiwan. With continued expansion, Uniqlo has since 2002 provided shareholders a return of nearly 1,000 percent, increasing its market capitalization by $39 billion.

Uniqlo is the dominant apparel retailer in Japan, and is three times the size of its nearest rival. Outside of Japan, growth has also been impressive. Since opening its first Shanghai outlet in 2002, Uniqlo now has more than two thousand stores, over half in international locations. While traditional retailing overall seems to be in a tailspin, as we saw in chapter 1, Uniqlo appears to be the exception that proves the rule.

The biggest change is yet to come. In 2017, the company announced plans to increase annual revenue to $26 billion by 2021, a nearly 70 percent increase. If Yanai can pull it off, it will make Uniqlo the world's biggest clothing retailer.

To succeed, Uniqlo will need to execute a successful pivot outside of Asia, and in particular to major expansion in the United States. It won't be easy. Casual apparel is already a crowded market, with sales growth of only about 1 percent a year. Respected brands such as Abercrombie & Fitch, BCBG, Eddie Bauer, Guess, J. Crew, and True Religion are either shuttering some stores or closing down altogether, as online retailers grab a larger share.

An earlier attempt by Uniqlo to break into the US market fared poorly, brought low by the fall of the suburban shopping malls where Uniqlo was located. So, as it did in Tokyo, the company's new strategy is to lift its brand image by opening stores in expensive, premium locations in New York, Boston, and Washington, DC.

E-commerce will also be a focus in Uniqlo's US expansion, but the company wants customers to keep buying at brick-and-mortar stores, about half of which are being completely remodeled. Yanai has long promoted a "click and collect" strategy, in which consumers purchase outfits online and pick them up at stores. Uniqlo believes this hybrid model actually increases sales at physical stores when customers come to pick up orders and end up buying other items that go well with their online purchase.

Beyond retail innovation, the company is also using the latest technologies to improve its integrated supply chain. In 2016, Uniqlo's parent company opened an eco-friendly Jeans Innovation Center in Los Angeles to create "the perfect jeans," with the goal of reducing design-to-production times of three to six months to only one or two, and to do so using more sustainable technologies.

Eventually, Yanai wants to trim that window to two weeks. Uniqlo is betting, and betting heavily, that speed in supplying its stores with the latest denim products will allow it to meet his aggressive goals.

Improving the speed of production, even dramatically, is only half the battle, however. The company will also have to drastically improve its inventory management capabilities.

That too is requiring a major adjustment. While fast fashion companies including Zara grew by responding rapidly to fast-changing fashion trends, Uniqlo took the opposite approach, planning production up to a year in advance. And unlike competitors that sell a wide variety of trendy fashion inspired by the global runway, Uniqlo produces only a few styles of practical urban basics.

That means it can take from six to twelve months from initial design to products actually appearing in stores. By then, however, tastes may have changed, resulting in lost sales and excess inventory.

To reduce those risks, the company is placing RFID tags on all their goods—collecting real-time data on the movement of merchandise that can be immediately analyzed. With the new system, Uniqlo can make accurate daily sales forecasts at each retail store, thereby planning and producing products more efficiently. The next step will be to automate the production process further, using IoT technology to collect and share data across the entire supply chain, from production through retailing.

To achieve these goals, Uniqlo partnered with Accenture in 2015 to create a cloud-based platform that optimizes its supply chain and improves customer service. Over the next three years, Uniqlo became a digital-first business, providing secure and personalized consumer experiences. As a result, both in-store and online sales increased.

Digitization is also helping Uniqlo pursue hyper relevance, for example, by offering shoppers customizable items and same-day delivery. A new factory complex in Tokyo supports this strategy by connecting a thousand employees from four divisions—planning, marketing, production, and logistics—through a common digital platform and by sharing data. The integrated system facilitates faster decisions and a more efficient supply chain. With Accenture's help, Uniqlo is working to collect and analyze even more store-level customer data and feed it back to the factory through the supply chain.

As part of its pivot, Uniqlo is spending nearly a billion dollars on new warehouse and distribution systems. Yanai believes these investments will pay for themselves by minimizing storage costs, reducing excess inventory, and delivering products faster around the world. While expensive, the integration of planning, manufacturing, and sales using digital technology is essential if Uniqlo is to succeed in changing its business model from, as Yanai puts it: "made for all" to "made for you."

Uniqlo's human capital strategy is also being leveraged as part of its retail expansion. The company practices the Japanese concept of *kaizen*, which translates roughly as the continuous search for perfection. While its competitors sometimes treat employees as easily replaceable, Uniqlo instead considers them valuable assets, encouraging workers to suggest ideas for improving productivity.

As part of the *kaizen* philosophy, Uniqlo prescribes, records, and analyzes every employee activity, from the way clothes are folded to the way credit cards are returned to customers (Japanese style, with two hands and full eye contact). All customers are greeted with "Welcome to Uniqlo!" and employees are taught to interact with shoppers using six standard phrases, including "Did you find everything you were looking for?"

Training is a priority. New employees go through Uniqlo University's basic curriculum three times in their first three months, with continuing education as they move up the ladder to management and supervisory roles. Interns work closely with experienced staff, in part to see if their personal goals align with the company's. Interns perform real tasks, easing the transition to actual employment.

THE FINANCIAL PIVOT

Uniqlo applied its unique capabilities to find and release trapped value, turning retail locations, which for other retailers have become liabilities, into strategic assets where customers get precisely the fashion solutions they want, where and when they want them, and at the best possible price. Uniqlo embodies many of the seven winning strategies, including technology propelled, hyper relevant, data driven, talent rich, and asset smart.

Uniqlo's ongoing global expansion likewise underscores how the conventional wisdom on how to respond to disruption can work against efforts to find and release trapped value. In retail, management experts are telling CEOs to get rid of stores, inventory, and, where possible, employees, in order to compete with e-commerce competitors. Amazon, after all, doesn't need them, so the theory is that incumbents don't either.

But what is right for one competitor is not right for all. Uniqlo's pivot proves continued investment in retail infrastructure, supported by improved information systems and new technologies, can make existing assets more, not less, valuable. Applied with creativity and determination, capital investment in the old can be a differentiator, and a rich source of competitive advantage.

Uniqlo has continued to make bold investments in fixed assets, including stores, innovation hubs, and training centers. Its retail outlets are being redesigned to accommodate digital technology and digital-first customers, but they are not being abandoned. Real estate is expensive, but that cost is offset by Fast Retailing CEO Tadashi Yanai's belief in cross-channel selling through click-and-collect. Automated factories are likewise a major investment, but they pay for themselves with lower inventory costs and more personalized products for customers.

The company also rejects conventional wisdom that says fashion inventory should be both ready to wear and produced in volume, even if that leads to overproduction. Uniqlo believes instead that higher sales can be generated through apparel that users can customize and then receive directly from the company on the same day. To achieve that goal of course requires significant technology investment in the now, including automation, analytics, and AI.

Uniqlo's pivots in fixed assets and inventory, finally, are supported by employee training and promotion as part of its commitment to *kaizen*. The result is a dedicated workforce that sets Uniqlo apart from other clothing retailers.

As the Uniqlo story suggests, the financial pivot is built around new strategies for managing three key capital assets: fixed assets (including infrastructure), working capital, and human capital.

Your approach to managing each is likely already being challenged by big bang or compressive disruption. In many industries, at least some aspect of physical infrastructure has become suddenly uneconomical compared to low-cost virtualized services, driven by cloud computing, high-speed mobile networks, and other rentable technologies that are increasingly faster, cheaper, and more reliable.

The proliferation of these technologies also generates rapid changes in customer expectations—such as having items delivered rather than going to the store—that can suddenly devalue physical assets such as retail outlets and distribution networks optimized to supply them.

Working capital, already a key factor in profitability, likewise takes on an even more strategic role as new technologies knock down barriers of time and competitive insight. For example, advanced analytics are giving some competitors early knowledge of demand—sometimes even before customers are fully aware of what they want—allowing retailers to reduce the risk of unsold inventory or lost sales due to inventory not being available.

You'll also need to reconsider how you develop human capital. The requirements for jobs that may once have been well defined and easy to fill are being disrupted as the new technologies unexpectedly reduce the life span of many business skills. In many industries, we risk the obsolescence of a generation of workers, even as demand for employees with new abilities grows rapidly, leading to unfilled openings.

Accenture, as a company that relies on the expertise of professional staff as the principal source of our revenue and differentiation, has always been obsessed with continuing education. That imperative, however, is becoming urgent for more companies in nonservice industries, including manufacturing, utilities, and natural resources.

How will you adjust your commitments and allocations to capital assets as part of a wise pivot? In this chapter, we'll address the three levers of the financial pivot: fixed assets, working capital, and human capital.

- **FIXED ASSETS.** Shedding fixed assets lowers ongoing costs, reduces the risk of obsolescence, and offers greater agility to quickly shift business offerings and operating models when new technologies make doing so attractive. At the same time, embracing the "as a service" model—where manufacturing, distribution, retailing, and technology capacity are acquired as needed from others—can dilute your uniqueness as a company and undermine your ability to develop your own innovations.

- **WORKING CAPITAL.** Reducing inventory-handling costs minimizes the risk of accumulating storage fees or being forced to offer clearance sales when you make too much too quickly, improving overall profitability. But having too little inventory reduces economies of scale, for example, when buying materials from suppliers. It can also cause damage to the brand if you underestimate demand, leaving customers unable to buy when and what they want.

- **HUMAN CAPITAL.** Employee skills, regardless of industry, are a critical asset: the ultimate differentiator. They are the hardest asset to buy on an as-needed basis. Disruption caused by an expanding trapped value gap, however, is rapidly erasing the advantage of having full-time workers. At the same time, the need for new skills in new technologies is urgent, with qualified workers in short supply. As part of your wise pivot, how can you balance the enhancement of employee skills with the purchase of expertise through part-time engagement?

THE FIXED ASSETS LEVER: WHEN DOES INFRASTRUCTURE CHANGE FROM ASSET TO LIABILITY?

Companies in capital-intensive industries (such as heavy manufacturing, utilities, natural resources, retailing, travel, and financial services) have historically achieved and maintained competitive advantage on the quality of their fixed assets, including property, infrastructure, and factories. The infrastructure, and the cost of duplicating it, at one time created a major barrier to new entrants.

While these assets may be both necessary and a source of differentiation, they require ongoing maintenance and modernization to remain relevant. And when demand slows, as it inevitably does in so-called cyclical industries such as commodity chemicals and airlines, overinvestment in new or expanded infrastructure can prove catastrophic.

In news and entertainment, printing presses were once not only an essential cost, but also one high enough to act as a barrier, discouraging new entrants. With the advent of better and cheaper content distribution through digital channels, however, those assets have increasingly become liabilities. They hold incumbents back from a pivot to the new and the chance for an even more valuable second incarnation as trusted information sources in an expanded global conversation.

Consider also the fate of South Korea's Hanjin Shipping Co., which sank into bankruptcy in 2016. Hanjin's problem was too many ships and not enough cargo. The company's troubles began a decade earlier, when many shipping companies sought to quickly replace older ships with more fuel-efficient vessels in response to rising fuel prices.

Ship builders, port operators, and container companies likewise geared up in response to fast-growing demand in China for industrial and consumer goods. But when the global economy sputtered, China's growth slowed. All that investment in new infrastructure proved to be not strategic, but fatal.

Sears, too, collapsed into bankruptcy, at least in part from the weight of its own once-valuable fixed assets. While anchor-tenant locations in malls once gave the retailer a competitive advantage, the company relied too heavily on its brick-and-mortar stores to drive sales without supplementing its shopping experience with innovative, engaging digital tools.

Adjusting the lever dramatically away from ownership, however, isn't necessarily the only solution. In retail, as Uniqlo's pivot makes clear, brick-and-mortar stores can still be valuable assets when deployed as part of a balanced portfolio of online and offline innovation.

Apple has likewise expanded rather than contracted its physical footprint. Apple Stores are the most profitable retail spaces in the United States, earning on average over $5,000 per square foot at more than five hundred global locations. From the stores' minimalist design to their limited product selection, Apple stands out from traditional retail spaces. Their most important distinction, however, is Apple's hyper-relevant customer experience. Low-value tasks such as waiting in line and paying have been totally automated, leaving employees free to focus entirely on individual customers.

Other companies, especially start-ups, can achieve success another way: using digital technology to virtualize business operations and remove the need for ownership of (and in some cases even the existence of) hard assets. Airbnb owns no hotels; Uber owns no taxis.

What they do own are software platforms, large user bases, and mountains of valuable transaction data. That allows them to overcome once-insurmountable barriers to entry, turning ownership of expensive real estate and vehicle fleets, respectively, into liabilities for incumbent hospitality and transportation companies.

Regardless of how you adjust the lever on fixed assets, our own experience, and that of our clients and the companies in our study, has taught us that the key to a successful financial portfolio is making the best use of whatever assets you decide you must control. That, after all, is one of our seven winning strategies: becoming asset smart. To some extent, it's a strategy every company must embrace.

To understand what we mean, consider the asset-smart strategy of Indian mobile network operator Reliance Jio Infocomm, better known as Jio. India is now the world's second-largest smartphone market, with 1.2 billion mobile subscribers, behind only China. But in 2010, some might have looked at the fierce competition between Bharti Airtel, Vodafone Group's India unit, aluminum billionaire Kumar Mangalam Birla's Idea Cellular, and some half dozen other carriers, and seen little room for growth. (Vodafone India and Idea Cellular have since merged.)

Mukesh Ambani, India's richest man, saw something different: a growing trapped value gap. A digital divide had cut off much of India's growing middle class and its poorest citizens; a divide Ambani felt was not shrinking fast enough. He decided to close it, pursuing an inclusive strategy that involved a major investment in fixed assets.

While another entrepreneur might have opted to rent the mobile assets of other providers, Ambani believed India's disbursed population and changing demographics required a dedicated, reliable, and high-speed network that could provide connectivity everywhere— features that existing networks didn't support. So with key radio frequencies he had acquired in 2010, he built Jio, the world's first mobile network based entirely on then state-of-the-art 4G LTE technology.

Using cash from Reliance's petrochemical businesses, Jio went on a $30 billion asset-buying spree, installing more than 100,000 cell towers, laying 155,000 miles of fiber-optic cable, and building 500,000 square feet of cloud data centers.

At the time of Jio's launch in late 2016, India's mobile consumers were paying as much as $60 per gigabyte for data transmitted over older, slower network technology. Jio charged less than $1 per gigabyte, initially giving away its service for the first seven months. Today, Jio's rates are a third of its competitors' prices, with larger data allowances.

That kind of price competition could only work with rapid growth in new subscribers, including many who hadn't previously been able to afford mobile service. And while Jio's low prices were appealing to middle-class customers, signing up less wealthy Indians required a solution to the high cost of the 4G devices themselves. So Ambani introduced the JioPhone, a basic 4G handset the company sold for a refundable deposit of about $23.

Marketing went into overdrive. Billboards with the Jio logo featuring Bollywood stars and the slogan "Come on India" appeared across the country. Jio's message was that it was more than just a business. It was a push to "democratize the digital culture in India." Ambani was on a mission to disrupt the industry by connecting millions to the internet for the first time. His pivot aimed squarely at trapped value in all four dimensions: enterprise, consumer, industry, and societal.

It worked. By December 2016, less than four months after its launch, Jio had 51 million subscribers. By late 2018, that number was 200 million, nearly 20 percent of the market.

Jio's competitors didn't see the urgency in upgrading to 4G LTE technology, pointing to slow adoption rates across the country and a customer base unwilling to pay a premium for faster speeds. What Ambani saw was trapped value, and lots of it. Indians wanted fast data and the latest mobile technology, so long as it was affordable.

Jio also invested in irresistible content, driving up network usage. After cricket, India's second-biggest passion is Bollywood. So JioCinema, one of the company's apps, streams high-definition movies. The network also offers a live TV app, music, messaging, online payments, and other must-have services. Equipment supplier Ericsson reported in late 2017 that Jio's entry into the Indian market had "pushed up global [mobile data] traffic noticeably."

Jio's success stunned and stung rivals. Since its 2016 launch, smaller incumbents without Jio's asset-smart advantage have sold out, closed down, or filed for bankruptcy. The rest are scrambling to compete, with two providers deciding to merge. Competitors are scrambling to replicate Jio's strategy, belatedly upgrading to 4G LTE and lowering data rates to stay competitive.

Ambani's solution was to build an all-new mobile infrastructure that duplicated what competitors already had, known in the communications industry as "overbuild." He bet big on his belief that what appeared to be a saturated market was actually masking considerable unmet demand—demand that could release trapped value for consumers by pairing the newest mobile technology with innovative applications to generate significant economies of scale.

Executing the plan was not without its complications. Initial launch dates were delayed as construction and operations proved more difficult than planned. The company's licensed frequencies were in three different bands, which meant harmonizing the network was difficult and time-consuming.

The 4G LTE protocols were, however, much more efficient users of bandwidth, supporting high-definition movies and voice communications better than the older standards used by Jio's competitors.

At the same time, 4G LTE was also relatively new, having only been adopted in leading global markets in late 2010. With no compatible devices to fall back on, Jio couldn't launch until its suppliers built new LTE devices, which didn't begin to appear in India until mid-2015. Jio's strategy, therefore, also required production of such devices at scale and the lowest possible cost.

What's more, a data network that could support huge data capacity required massive amounts of fiber-optic cable installed across the country. Cellular towers had to be erected. And regulatory approval in India takes time, as does attaching new antennae and other equipment to existing cell towers. (Around one-third of Jio's towers are company owned; the rest are shared.)

There was also the matter of interconnection, a critical component that ensures communications between networks is possible. In the months leading up to launch, Jio accused rivals of sabotaging initial testing by company employees and early customers. The company complained that other communications providers intentionally failed to offer enough interconnection points, leading to a high number of dropped calls for Jio users.

Despite these obstacles, Jio has been profitable since late 2017, earning $89 million between March and July 2018. If Jio continues offering substantially lower prices than competitors, the company will increase its share of the market, enlarging the economies of scale the network needs to be profitable.

Even now, Jio's counterintuitive positioning of the fixed-asset lever, according to Ericsson, has ushered in a new period of sustained expansion of mobile services in India. Ericsson predicts data consumption in India will increase fifteenfold between 2015 and 2021. Releasing trapped value at the consumer and societal level, Jio's pivot has improved the outlook as well for its ecosystem partners, who once struggled to expand their offerings beyond wealthy urban populations.

"It's changed the entire consumer habit," as one market analyst put it. "Everyone is now hooked on the internet."

THE WORKING CAPITAL LEVER:
HOW MUCH INVENTORY IS JUST ENOUGH?

Companies across industries that include apparel, consumer electronics, appliances, and even automobiles, all face a brutal trade-off when it comes to inventory management. Do they produce and stock lots of finished goods, risking surplus, or do they keep supplies lean and risk the chance buyers won't be able to purchase what they want, when they want? The answer can profoundly impact accounts payable, receivable, and inventory, or what is known generally as working capital.

More conservative enterprises err on the side of possible stockouts, producing only what they know they can sell. That approach prevents the buildup of unwanted inventory that may depreciate rapidly, but it also makes companies vulnerable if demand surges unexpectedly, perhaps generated by positive user reviews on social media or other electronic word of mouth.

A few key facts from industry research underscore the trade-off. Sales lost due to out-of-stock conditions reduce potential revenue by as much as 4 percent worldwide, with estimates of over $125 billion annually in North America alone. In general, customers find that the item they want to buy is unavailable nearly 10 percent of the time. And only 15 percent are willing to delay their purchase until supplies are replenished.

That global inventory management problem is about to get even worse. In markets subject to big bang disruption, consumers who find new products and services they like are using social media to tell everyone they know, and don't know, generating sudden spikes in demand. If you're not prepared for that kind of free advertising, you may find yourself selling the thing everyone wants but no one can get, a crisis we call "catastrophic success."

Consider the cautionary tale of artisan apparel start-up American Giant. In 2012, a favorable review on online magazine *Slate* of the company's new all-cotton hoodie ("the best sweatshirt known to man") unexpectedly launched demand into the stratosphere. In a single day, American Giant received five thousand orders—orders that the company, which prides itself on obsessive attention to detail in design and customer service, couldn't possibly satisfy. "Four days later we had nothing left," Bayard Winthrop, the company's embarrassed founder, told the BBC. "We were down to the sticks in our warehouse."

Like any business, American Giant must do its best to predict future demand, ordering the raw materials it needs to produce goods that, in its case, take three months to finish. The *Slate* review blew away the company's sales forecast, generating an enormous backlog.

Filling the accumulated orders meant choosing between two dangerous paths. By the time American Giant could sufficiently increase production capacity, many customers would likely have grown tired of waiting. Worse, the company had no way of knowing if the spike in sales was more than just a onetime blip, risking the possibility that expansion now would saddle the company with unmanageable debt later.

Being caught unprepared for a catastrophic success can hurt established companies just as badly, if not more. When Switch, Nintendo's latest gaming console, began flying off store shelves, disappointed fans accused the company of intentionally holding back shipments to inflate demand. An urban myth even circulated that Nintendo was safeguarding a warehouse full of Switch consoles, selectively releasing just a few at a time to retailers around the world.

The reality was much less dramatic. Nintendo was just being cautious—perhaps too cautious. Given the modest success of the Wii U, its previous product, Nintendo deliberately avoided manufacturing too many Switches for the March 2017 launch. Executives were hoping for, but not in truth planning on, a hit.

As the old saying goes, be careful what you wish for. The Switch became the fastest-selling Nintendo console of all time. By the end of the first month, nearly 3 million had been sold, along with nearly 5.5 million games. Nintendo immediately ramped up production, but soon found itself competing for components against companies such as Apple that had insatiable demand of their own to satisfy. Flash memory, LCD screens, and the motors used to create the Switch's vibration feature were all in high demand, forcing Nintendo into a bidding war for parts.

Just as Nintendo was caught unaware by the spike in demand, the company could have just as easily made far too many Switches or, worse, made them at the wrong time. In fact, as we saw in our brief discussion of Nintendo's product strategy in chapter 6, the very nature of big bang disruption is that instant adoption across market segments invariably means demand will reach saturation sooner rather than later.

Time your production right and you capture the entire market. Time it wrong and you either leave money on the table for more nimble competitors, or wind up with a warehouse full of inventory everyone wanted but already has.

Accurately forecasting the timing and magnitude of demand for new consumer products has until recently been nearly impossible. For companies that sell relatively low-cost goods, the model has long been to overproduce and write down or write off unwanted inventory. For many sellers in the retail apparel industry, for example, the mantra is "Stack 'em high, sell 'em low." Even in fast fashion, where the goal is to get new designs from the runway to stores as quickly as possible, followed immediately by the next fashion trend, that sometimes means overproduction and discounts.

Premium fashion brands don't have the option of discounting, however; at least not if they want to maintain premium prices in the future. Some luxury goods makers go so far as to destroy their excess inventory. One brand came under fire in 2017 for burning $38 million worth of unsold clothing and beauty products rather than discount them. The company has since stopped the practice.

Companies selling consumer electronics, which can be almost as fad driven as fashion, have the same problem. In 2012, for example, Microsoft wildly overestimated consumer demand for its Surface RT tablet by about six million units, leading to a whopping $900+ million write-down. A dearth of third-party apps and no included keyboard irked potential buyers, leading the company to slash prices as much as 30 percent for the entry-level model, from $499 to $349.

A year later, the problem was just the opposite. The Surface Pro, which delighted customers and became a big seller, experienced strong demand at launch. By then, however, an understandably cautious Microsoft had underproduced early versions, quickly generating serious out-of-stocks.

As these examples suggest, it's especially difficult to forecast demand for goods, like fashion and consumer electronics, marketed as novel or even revolutionary. You either get a spike in demand or you get nothing at all.

Fortunately, having to choose between too little or too much inventory, and basing that decision largely on intuition, is increasingly unnecessary. With advances in technologies like machine learning, simulating demand even in the most uncertain markets is getting more accurate. And as the internet of things connects more parts of more supply chains, companies will have instant visibility into how and where products are selling best—and where they aren't—allowing for faster adjustments in either direction.

The value releasers in our study combine these technologies with the seven winning strategies to postpone production as long as possible until demand is better known, then apply innovative marketing approaches, as Uniqlo and others are doing, to maximize customer satisfaction through better targeting and personalization.

When manufacturers do wind up with more inventory than anticipated, other digital tools can lessen the impact by connecting them with specialty online overstock sellers to clear the excess. They can even use technology to do so at the best possible prices.

To improve results for one overstock seller, for example, Accenture built a prediction model that allows the company to use historical data to improve its predictions of sales volumes and sales velocity at different price points. Within seconds of offering a new overstocked product at a given price, the tool recommends the amount and timing of price changes that will optimize profits and ensure the product sells out, in many cases with just one adjustment.

Already, AI-driven optimization algorithms look more broadly for and exploit observed patterns, correlations, and relationships among data elements, yielding better supply chain decisions.

These new tools predict when to order particular models, how many to order, where to sell them, and in what colors, sizes, and so on. Soon every industry will be able to offer its own version of fast fashion, rapidly introducing new products to satisfy quick-changing customer tastes, supported by software that recommends the best places to sell and the prices that will minimize excess inventory.

The algorithms can also be tested using past data, then automatically evaluated and corrected based on actual realizations of customer demand, literally learning as they go. As with our overstock client, they can immediately identify inventory that is not in demand and sell it off quickly.

Adopting these tools is essential for public companies in particular. Market analysts keep a keen eye on working capital. Spooking the market with inventory problems can prove highly detrimental to the health of your stock price.

That's what happened in 2017 to Nike, the world's biggest sports brand. The company set what may have been too ambitious a revenue target—$50 billion by 2020—that in turn led to overproduction. Excess inventory had to be discounted, and that hurt the bottom line. Citing "fundamental challenges" in the sportswear and apparel industry, including excess inventory with Nike's retail partners, Goldman Sachs downgraded the company to a "neutral rating" in a note to investors. Shares sank.

It wasn't as if overall demand had waned; in fact, with the advent of "athleisure," clothing that can be worn at the gym or as casual attire, industry sales have increased. Competition was, however, incredibly fierce, with innovative brands such as Athleta, Under Armour, lululemon athletica, and celebrity-branded lines gaining traction.

Nike recovered quickly, accelerating data-driven and hyper-relevant strategies already in process. In the short term, management committed to a 25 percent reduction in the number of styles it brought to market, in order to focus on its best sellers.

Nike then dramatically shrank its retail partners from thirty thousand companies with 110,000 points of distribution to just forty key retail partners. The chosen retailers include Foot Locker, Nordstrom, and a select group of others that manage unique, branded Nike spaces within their stores, and which have specific Nike-trained employees to assist with sales.

With fewer retail partners to manage, Nike turned its attention to collecting more and better data from customers. In exchange it offered a more relevant and customized customer experience, the cornerstone of its working capital adjustment.

In what it calls its "consumer direct offense," for example, Nike is converting anonymous online buyers into NikePlus "members" with accounts at Nike.com or on one of its apps. Already, Nike has signed up more than a hundred million users, who spend on average almost three times more than unregistered Nike.com "guests." The company's goal is to triple membership over the next five years.

Leveraging data about the buying habits of hundreds of millions of customers, Nike can improve its ability to predict what it should make, for whom, and how to best sell it, whether in a store or online. As part of its commitment to an ever-improving consumer experience, at the same time, Nike will double the speed with which it brings its reduced line of new products to market.

Even more impressive, the company is developing tools that localize inventory control, with stores carrying only the products customers in those locations want. Consider "Nike by Melrose," an innovative pop-up-like store the company opened on the famous West Hollywood avenue in the summer of 2018.

The company is using data from local NikePlus members to determine how to stock the new store. Nike by Melrose offers city-specific styles, regardless of the company's broader seasonal priorities. The low-cut Nike Cortez sneaker, for example, is a popular purchase in Los Angeles, so the store stocks more of that sneaker in an assortment of colors. To keep Nike by Melrose hyper relevant, the company tailors the inventory every two weeks to respond to changing local trends.

Advancing its inventory optimization even further, location sensors in the stores help identify NikePlus members when they come in. Based on purchase history, the store can then reserve special items for each member, whether they have requested them or not.

Selling directly to consumers, and doing so more quickly than in the past, is part of a larger strategy to enhance the company's brand, offering not just products, but a customized experience—a lifestyle, if you will—for its most loyal shoppers.

While Nike's pivot is still in its early stages, its laser focus on collecting, analyzing, and operating based on more and better data highlights how companies across industries are adjusting the working capital lever. We believe businesses of any size can use new technologies not only to more accurately manage inventory, but also to turn inventory management expertise into a competitive advantage. With ubiquitous communications networks, low-cost cloud-based capacity, and increasingly reusable data sources, companies can have their cake and sell it too.

THE HUMAN CAPITAL LEVER:
HOW MUCH DO YOU REALLY VALUE YOUR PEOPLE?

The pace of technology-driven disruption is forcing companies across industries to rethink a third major category of financial assets: the collected skills and expertise of their employees.

No matter what your business, it's likely you've invested heavily in training, whether in specific techniques and equipment, business processes, professional and interpersonal development, or licensing and continuing education.

New technologies, however, can change the calculus of those investments, sometimes slowly and sometimes very quickly. Disruption doesn't just require you to replace old equipment and outsource infrastructure. It also compels you to reskill or retire workers once expert in those assets. Ironically, just as older skills become obsolete, high demand for employees trained for work in the new is creating large gaps in availability.

In transportation, for example, we are on the verge of autonomous long-haul trucking, where vehicles can be "platooned" in close configurations to deliver goods more efficiently, quickly, and safely. So what happens to career truck drivers in the process? And how will you hire and retain experts in the implementation and operation of the new technology who will, at least initially, be hard to find and retain?

Although a skills inventory of your company's employees may not appear directly on your balance sheet, human capital is an increasingly important asset, and the most volatile of all.

We know this from personal experience. Since 2015, Accenture has built, largely from scratch, a $2 billion cybersecurity practice as part of our pivot to becoming digital first. Today, we have nearly six thousand security experts working around the world, including cyber centers in Manila and Prague. Much of the influx of specialized talent has come from acquisitions, including Arismore, iDefense, Defense Point Security, and security firms in Australia, Israel, and India.

But even that high level of merger and acquisition activity wasn't enough to build the kind of practice our clients in the now already need, let alone to give Accenture the scale essential to our pivot to the new. We remain propelled by organic growth, committed to continual investment in the abilities of our people, regardless of how they first joined us. That's why, in 2016, our facility in Bengaluru, India, automated a number of lower-level tasks, both to increase capacity and to shift our employees' work to higher-level problem solving.

One of the top priorities for Accenture's human capital portfolio is the rapid expansion of highly specialized skills. During fiscal year 2018, we spent more than $925 million on employee development, offering continuing education opportunities customized for the individual in an on-demand, digital environment. We also made substantial investment in reskilling, with over 290,000 people trained in new technology skills, including automation, agile development, and intelligent platforms.

Technology is driving the need to rethink the human capital lever, providing new tools, and new imperatives, for companies embracing the talent-rich, asset-smart, and network-powered winning strategies as part of their wise pivot. Training is moving from classroom to cloud, enhanced by high-definition video and advanced teleconferencing, holography, machine learning, and new human interfaces built with augmented and virtual reality.

We've described the role adjusting the human capital lever has played in our own reinvention. Now let's look at how another leading company, one of the oldest and largest in the world, is turning the skills lever as its industry undergoes both big bang and compressive disruption. In this case, we're talking about modern media giant AT&T.

The rapidly converging communications and media industries, as we've noted in earlier examples, are experiencing some of the most intense disruption of any industry. It wasn't that long ago that voice communications used its own analog-switched network, while video entertainment relied on over-the-air broadcasting. In many countries, both services were offered exclusively by government agencies, and later by closely regulated monopolies. Prices and services, entry and exit, and requirements for universal coverage were all set by complex proceedings, often conducted by local authorities.

As new production and delivery technologies, including cable, cellular, fiber-optics, and satellite, became commercially viable, they were initially shoehorned into the old network and regulatory schemes, some less comfortably than others.

Some countries, for example, kept new data communications services legally separated from government or regulated providers. This meant that as the technology continued its journey into the realm of the better and cheaper, there was little to constrain the companies building and deploying it from adapting their networks to new and old uses. These included new hybrids such as text messaging, video chat, and social networks.

One result of that freedom was that the largely nonproprietary standards of the internet infiltrated every older networking technology, delivering voice, video, data, and new combinations of the three in a matter of only a few decades.

That revolution and the growing trapped value gap it creates has put profound pressure on incumbents, especially companies once closely regulated, to execute a rapid and accelerating series of pivots. We've already talked about how some industry leaders and new entrants including Comcast, Jio, Google, Microsoft, and Amazon have pivoted both their innovation and infrastructure strategies in response.

Now let's look at how AT&T, one of the world's largest employers, is fueling its own pivots by adjusting the human capital lever.

As of this writing, AT&T is in the middle of the most significant strategic challenge in its nearly 150-year history. Customers have almost completely abandoned legacy telephone service, even as they display nearly infinite demand for content-rich wireless voice, video, and data services. From the 2007 introduction of Apple's iPhone through 2015, data traffic on AT&T's mobile network increased by more than 150,000 percent!

Enterprise communications services have also boomed, as companies beam ever-larger amounts of data between offices and to the cloud infrastructures of Amazon, Google, and Microsoft. Every day, AT&T's increasingly fiber-centric network handles 130 petabytes of data (in bytes, that's 1.3 followed by seventeen zeroes), equal to more than forty times the digital holdings of the Library of Congress.

Still, growth is slowing as consumers anticipate the introduction of 5G networks, a next-generation protocol offering dramatic improvements in speed, reliability, and capacity, but which will require billions of dollars in new infrastructure investment that must be raised in the midst of a protracted price war among the four major US mobile network operators.

On the entertainment side of AT&T's business, pay-TV customers are moving from fixed cable and copper network technologies to satellite-based services, and from satellite to over-the-top internet streaming content from a large and growing base of new entrants, including many of AT&T's suppliers and content partners.

Under CEO Randall Stephenson, who took the helm in 2007, AT&T has been pivoting constantly. The company acquired satellite provider DirecTV for $63 billion in 2014, and in 2018 completed a $85 billion merger with content giant Time Warner, giving the company access to the creative talents and catalog of HBO, CNN, and the Warner Bros. Studio.

At the same time, the company's legal team has been working with national and local governments to facilitate the shutdown of what remains of its analog voice network, moving customers old and new to better, faster, and cheaper internet-powered fiber-optic and mobile communications.

But do AT&T's employees have the skills needed to work at the reinvented AT&T, let alone lead it into emerging markets at the scale needed to catch Silicon Valley's fastest and strongest competitors? That, in any case, is Stephenson's challenge.

AT&T employs about 250,000 people, most of whom got their education and job training in a different era, for a different AT&T. On the one hand, those workers retain considerable institutional and cultural knowledge the company can't afford to lose. Setting aside call-center workers, the average tenure of an AT&T employee is an astonishing twenty-two years.

On the other hand, the new business landscape demands skills few current employees have in cloud-based computing, software development, data science, and other digital-first capabilities. Many of these fields are advancing so quickly that traditional methods of on-the-job training and development cannot keep up. And, outside the company, demand is high and supply is low, driving up salaries.

Internal research in 2013 showed that only about half of AT&T's employees had the necessary science, technology, engineering, and math skills the company already needed, a percentage that would drop to 5 percent by 2020. A hundred thousand workers were supporting hardware the company would likely have retired by then.

That left AT&T between a rock and a hard place. The company could try to hire new technology talent to fill current needs in digital-first skills and emerging requirements in digital entertainment, analytics, computer security, mobile app development, autonomous vehicles, and the IoT. But even paying premium prices, the company would likely still face a talent deficit as it tried to fill tens of thousands of software and engineering jobs.

And what about current employees? Replacing workers is not only traumatic for them, the enterprise, and the communities in which they live and work, it's also expensive. According to a 2012 study, the median cost of replacing a worker is more than 20 percent of an employee's annual salary, a percentage that rises as the base salary increases.

So, instead, AT&T opted to retrain the existing workforce, giving them the skills to run the company's business in the new. The process began with Workforce 2020, a massive reconstruction of AT&T's organization chart. More than two thousand job titles were reduced to a more manageable size, combining jobs with similar skills into a single description. Seventeen different programming titles became simply "software engineer."

Next came systems for retraining hundreds of thousands of employees. AT&T invested $1 billion in a multiyear effort called Future Ready, which includes online courses and collaborations with digital education companies such as Coursera and Udacity, as well as leading universities.

Other tools help employees figure out what kinds of jobs the company needs to fill in all three lifecycle stages, allowing them to structure their training accordingly. To help with that planning, an online portal shows what jobs are available and their requirements, the potential salary ranges, *and* the likelihood for each job category to either expand or contract.

The system also evaluates each employee's current skills and recommends a specific job they could obtain in the future with additional training. Employees can choose a different target, then set the system to alert them as jobs matching their preferred skill set become available.

As of 2017, more than half the company's employees have completed nearly three million online courses in data science, cybersecurity, agile project management, and computer science. To earn a master of science degree, another five hundred AT&T employees enrolled in the online computer science program at Georgia Tech, a leading engineering school. Almost a hundred have graduated.

In practical terms, according to a CNBC report: "Employees that are currently retraining are two times more likely to be hired into newer, mission-critical jobs, and four times more likely to make a career advancement."

John Donovan, CEO of AT&T Communications, which is responsible for the bulk of the company's global communications and video services businesses, told CNBC in 2018 that the organization is now relying much less on outside contractors for technical skills. "We're shifting to employees, because we're starting to see the talent inside," he said.

To manage the realignment of skills, Donovan, in a 2016 article for *Harvard Business Review* co-authored with Cathy Benko, described three ways AT&T redesigned talent practices:

- Performance metrics were simplified to focus on how individuals contributed to business goals and to better recognize the market value of jobs. This has increased the financial rewards for individuals with skills in high demand, including cybersecurity, data science, and computer networks.

- Performance expectations were also raised. In AT&T's technology and operations unit, the number of managers receiving the two highest performance ratings on a five-point scale declined by 5 percent, while the bottom two ratings increased by 37 percent.

- Redesigned compensation plans deemphasized seniority, added more variable compensation to motivate high performers, and gave weight to in-demand skills.

For professional staff, the company has made it clear that reeducation would require some investment of the employees' own time and money. Motivating that kind of commitment has been a key challenge.

About half of AT&T's career employees, moreover, are unionized—the largest full-time unionized workforce in the United States. So, starting around 2013, new contracts have included details on training and development programs. The company has worked in partnership with the union, which recognizes the risks to its members of failing to keep their skills current.

AT&T is only midway through its plan to meet its aggressive 2020 goals. The company still has tens of thousands of employees to retrain to satisfy its goal of having a technically proficient workforce for the next decade. At the same time, more than half the network still needs to be shifted to digital technology, meaning skills in the old are still very much in demand.

Regardless, there are promising signs of success. In 2016, more than 40 percent of forty thousand open jobs were filled by internal candidates. In early 2017, the company estimated that 140,000 people were preparing in some way for a different job within the company.

AT&T's bold adjustment of the human capital lever is using the power of technology to reskill and augment current employees cost-effectively, achieving the best of both worlds. It also reflects a substantial release of both enterprise and societal trapped value.

That example should put to rest any doubt you may have that your company is too big or too set in its ways to move quickly when the need for a wise pivot arises. "Technology shifts have become somewhat routine," AT&T CEO Randall Stephenson told *Fortune* magazine in 2017. "But who can transition their talent at scale as the technology changes?"

AT&T's dramatic approach to human capital highlights some other important questions that many companies are grappling with today, and that our research addressed:

- What is your responsibility for retraining employees whose skills become obsolete as a result of compressive or big bang disruption?

- How much should you invest to develop workers who are highly skilled or unique in their capabilities, knowing they may leave or, if they stay long enough, require reskilling?

- Should you instead minimize uncertain and unpredictable skills investment and just buy the talent you need, understanding, however, that the freelance market suffers from a short supply of the most current technical skills?

There are of course no easy answers to these questions, and there are many trade-offs specific to your business and strategic position to consider. An ample supply of right-skilled employees may lower profits, while underskilled workers can raise costs through errors and poor customer service, not to mention lower levels of the kind of bottom-up innovation a wise pivot relies on.

Still, as AT&T's story shows, no matter how you balance your financial portfolio in the old, the now, and the new, the successful execution of a wise pivot requires a thoughtful and strategic management of one of your most value assets: your people.

A subject to which we now turn in the next and final chapter.

chapter 8

THE PEOPLE PIVOT
Leadership, Work, and Culture

WE ENDED OUR REVIEW of the financial pivot by looking at how companies in different industries are managing the costs and risks of keeping employee skills up to date in the face of accelerating technology-driven disruption.

This chapter dives deeper into the human equation and the role it plays in a wise pivot. We'll move beyond the quantification of skills and talk more specifically about human resources. As anyone who has ever worked for a business large or small knows, nothing changes if the people don't change first.

We'll look in particular at how successfully managing businesses in the old, the now, and the new affects how you bring together a wide range of people and cultures, uniting them for a common purpose, while still respecting individuality. At Accenture, we refer to that goal as becoming "truly human," a holistic approach that focuses on nurturing people's whole self—their mind, body, heart, and soul.

Making that aspiration a core tenet of your business, as it is for us, requires adoption of an expansive approach to human resources that includes diversity, inclusion, mindfulness, and continual learning. Creating a balanced people portfolio is not just good business; it's the only way to operate successfully across all three lifecycle stages. It is an essential component of our corporate culture and a key success factor in our wise pivot.

Here we explore the three final levers, targeted respectively on leadership style, the fast-moving frontier converging around humans and machines, and corporate culture.

First, let's look in detail at one more company in the volatile communications industry, and how the unconventional leadership style of the CEO at one of its subsidiaries had an impact far beyond the company's bottom line.

UNLIKELY ALLIES

Germany's Deutsche Telekom, the communications giant, made a critical decision in 2012. If mobile network provider T-Mobile, the company's major US asset, was going to survive in a market with fewer, stronger competitors, new leadership would be needed.

T-Mobile was at the time last in a field of rapidly consolidating US carriers, behind Verizon, AT&T, and Sprint, which itself is controlled by Japanese investor SoftBank Group. Deutsche Telekom had stopped making major asset investments in T-Mobile, lealving the carrier unable to compete successfully as technology shifted from 3G to 4G LTE.

A $39 billion merger with AT&T looked like Deutsche Telekom's best option for T-Mobile. The deal was blocked, however, by US regulators, T-Mobile ended up with a $4 billion breakup package that included $3 billion in cash and some of AT&T's best radio frequency licenses, but no strategy for making use of either.

Enter John Legere, the self-styled maverick hired to turn T-Mobile around. Legere quickly proved his worth. In 2013, his first full year as CEO, T-Mobile added an impressive 1.65 million subscribers. And after losing billions of dollars the preceding two years, it even eked out a profit.

But Deutsche Telekom CEO Timotheus Höettges, who took over in 2014, faced continued pressure to find a buyer for T-Mobile despite Legere's gains. For one thing, subscriber growth and a return to profitability would likely be short-lived amid an escalating price war among US carriers. To truly take on Verizon and AT&T, T-Mobile would need much more investment to update its out-of-date infrastructure, a requirement likely to reappear a decade or so later, when 5G technology matured.

Selling T-Mobile would also bring much-needed cash to help Deutsche Telekom fend off disruptive threats at home in Europe.

Timotheus Höettges and John Legere were the telecom odd couple. Höettges, stoic and straightforward, is known as an intense negotiator who immerses himself in details while keeping one eye on broad strategy. Legere is brash, combative, and sometimes less than polite, taking to Twitter to attack rival CEOs.

Höettges decided to take a chance on a pivot to the new, one that first required considerable investment in the old and the now. Deutsche Telekom's leadership accepted Legere's assessment of the need for an overhaul of everything about T-Mobile, from the product to the corporate culture. Legere was given free rein to remake T-Mobile in his own swaggering image, including allowing employees to have facial piercings and tattoos.

Under Legere, T-Mobile uncovered vast troves of trapped value for the company's customers. He ended long-term cell phone contracts and replaced them with simple, transparent pricing. He made it easier to upgrade devices and eliminated charges for global roaming. He offered to pay off early-termination fees for competitors' customers who were willing to switch. He made it easy to make free phone calls over Wi-Fi networks. Legere also struck a deal with Apple to sell the iPhone, the last of the four major US carriers to do so.

And as streaming video became more popular, T-Mobile launched Binge On, which allows customers to enjoy YouTube, Netflix, and other music and video content without deducting it from their data allotments. Looking to both the now and the new, he won government auctions for more spectrum, improving T-Mobile's 4G LTE network, and at the same time providing a clearer path to 5G.

Legere was driving unprecedented growth in subscribers, sales, profits, and share price. So long as he continued to do so, Höettges saw no need to divest T-Mobile. "This team is doing a great job," Höettges said on his first call with analysts in 2014. "There is no urge, no hurry, no—any kind of desperate, a must M&A activity from our side."

While Legere's management style would, as Höettges acknowledged, never work in Germany, the T-Mobile CEO's competitive nature did synch up perfectly with Deutsche Telekom's culture. "I like people being disruptive," Höettges said in an interview. "I like people who are brave. He is very much fitting to our DNA, how we want to be, even if he is very American in his approach."

The American approach paid off. In 2018, after five years of turnaround and reorganization that saw T-Mobile become a real competitor to Verizon and AT&T, the company announced a merger with Sprint, a deal that valued the combined company at $146 billion. To preserve the leadership engine that saved T-Mobile, its executives will hold the top roles in the new company, which will retain the T-Mobile name. As of this writing, the deal looks likely to be approved by regulators keen on robust 5G competition.

For Deutsche Telekom, empowering Legere was far from a one-off experiment. To prepare for a future where communications companies (as we have seen with Comcast, AT&T, Jio, and others) must pivot to become content, application, and technology innovators, Deutsche Telekom will need more business creators and risk takers, at home as well as abroad.

Höettges and his leadership team have embraced a new outlook, including a training program for executives worldwide focused on successful leadership in the digital era. Called levelUP, the yearlong course offers customized content on managing digital-first enterprises, including strategies to expand today's core business while creating space for scalable new businesses.

Seven hundred Deutsche Telekom managers from Germany and abroad participated in the program in 2017, which has instilled increased urgency about the need to change the company.

But management knows it needs to be careful not to push the lever too far toward the new. "It is simply not possible to manage a group like Deutsche Telekom, with its 230,000 employees worldwide, in the same way you would a start-up," then chief human resources officer Christian Illek said in a 2017 blog post. "The trick is to manage core business efficiently while developing new digital business areas successfully, like the cloud, for example."

Ilek's point is that while start-ups only have one business to worry about, incumbents need to run multiple businesses at different stages in their lifecycle. This means managing different business cultures—more traditional in the old, more open in the new.

So in response to the big bang and compressive disruption the company recognizes as endemic in the communications industry, Deutsche Telekom has changed how they acquire and manage talent, from company CEOs to entry-level call-center workers.

That includes taking direct action to improve diversity, both in the company's leadership and in its culture. For much of the past decade, the company has strived to hire more women for management and leadership positions, going so far as to establish quotas. The percentage of women in management increased groupwide to 25 percent in 2017, up from only 19 percent in 2010. The company also raised the percentage of women on supervisory boards to 40 percent. (German law requires companies to have these second boards, made up of shareholder representatives and company employees, a substantial portion of whom must be women.)

Increasing women's representation in company leadership and reducing gender gaps in salary and in professional opportunities have been thorny political issues in Germany, but Deutsche Telekom has embraced rather than resisted regulatory intervention.

Whether mandatory or voluntary, establishing quotas may not be an optimal solution but for now, at least, they are necessary. "I certainly like what it does," Dr. Elke Frank, head of HR development at Deutsche Telekom, says on the company's website. "I would be delighted if we could get the same results without quotas. But that just doesn't seem to be possible in Germany. So, we should just be pragmatic and use quotas."

Developing diverse talent for management positions has also meant changes to general work conditions. Deutsche Telekom has expanded parental-leave programs for all employees, for example, and introduced more flexible working hours for managers. The company also allows more part-time work arrangements. Employees can either start their employment on a part-time basis or switch from full time to part time; and once they go part time, they can return to their original number of working hours at any time.

New technologies are also changing the kinds of tasks Deutsche Telekom employees do and do not do. The company wants to grow revenues by 1 percent annually through 2021, in part by streamlining the workforce in favor of automation and digitalization.

The company is developing AI solutions such as "chatbots" to make customer service more efficient for customers and human workers. The chatbots, which simulate human conversation through text or audio, are designed to relieve human call-center agents of standard tasks, giving them more time to handle work only they can do. Tinka, a "virtual employee" at T-Mobile Austria, knows more than fifteen hundred answers to typical customer questions, and can handle about 80 percent of all queries put to her. When she can't answer a question, she forwards it to a human agent.

THE PEOPLE PIVOT

As Deutsche Telekom's story illustrates, companies hoping to optimize their workforce across all three lifecycle stages—the old, the now, and the new—will need to make a people pivot, adjusting the way they approach hiring and retaining talent.

The people pivot doesn't apply just to the "troops." It includes having the right combination of leaders across all three stages, and being open to contributions from talent sources well outside the confines of your own offices.

Your particular industry and the size of the trapped value gap pressuring it to change may also lead you to create new employee roles, harnessing the power of humans working with increasingly intelligent machines.

How will you integrate different leadership styles and levels of automation into an inclusive corporate culture, one that still maintains a coherent brand and customer experience?

Deutsche Telekom, for one, has struggled to embody an inclusive strategy. Not only does it need to motivate employees, it also has to follow fast-changing employment laws, including how it collects and uses employee data, a challenge for many global companies.

Accenture's own wise pivot likewise required new thinking about managing hundreds of thousands of employees in a business being run as a portfolio across the old, the now, and the new. Given the different objectives we had in each time frame, we needed to develop the skills to juggle optimal work styles and talent mixes that differed dramatically.

This included geographic, cultural, and generational differences that couldn't simply be ignored. In some countries in which we operate, millennials represent more than two-thirds of our workforce. Getting the best out of our youngest generation of employees required us to adapt our leadership, training, and evaluation processes to them, rather than force-fit them into a culture optimized for an earlier era.

Our particular challenge, as noted earlier, was to find better ways to attract and integrate leaders from organizations and cultures not native to Accenture, an extraordinarily important and valuable skill essential to growth through acquisition. That required us to reengineer management down to the deepest levels—a significant evolution of our leadership DNA.

When acquiring companies, we now look for cultures we want to "infect" us; that is, people who have behaviors and skills—technical, entrepreneurial, creative, and otherwise—we can learn from. The challenge then becomes creating the space for them to teach us.

It wasn't just outside talent that needed a more welcoming environment. The kind of growth we have achieved in the last five years, particularly in new businesses such as digital marketing, AI, and customer experience design, demanded a broad rethinking of traditional employee roles, work definitions, and hiring strategies. It also required the creation of a more flexible workplace with practices and approaches that welcomed as wide a range of talent and contributions as possible.

What's more, given an expanding trapped value gap, keeping our employees' expertise current is essential to delivering superior client service in the future. Beyond the reskilling we described in chapter 7, our wise pivot leans heavily on empowering employees with the very technologies that continue to disrupt our industry.

As noted, we've invested heavily in training programs. Over the past two years, we retrained tens of thousands of people whose traditional roles were likely to be automated. These employees are now performing higher-value work, in some cases using AI and other technologies to provide state-of-the-art services to clients.

Professional service firms haven't historically been thought of as being high tech. But the new technologies are quickly changing that reality. For us, that meant adopting the most advanced tools and techniques for data design and visualization, reinventing software development, and becoming expert in the latest computing architectures. We've also made substantial investments in leading-edge video conferencing, collaboration software, and other tools that improve teamwork.

The elephant in the room in any analysis of a company's talent pivot, however, is artificial intelligence. Many AI promoters and developers believe AI will soon make using automation to replace knowledge workers a cost-effective option, particularly for start-ups looking for rich supplies of trapped value in mature service-oriented industries.

Much of the popular conversation about AI is, however, unhelpful. The underlying assumption is that humans and machines are competitors and that AI, with superior speed, fast-growing processing power, and inexhaustibility, will replace workers at all levels.

We don't agree. As our colleagues Paul R. Daugherty and H. James Wilson argue in their recent book, *Human + Machine*, the more likely future is one in which employees and technology will work together in new ways. We'll still need people, albeit with new, different, and constantly evolving skills.

What is true is that AI is already a significant contributor in more nuanced ways to the increasing pace of technological disruption, upending conventional workforce roles, hierarchies, strategies, and leadership styles.

An important finding of our research is that there is an enormous opportunity to *enable* workers with technology rather than using it to replace them, a recognition that features prominently in Deutsche Telekom's pivot.

Few companies, however, are following its lead. Our surveys reveal the vast majority of senior executives plan to use AI over the next three years to automate tasks, differentiate their offerings, and enhance human capabilities. But almost none plan to enable those activities by increasing their companies' investments in training and reskilling during the same period.

How will you bridge that gap as part of your wise pivot? How can you manage talent from top to bottom as you navigate between the old, the now, and the new? And how will your company's culture need to change in all three, responding to the pressures of changing social values, the preferences of younger workers, and an increasingly global workforce and customer base?

We'll answer those questions in a close look at the three remaining wise pivot levers: leadership, workforce, and culture:

- **LEADERSHIP.** There is an inherent trade-off between leaders focused on business creation (entrepreneurs) versus leaders focused on business running (operators). In an environment characterized by continual disruption, you'll need both. It's the rare executive who can juggle the two at the same time, meaning you'll likely need multiple leaders with different skills and styles. In distributing leadership talent across the three lifecycle stages, true stewardship comes from knowing how to invest in and manage just the right mix.

- **WORK.** The fear of machines taking away jobs goes back at least as far as early nineteenth-century England, when Luddites (said to be following Ned Ludd's example) smashed early industrial textile machines. Those fears have always been if not overstated then certainly misplaced, masking opportunities to improve the nature of human work by finding what Accenture Research calls the "missing middle"—technologies that empower workers rather than diminish them. The exact contours of the workforce of the future may remain unclear for some time to come, but you'll need to engage, sooner rather than later, your own potential in the missing middle.

- **CULTURE.** Pivoting to the new often requires companies to adopt more of the kind of open and entrepreneurial culture that spawned the information revolution, including the social values and work ethic of a younger generation of workers. Having employees who simultaneously work in and serve customers in a global marketplace, moreover, is challenging businesses to move from a single set of uniform operating principles toward a more inclusive model: a culture of cultures. In doing so, leaders must take care not to lose sight of the principles that distinguish their brand, including a shared mission everyone believes in.

THE LEADERSHIP LEVER:
FROM OPERATORS TO ENTREPRENEURS

Novelist F. Scott Fitzgerald wrote in a 1936 essay that "the test of a first-rate intelligence is the ability to hold two opposed ideas in the mind at the same time, and still retain the ability to function." That's an especially appropriate insight for today's occupants of the C-suite, where two types of leadership must coalesce to manage large-scale pivots to the new: operators who run the business, and entrepreneurs who make new business. True to Fitzgerald's paradox, a wise pivot demands both leadership types.

The successful working relationship of Timotheus Höettges and John Legere illustrates Fitzgerald's point beautifully. Business runners like Höettges are detail oriented, understanding how even small shifts in performance can multiply to the bottom line. Operators to their core, business runners are hardwired to find opportunity not so much in disruptive change, but in incremental improvement of existing businesses, processes, and systems. They are the perfect leaders for managing your wise pivot portfolio in the old and the now.

Business makers, on the other hand, revel in violating rules in the name of innovation, creating bigger and bigger bangs. Entrepreneurs at heart, they are wired to scan constantly for the next big thing and scale it like crazy when they find it. Where business runners motivate high performance, business makers inspire innovation—just what you need to manage the new part of your portfolio.

Accepting the need for different kinds of leadership can be one of the hardest things for managers in today's business, especially when their own style doesn't fit with their companies' requirements in the new.

Accenture experienced exactly that challenge in the execution of our own wise pivot. Our mature systems integration and outsourcing businesses were expertly run, and our consulting and strategy practices were developing nicely. But where were the entrepreneurs we would need to scale the new digital-first businesses we knew would be our future and our salvation?

The kind of leaders we really needed, frankly, operated under paradigms foreign to our carefully crafted corporate culture, which emphasized repeatable quality and superior client service over the kind of nonconformity revered by Silicon Valley.

Our solution was to embrace fully the winning strategy of inclusion, breaking down physical and virtual barriers that would have made life at the old Accenture seem constrained and regimented to someone like John Legere.

We have been able to do so with the help of entrepreneurial leaders from many of the companies we acquired in the last five years. We not only retained these talented people, but also, like the management of Walmart, integrated them into executive roles, allowing them the freedom they need to scale our new businesses.

The new mix of senior talent has dramatically increased the diversity of Accenture's leadership and its thinking. Our corporate DNA now demands senior executives who can embrace both operating and entrepreneurship objectives, with a new emphasis on the latter, including contributing to innovation, internal and external collaboration, and delivering solutions for our clients that go well outside the box.

To power our reinvention and expansion, we substantially increased the size of our gene pool. For example, during fiscal 2018, even as we promoted nearly seven hundred new managing directors, we also hired almost three hundred more from outside Accenture—often senior business leaders from industry—adding significant specialization to our leadership ranks.

At the very top, though, it's the rare leader who can guide a company through successive wise pivots as both business runner and business maker, shifting their emphasis between operator and entrepreneur as disruption appears in the three lifecycle stages, sometimes all at once and always unpredictably.

Consider Michael Dell, who first disrupted the personal computer business with a model of customizing every product based on customer preferences. Dell's make-to-order production, launched in his college dorm room, soon beat out giants like HP, Compaq, and even IBM. In 1992, at the age of twenty-seven, Dell became the youngest-ever CEO of a Fortune 500 company.

By the mid-2000s, however, two forces were challenging Dell's core business: a glut of low-cost PCs from new overseas competitors and the shift to smartphones and tablets. In 2006, the company lost its number one position in the industry.

So in 2007 Dell pivoted back to the role of CEO, having relinquished day-to-day operations only a few years earlier. The shake-up was necessary. The company, operating successfully for years, needed its entrepreneur back.

Dell set about reinventing the company into a more sustainable enterprise, a multifaceted technology empire with investments across all three lifecycle stages. Over the next few years, he spent billions acquiring businesses in areas where demand was ramping up, including IT service giant Perot Systems, cloud players Boomi and Wyse Technology, and companies specializing in computer security.

In 2016, Dell made his biggest pivot, spending $67 billion to acquire EMC Corp, the leading producer of data storage and data management hardware and software, in hopes of scaling up fast in the emerging market supporting ever-larger collections of business and customer information. The deal also included EMC subsidiary VMware, a leader in "virtualization" technology that allows applications to run in multiple hardware and operating system environments.

All in all, Dell has overseen a profound series of pivots, from personal computers to industrial-strength data storage, to cloud hardware and software solutions. The company that started out producing make-to-order PCs now provides the complete IT needs of some of the largest companies in the world.

Leaders like Michael Dell are hardly the norm. Nor are they limited to high-tech industries, or to locations in Silicon Valley and other technology hubs. As we saw, Toyota's leadership was able to create a mass market for hybrid vehicles while maintaining growth in traditional internal combustion cars.

Our wise pivot research identified a few other leaders who can operate today's core while rebuilding it for tomorrow, often relying on unconventional means. What distinguishes senior executives who, like Dell, embody the roles of both business runner and business maker? Consider three unique characteristics:

- Instead of turning inward, applying old theories of strategic planning to find and extend their "core competencies," they set their sights on closing the trapped value gap, collaborating with the sometimes unusual characters who prefer to live nearby: venture investors, entrepreneurs, and next-generation technology developers.

- Instead of strategic plans, they solicit ideas from customers, suppliers, students, and anyone else who feels strongly about the kinds of products they produce. Like GEA's FirstBuild lab, they hold hackathons, inviting outsiders to collaborate on future products without limitations or nondisclosure agreements.

- They risk showing their hand to potential competitors, trading secrecy for the chance to engage in creative experimentation. To scale quickly in the new, that trade-off makes sense, even if all they get from more open innovation is the insight needed to move quickly into new markets that can't be discovered by focus groups or other marketing techniques aimed at incremental improvement. They minimize the risk by becoming expert at knowing when and how to launch new offerings and ventures.

In most of the companies we studied, of course, it takes a combination of leaders and leadership styles to navigate a successful pivot—achieving just the right setting for this critical lever. That works too, as we can see most clearly by returning to Walmart.

When Doug McMillon became the company's CEO in 2014, the kind of forward and backward expertise Michael Dell personifies didn't exist at the company. But McMillon, who started his career at Walmart as a teenager unloading trucks, had the foresight to know he needed the stimulation of entrepreneurial thinking.

To take on the existential threat of online retailers, including Amazon, McMillon needed more business-making capacity than he had available. So Walmart's new CEO decided, with the strong support of the Walton family, to pull the leadership lever sharply toward the new.

To jump-start Walmart's pivot in 2016, as we noted in chapter 6, McMillon acquired internet retailing innovator Jet.com, led by its founder, Marc Lore. Rather than leave Lore to continue building Jet.com as

Walmart's hedge for a scalable new, however, McMillon appointed him the head of e-commerce.

Despite the relatively small size of his business unit, that meant Lore became one of four CEO/presidents on the executive leadership team, a peer of the CEOs of Walmart US, Sam's Club, and Walmart International. (With the acquisition of Jet, Lore is also the fourth-largest individual shareholder of Walmart stock. He owns more shares than the rest of the executive team combined.)

Together, McMillon and Lore completed a steady stream of digital retailing acquisitions, including India's largest online retailer, Flipkart, at a cost of $16 billion; as well as the outdoor clothing and gear site Moosejaw; the vintage-style fashion retailer ModCloth; Shoes.com; and menswear site Bonobos. Many of Walmart's digital acquisitions are now managed by Bonobos co-founder and CEO Andy Dunn, who reports to Lore and holds the title of senior vice president of "digitally native vertical brands."

McMillon's acquisition strategy is as much a people pivot as it is an innovation pivot. Walmart needed the scale and trajectory the start-ups had already achieved, to be sure, but just as important to Walmart were the entrepreneurship skills the leaders of these companies had clearly mastered.

Jet was allowed to continue developing on its own path, in large part because Walmart needed it to clear the way for the larger pivot to the new. Jet's leader, however, was tasked with helping Walmart become a digital-first business.

In addition to promoting Lore, McMillon approved his proposal to assign several Jet executives and other former colleagues to leadership positions in Walmart's e-commerce business. McMillon not only let him—he was effusive about the idea.

These were no empty gestures. McMillon was determined to re-align Walmart's existing leadership to better match the evolution of consumer retailing, not just at its stores but also on its websites. Separate digital efforts were combined, including the company's Arkansas IT team and its e-commerce group in Silicon Valley.

Walmart also pivoted its compensation model. To contend with digital-only competitors, the company moved away from tying executive salary directly to the amount of revenue overseen, applying other measures of value creation that better fit the contributions of executives running digitally native vertical brands.

The company now pays the leaders of some of its acquired e-commerce companies, and other start-up talent they've hired, significantly more than what a traditional Walmart exec running a retail store with similar revenues might make. Some of the highest-paid leaders of Walmart's e-commerce businesses, in fact, are running sites earning barely any revenue, a major cultural shift for the company.

Walmart's pivot to the new required nothing less. And there was more realignment to come. In a 2017 memo to employees, McMillon called for "more speed and less bureaucracy" to accelerate Walmart's core mission of saving shoppers time and money. To stay "lean and fast," he wrote, some positions would be eliminated, while new ones would be created.

Walmart's people pivot is already paying dividends. Thanks to changes made by Lore, including online grocery pickup, expanded inventory on the company's website, and free two-day shipping on larger orders, e-commerce sales have grown substantially. In 2017, a year after the Jet acquisition, online sales growth jumped from the previous year's 7 percent to 40 percent, totaling over $11 billion for that year.

In mid-2018, Walmart reported its best overall quarterly sales growth in more than a decade. It posted particularly good numbers in e-commerce and grocery, throwing down the gauntlet to Amazon, which leads in the former and which, through its own acquisition of organic grocery chain Whole Foods Market, has clearly set its sights on the latter. Walmart supports online order pickup at twenty-one hundred locations and expects to reach 40 percent of US households with home delivery by the end of 2018.

At the end of 2017, Amazon still accounted for about half of all online sales, compared to Walmart with less than 5 percent. But Walmart's percentage has grown significantly in the last three years; by late 2018, the company was on track to achieve 40 percent e-commerce growth for the year and overtake Apple with the third-highest online market share. Adjusting the lever from business running to business making was the right strategic choice for Walmart CEO Doug McMillon.

Does your company, like Deutsche Telekom and Walmart, require separate operators and entrepreneurs—business runners in the old and the now, and business makers in the new? Or can today's leadership team straddle all three lifecycle stages at once without losing their balance?

The answer, as always, will depend on the state of disruption in your industry, and the size of its trapped value gap. It will also depend, as at Dell, on how ingrained the idea of continuous pivoting already features in your corporate culture.

Most of all, your optimal leadership setting will change with the nature of the work you need to perform to satisfy customers, and the level of disruption new technologies are exerting to change it—the subject of the second lever in the people pivot.

THE WORK LEVER: ADJUSTING THE BALANCE
BETWEEN HUMANS AND MACHINES

We live in a time when the worlds of sci-fi movies and TV shows like *Robocop* and *Knight Rider* are becoming reality. Intelligent machines and autonomous vehicles are here now, even if their costs haven't yet fallen to the point needed for mass adoption. A question many are asking, in Hollywood scripts and serious journalism alike, is whether there will be a robot uprising.

The short answer is no. Accenture's research shows that machines are not replacing humans. Nor are they obviating the need for humans in the workplace. In fact, machines and humans are coming together in new roles and new kinds of collaborative partnerships. We call these new forms of work the "missing middle," mainly because they are largely absent from current economic research and reporting. (Labor reports tend to use metrics based on industrial models, rather than measures suited to the information age.)

For years, traditional analysis of automation has viewed humans and machines as rivals, pitting jobs on the one hand with productivity and (in some cases) safety on the other. But that binary perspective is a gross oversimplification, neglecting the powerful collaborations that occur in the missing middle.

Succeeding in the missing middle, however, requires a significant investment both in AI applications and in reskilling the employees who will work with them. As we noted, few companies report being prepared to take on the second part of that equation.

The good news is that it can be done. For the early adopters, doing so can yield big boosts in performance when humans and machines work together as allies, not adversaries, taking advantage of their complementary strengths.

Humans can thrive in situations where there is little or no data, while machines excel in those where there is lots of information. Businesses require both capabilities. In the missing middle, the two can come together, enhancing the nature of work for humans in the process. If health-care providers utilized intelligent systems to minimize paperwork and data entry, for example, more of their employees' time would be freed up for patient care.

Pivoting to the missing middle means certain human skills, like empathy and communication, will rise in importance while others, like administration, will decline. Humans can develop, train, and manage AI applications, enabling those systems to function as part of true human and machine partnerships. The machines, meanwhile, can augment human capacities, particularly by processing and analyzing ever-larger quantities of data available from more and more sources.

But few companies, according to Paul Daugherty and H. James Wilson, are developing solutions aimed at the missing middle, especially with respect to fast-evolving AI technologies, which include advanced robotics, machine learning, and speech recognition.

How big is the opportunity? Our research found that if every company invested in AI and human-machine collaboration at the same rate as the top-performing businesses are already, they could boost revenues by 38 percent between 2018 and 2022, lifting global profits a total of $4.8 trillion. For the average S&P 500 company, this equates to $7.5 billion of new revenues and $880 million in additional profit during that period.

And employment wouldn't decrease. It would actually grow by 10 percent.

Those collaborations won't always be easy to implement. The truth is that many jobs will have to be reconfigured as technology drives change down to the task level. "To tap the full potential of a human-machine workplace," Daugherty and Wilson write, companies will need to engage in "a complete reimagination of business processes."

E-commerce start-up Stitch Fix, launched from a Cambridge, Massachusetts, apartment in 2011, offers a good example of how reimagining human and machine collaboration can lead to rapid scale in the new—the missing middle in action.

The company's mission, according to its website, "is to change the way people find clothes they love by combining technology with the personal touch of seasoned style experts." Stitch Fix's stylists pick items for you based on data you provide, including survey responses, measurements, brand preferences, and photos of items you like, then send products directly to you.

The stylists are assisted by machine-learning algorithms that help them analyze the data and narrow down potentially millions of options to a manageable number. Stitch Fix is pursuing a hyper-relevant strategy, releasing trapped value by using AI to identify ultrapersonalized solutions adapted to the changing style preferences of its customers, selling not so much the clothing as a new look.

Each order, called a "Fix," is first processed by five to ten styling algorithms. Another algorithm matches the Fix to a human stylist, based on the best match with the human's expertise. Fixes are then routed to a specific warehouse, directed by yet another algorithm. If the customer doesn't like any of the items, they just send them back.

Growth has been impressive. By 2018, Stitch Fix had over four thousand employees, including one hundred data scientists. It has changed the look of nearly three million customers, approaching $1 billion in annual sales.

Stitch Fix's business model is only as valuable as the quality of its clothing suggestions. So humans and machines must work together to get it right. The software manages the more structured data, such as measurements and survey responses. Human stylists focus on the unstructured data, including images tagged in social media and notes from customers prescreened by machines using natural language processing.

The performance of this hybrid workforce is measured in a variety of ways, including how quickly a collection gets put together, how much a customer spends, how many items in a shipment the customer keeps, and how satisfied they are.

Both human and machine constantly learn and update their deci-sion-making skills. The client's choice to keep an item of clothing or not, for example, trains the algorithm to suggest more relevant items in the future. At the same time, the stylist improves and adjusts recom-mended Fixes based on notes from the client and with insights gained from previous interactions.

"We consider our algorithms to be composed of both expert hu-man judgment and machine," Chief Algorithms Officer Eric Colson told *Forbes* in 2018. "When clients request a Fix, the selection is nar-rowed down and ranked using a set of algorithms, but final selections are always made by a human."

Stitch Fix is distinguishing itself as a company that understands the importance of improving the quality of work performed by profession-als. In the missing middle, the software works for the humans, in other words, rather than the other way around. So even with regular mon-itoring and measurement of their performance, it's no surprise that Stitch Fix stylists are mostly satisfied with their jobs, in large part be-cause they spend more time on the creative aspects and less on routine.

In a very different context, premium auto leader Mercedes-Benz is also pursuing a hyper-relevant strategy by applying AI in the missing middle, differentiating its vehicles with customization and individual-ization. Whether it's cupholders or the caps for tire valves, each Mer-cedes model is tailored to a customer's personal specifications.

That strategy translates to a need for Mercedes' human workers to play a much larger role on the factory floor. While robots are good at repeatedly performing defined tasks, they are not very good (yet) at adapting to customizations. Mercedes needs adaptability and flexibil-ity, traits where humans still outperform robots.

"Robots can't deal with the degree of individualization and the many variants that we have today," Markus Schaefer, the automaker's head of production, told a trade publication in 2016. "We're saving money and safeguarding our future by employing more people."

The automotive industry is one of the largest users of industrial robots, but with increasing competition in the luxury car market, cus-tomization is paramount. So Mercedes is investing in a different kind of automation, where robots work side by side with humans. As part of Mercedes' adjustment of the work lever, the company has over the last few years been equipping workers with smaller, lighter, more flexible machines to enhance their capabilities, or what the company calls "robot farming."

For the Mercedes E-Class, the company replaced two fixed machines with smaller, more flexible robots that augment the work of human engineers performing such precision tasks as aligning the car's new heads-up display, which projects speed and directions on the windshield.

According to Schaefer: "We're moving away from trying to maximize automation with people taking a bigger part in industrial processes again. We need to be flexible. The variety is too much to take on for the machines. They can't work with all the different options and keep pace with changes."

Fashion stylists, carmakers, and others must strike a careful balance between humans and machines. To achieve "zero distance to the customer" in markets growing more competitive all the time, businesses must close the trapped value gap by becoming hyper relevant, providing customers ever-more granular personalization. But to keep some of the value you release, you'll need to employ technologies, such as AI, that improve worker productivity along the way.

When considering possible adjustments to the work lever, in other words, it's still important to weigh the impact of new technologies on work roles, and to do so across all three lifecycle stages. Look at them through the lens of the missing middle, however, not the zero-sum game of man versus machine.

THE CULTURE LEVER: BALANCING ONE CULTURE AGAINST A CULTURE OF CULTURES

Executing a successful wise pivot will mean reconsidering many aspects of your company's culture.

That's especially important, and especially difficult, the longer your company has been around. The teachings of your founders may rightly be held in high esteem, your previously successful products and services considered touchstones for future R&D, and your values and brand fiercely protected as the valuable assets they are.

Yet faced with big bang or compressive disruption, or both, even the most venerable businesses have been challenged to pivot wisely, adopting the portfolio model across the three lifecycle stages. Sometimes, scaling to the new requires you to strengthen the foundation of your culture with new technology building blocks. Or perhaps to rebuild them from scratch, as we found in a unique experiment in national identity ongoing in EU member country Estonia.

Estonia only regained its independence in 1991, after decades of occupation during which the country's history, language, and documents were destroyed or suppressed. The country was nearly broke, with little in the way of infrastructure or economic development.

Accenture has worked closely with Estonia's government to establish a unique national identity for it as one of the world's first fully digital societies. Well over 90 percent of the country's 1.3 million residents are regular internet users, for example, with access to high-speed broadband.

The e-Estonia project goes much further than just inclusion, comprising a complete reimagining of government services, with the goal of making them easily accessible, efficient, and transparent. All the data the country collects about its citizens is being stored in the cloud. The information is primarily maintained by the schools, hospitals, and other agencies collecting it, but is also accessible to other agencies when needed.

The core of e-Estonia is a digital ID system the country's population uses to access everything from health records to voting and paying taxes. Every resident has a state-issued digital identity. The IDs are used for nonpublic activities as well, assuring, for example, that comments posted on the websites of Estonian newspapers are authentic.

Securing the digital ID, needless to say, is a top priority. So Estonia turned to blockchain technology. Every interaction involving the digital ID is cataloged on a distributed and encrypted virtual ledger.

That design guarantees not only security but, even more important, complete transparency. Estonians can see every interaction in which their information was accessed, and by whom. Rather than using technology to scale up the government's ability to police its citizens, the system actually does just the opposite, giving Estonians an unprecedented ability to monitor the government.

Trust and transparency are core features of the new national identity Estonians have been building together. Toomas Hendrik Ilves, Estonia's president from 2006 to 2016, goes so far as to say the role of national governments in the digital age is not just to authenticate the identity of their citizens, but to protect it.

And not just from the government itself. In a world where global data collectors and information brokers are becoming ever-more powerful, Estonia is determined to create a trusted and secure system for every information exchange. "Somebody knowing my blood type isn't a big deal," Ilves explained to author Andrew Keen in his book *How to Fix the Future*. "But if they could change the data on my blood type—that could kill me."

The evidence suggests that Estonia's efforts to create a new identity for itself are working. Surveys find that a majority of citizens say they trust their government, a percentage close to double that of the rest of the EU.

The country's leaders are working to scale rapidly, leveraging Estonia's singular commitment to trust into a competitive advantage. It is the first country in the world to outsource government services to noncitizens, offering "e-Residency" to any individual interested in doing business from Estonia, and by extension the EU. A digital passport is issued to e-residents, making them eligible for some of the same services as residents; they can, for example, apply for secure electronic banking, access international payment services, and digitally sign and transmit documents, all authenticated by a national government.

Estonia has set an ambitious goal of signing up ten million e-residents by 2025—eight times the country's actual population. It hopes to become a kind of modern Switzerland: a neutral country, in this case one uniquely positioned to offer secure digital identity and data verification to the world.

The example of Estonia is remarkable for several reasons, but in particular for its focus on using the country's national identity technology as a kind of uniform digital brand. More often, the culture lever moves in the other direction, with business leaders rebalancing a strong shared corporate culture in the old with a looser, more open approach in the new, or what we call a "culture of cultures." We've already seen examples of leading businesses, some more than a century old, adopting a more fluid approach to corporate culture.

Philips, remember, broke from a tradition of over a hundred years as a leading producer of incandescent lights, where profits were determined by strict adherence to operational efficiency and incremental improvement.

But in the face of new technology that signaled unequivocally the eventual, perhaps imminent, replacement of incandescent technology, the company's leaders had little choice but to pivot. Not just to new products, but to a culture of entrepreneurship and disruptive innovation, not only in lighting, but also in the faster-changing, technology-dominated health-care industry.

Automobile companies, likewise, were initially hesitant to invest in autonomous vehicle technology. But they have now recognized the opportunity and risk of leaving self-driving innovation to start-ups, necessitating a reconfiguration of their historically buttoned-down cultures to become more experimental.

Earlier in this chapter, we saw how Walmart, still the largest company in the world by revenue, adapted to the very real challenges of e-commerce companies, first by acquiring and then by integrating start-up talent of their own, much of it from the most freewheeling technology hubs in the world, including the notoriously casual Silicon Valley.

Accenture's own reinvention likewise forced us to reassess the value and viability of our long-standing commitment to doing business and developing our people with a clear but uniform set of processes: our one-firm culture applied around the world.

As a professional services company, we had to accept a need to adapt, particularly in our new businesses, to the cultures of different regions, countries, and in particular the work styles and diverse social values of younger employees, rather than the other way around.

Given the accelerated pace of change in consumers' tastes, and their increased ability in a connected world to organize and communicate their preferences to stakeholders up and down the supply chain, a similar reconsideration is now underway in consumer products industries.

That has meant significant challenges for, among others, Procter & Gamble, the nearly two-hundred-year-old consumer products giant.

In 2015, new CEO David Taylor vowed to change the internal corporate culture; what he characterized in an interview with the *Financial Times* as a "big intervention."

P&G, he knew, *had* to change. Growth was slowing, and the company had been caught unprepared, as consumers shifted to shopping online or with mobile devices in hand at the store. Customers armed with powerful information-access tools were demanding more facts not only about the company's products, but also about how they were produced and by whom. They also demanded a wider range of personalized options and specialized ingredients.

Among Taylor's big adjustments to the culture lever was to give product managers in P&G more autonomy (and responsibility) to make decisions about product investments, supplier contracts, and more, eliminating an approval chain of command that longtime employees nicknamed "the thicket." Global product leaders were given control over sales teams, who previously reported to regional managers.

Another adjustment was to not only hire more outsiders, but also to expand the company's reliance on freelancers. This was no small pivot. P&G has a long history of promoting employees almost entirely from within. Taylor himself is a P&G lifer, having joined the company after college as a production manager.

With a new directive to shake things up, P&G's then head of human resources, Rich Postler, began experimenting with external talent marketplaces. He used digital tools to help the company tap into a global workforce of professionals with particular skills the company might need, on a just-in-time basis, as demand for specific expertise came and went.

The effort was explicitly aimed at speeding up innovation in a company well known for both its complex organizational structure and process-bound approach to development. As Taylor explained it in a 2016 interview: "In many organizations, including ours, there are processes that a company gets enamored with. Once a process is deeply ingrained, a company—and, by extension, its employees—can lose sight of the fact that it's no longer achieving the desired outcome."

P&G believes its shift to more freelance workers will help shake out which processes have outlived their usefulness. The hope is that outsiders not encumbered by the company's strong culture will work faster and question inefficiency, even as Taylor moves to unleash internal talent to do the same. "As a leader," as Taylor said at a 2018 leadership conference, "you have to create the environment that gives people the courage to step out and make the future different than the past."

By early 2017, the company completed a pilot program that tested the impact of minimizing hierarchy and bureaucracy in an open market for talent. P&G experimented with several software-based freelancer management platforms, including Upwork's service for businesses, Upwork Enterprise. Upwork allows companies to post job requests, which are then matched with qualified freelancers—kind of like an Airbnb for talent.

For projects in the pilot, P&G managers used the On-Demand Talent marketplace, a customized version of Upwork that lets project managers shop for freelancers. On-Demand Talent simplified and reduced the cost of contracting for a wide range of skills, including customer research, web and creative development, software engineering, graphic design, data analytics, core sciences, and even regulatory compliance.

The pilot, the company found, delivered products faster and at a lower cost than conventional methods 60 percent of the time. The quality of work improved by 33 percent, while the amount of time required to find needed staff dropped from ninety days to only four.

One challenge P&G has faced in its move to workforces who don't know the company's ways is teaching career managers to think in terms of projects rather than job descriptions. Where project leaders would traditionally call someone in-house to ask for help, they must now plan ahead for all the work that needs to be done, along with scheduling and identifying key milestones. Managers also need to learn new skills to supervise remote workers.

The company has likewise changed its R&D culture, from one based entirely on proprietary, internal invention to more open innovation. P&G now matches external problem-solvers with internal users looking for creative alternatives to specific design problems.

P&G's open innovation platform, Connect and Develop, has contributed to several recent product launches. In 2017, for example, in order to respond quickly to a sudden surge in demand for lip balms, P&G used the platform to facilitate a collaboration with OraLabs, a competitor in other product categories. Instead of developing the product from scratch, P&G licensed technology already developed by OraLabs, in effect trading secrecy for speed.

P&G efforts to embrace a leaner and more agile culture appear to be paying off. By 2018, the company had returned to stronger growth.

>

In concluding this chapter, the last in our journey through the wise pivot, we need to emphasize an important counterpoint to these last few examples.

Much of our discussion of the culture lever focused on the need to adjust it in the direction of a looser grip on uniformity, toward a culture of cultures.

That's because doing so is often essential to achieve rapid scaling in the new. Closing a fast-growing trapped value gap, as we've seen, requires creativity, experimentation, entrepreneurship, and other skills that often don't mix well with the kind of process-centric corporate cultures key to success in the old and the now, where the emphasis is on incremental improvement and predictable, efficient operations.

Still, achieving a wise pivot requires balance between, and focus on, all three lifecycle stages. You can't just abandon the old products and services generating most, if not all, of your revenue.

Neither can you jettison the culture that keeps them profitable. As companies in industries as different as those of Deutsche Telekom, Mercedes-Benz, and Walmart demonstrate, pivoting to the future requires you to blend the best elements of your existing core with the tools and techniques of today's most successful disruptors, along with the new technologies that drive them.

That blending includes features of your corporate culture, no matter how old or how different the customers it was built to serve. Though many of the value releasers in our study adjusted this final lever in the direction of a culture of cultures, no company in our analysis succeeded by giving up entirely on the guideposts and ethical principles embedded in powerful, trusted corporate brands.

Nor could they. You and those you interact with in the ecosystems of the new can't function, let alone scale new businesses, without the same mutual respect and shared values that keep you successful in the old and the now. Without that foundation, your brand doesn't stand for anything, let alone a commitment to deliver every day on promises that customers, employees, suppliers, investors, or regulators can rely on and trust. A culture of cultures still needs to have ground rules.

Another word for that kind of commitment is "mission." We don't mean the generic mission "statements" popular a few decades ago, largely meaningless platitudes such as "increase shareholder value" (that is, "raise our stock price"). Those may have looked good on plaques and posters, but ultimately they didn't oblige anyone to do anything, let alone rally stakeholders to strive for the same goal, using shared rules of engagement for achieving it.

That's what a real mission is—a promise we make to each other, inside and outside the companies at which we work, to continue identifying and releasing trapped value to the best of our abilities. Even when that means sharing the benefits with employees, customers, and society as a whole.

Absent a real and attainable mission every stakeholder believes in and pursues to the best of their ability, a business is just a collection of unrelated and disconnected resources.

At Accenture, for example, we still take with utmost seriousness our founders' commitment to deliver products and services that exceed client expectations, regardless of whether the project is to create an interactive customer experience, help a multinational company migrate legacy IT operations to the cloud, or provide cybersecurity incident response when a business finds itself under attack.

Likewise, no matter with whom or where we work, there's no compromising how we treat our people, or how we expect them to treat each other and those they work with. That's part of what we mean by "truly human."

From that standpoint, our one-firm concept has actually become more embedded during Accenture's rapid expansion in size, service offerings, and geographic diversity in our pivot to the new. We've grown not in spite of, but because of, that culture.

We've now covered all nine of the strategic levers you'll need to consider, and reconsider, as part of your own wise pivot. In a moment, some concluding thoughts and suggestions on how to get started putting it all together. For now, let's take a breath.

conclusion

FINDING YOUR BRICK

AS PIERRE NANTERME remarked at the very beginning of this book, "it takes courage."

There's a reason Pierre calls this out. Pivoting to the future can only happen if leaders are prepared to leave the safe harbor of today. And that takes courage.

Courage to accept that today's core offerings may be coming to the end of their profitable life.

Courage to engage with new technologies that aren't quite ready for problem-free adoption.

Courage to embrace some of the best innovations in business tools and management approaches that come out of Silicon Valley and other global technology hubs.

Courage to scale new offerings when market conditions align.

We know how hard that courage can be to find and nurture. We've lived through it. Maybe that's why our story seems to resonate so well in our continuing dialogue with CEOs struggling with the same issues. It doesn't seem to matter how old the company is, what industry it is in, or where its customers and employees live.

Even as we were finishing the last pages of this book, we met with nearly a dozen business leaders in different parts of the world. Nearly all of them asked the same questions. How can I avoid being disrupted in my core business? What is my company's new? How do we scope it? How can we pivot to it at speed and scale?

Other equally provocative questions kept coming up. Who on my executive team should be responsible for the customer experience? How can we convince today's investors of the need for increased investments in innovation? How on earth does my product company develop a services culture and mind-set? How do I continuously re-invest the trapped value we release into subsequent pivots, without alienating shareholders? How do I attract employees with highly sought-after skills in new technologies, who would rather work at a cool new start-up?

Some of those questions, we hope, have been answered. From the case studies in our research to the personal experience of our own pivoting, and that of the senior executives with whom we've worked, we have tried in these pages to give you as many specifics as we can on the dos and don'ts of embracing disruption.

No doubt there will be more questions that come to you as you begin your pivot to the future. We'll continue to answer them, both in our research and in our work with clients, as well as from what we learn in our own continued reinvention.

We hope you'll join us in an ongoing dialogue about the wise pivot, sharing your own experience and ideas. Please join us at www.pivottothefuture.com to continue the conversation.

We'd like to close with a few last pieces of advice. They are more intuition-based than the specific findings of research. Still, they are the kinds of insights we wish we'd had seven years ago when we started our own pivot.

BE PATIENT—There's an old saying in start-ups: "Being early is the same as being wrong." Companies that make the wise pivot find joy in the forward march of time, but they never rush the future. As an old commercial for Paul Masson vineyards used to put it: "Sell no wine before its time."

Look to the future without being beguiled by it. What looks to be a trapped value gap ripe for closing may only be a mirage, reflecting an oasis that, while real, is much further away than it appears. Toyota timed the market for hybrid technology, but it should be noted that the first hybrid car was designed in 1898 by Ferdinand Porsche (yes, that Porsche) when he was just eighteen years old. Production was canceled after eight years and only three hundred vehicles sold.

Likewise, consider the fate of Friendster, the first major social networking site, which, founded in 2002, predated Facebook by two years.

Despite heavy investment from one of the most powerful venture capital firms in the world, the market went elsewhere. Another Facebook competitor, MySpace, was owned by one of the most powerful media companies in the world, and at one point was so ubiquitous that the *Guardian* newspaper asked in a 2007 headline: "Will MySpace ever lose its monopoly?"

Patience doesn't mean doing nothing. It means recognizing experiments are just that: a way of testing the future without committing to move there. You still need the means to live in the now, not to mention to fund the new.

AB InBev, as we noted, is moving to produce the kind of microbrews newer customers want, but they are not abandoning mass-produced brands many still prefer, or the assets needed to make them. (The most popular microbrews will still need to be produced at some scale, after all.) Energy companies are likewise actively developing capability and capacity in more sustainable sources of power, but they won't be able to afford continuing to do so if they abandon fossil fuels prematurely.

Patience is required even when you have a better and cheaper product at hand. Amazon's Kindle was not the first e-reader to market, but not because Amazon couldn't have introduced it sooner. Amazon waited patiently until the right combination of factors, including manufacturing cost, screen contrast, battery life, and number of available titles, could be brought together to then seize the market quickly.

BE GENEROUS—Like water, trapped value, once released, finds its own path to the ocean. Along the way, your customers and industry partners will benefit from your labors, perhaps even more than you do. You may do more good for the world's most at-risk communities than for your own bottom line. You may even help your competitors, as their pivots may in turn benefit you.

That's okay. Be satisfied with your portion of the value released, and be glad for the overflow.

One of the key features our research revealed about value releasers—those who improved both today's bottom line and tomorrow's potential—was the strategies they devised to share the wealth. Doing so is likely necessary to attract the ecosystem participants needed to develop innovations that can scale rapidly. We found some of the companies that gave the most away also grew the fastest, becoming among the most valuable in the world, and in record time too.

One way to practice generosity is to focus on creating value rather than simply shifting it. Think of Amazon's and other leading retailers' experiments in technology that allows hands-free checkout, whereby radio technologies, sensors, and cameras make it possible simply to walk out of the store with your purchases and be charged automatically. For the store, hands-free checkout represents an enormous reduction in cost, allowing the human workers to focus on more valuable forms of customer service, such as answering questions and making recommendations.

But the customer also benefits from faster service, fewer errors, integrated loyalty rewards, and other conveniences. It's truly win-win.

BE REALISTIC—Not every pivot will succeed wildly. Some investments will fail to generate any returns.

That's okay too.

If you don't put all your eggs in the flimsy basket of corporate transformation, you can develop a living strategy that adapts to unanticipated new technologies, competitors, and customer demands. You can afford to stumble, redirect, and pivot again. Winning some and losing some is much more the norm, even for the most successful companies in the world. No one can be great all the time.

You can, however, improve your odds. Managing innovation, investments, and other assets as a portfolio, balanced and focused across all three lifecycle stages, offers the best possible insurance that investments that do fail won't bring on an existential crisis. You'll have other bets to fall back on, and an existing core, strengthened and expanded, to keep you going.

By adjusting some or all of the nine levers of the wise pivot, you can fine-tune the portfolio on the fly, measuring and refining your strategy continuously, rather than just once every few years, or even less frequently, as we often find when analyzing company strategies.

We end with the story of one company that faced a trapped value gap that loomed suddenly and seemed overwhelming. Rather than becoming discouraged and retreating, the company went back to its roots. It reconnected with its core assets and offerings, and its powerful culture of innovation and customer service, emerging even stronger than before.

About fifteen years ago, the nearly century-old toymaker LEGO Group was on the verge of bankruptcy, struggling to manage costs and come up with new products consumers wanted. Technology had made possible a new generation of affordable electronic and digital toys. Nothing, it seemed, was less cool than a plastic brick.

Instead of shrinking into ever-smaller markets of ever-younger children, however, LEGO pivoted to the future. From LEGO Digital Designer, a free computer program that allowed LEGO builders to plan out their creations before using physical pieces, to LEGO Boost, a robot-building kit that combined computer coding with physical building, to LEGO Life, an online network where children could share their model designs with peers in a safe and engaging environment, the company innovated like never before.

Kids loved the new LEGO, recharging their fondness for the original. And after years of double-digit growth, LEGO Group continues to pivot. The company's chief executive, Niels B. Christiansen, speaking to the *Wall Street Journal* in 2018, summed up the challenges and the opportunities of running a business close to the edge of the trapped value gap.

"The brick is at the heart of what we do," he said, "but we are, to an increasing amount, using digital to enhance it."

That's the essence of the wise pivot. Find your brick, then keep enhancing it.

index

Abbosh, Omar, 100–101, 108, 114–115,
  118, 167
Abercrombie & Fitch, 188
accelerators, defined, 6
Accenture
  becoming digital first, 19
  benefits of being asset smart, 78
  CEO as chief technology booster,
    65
  Corporate Citizenship agenda, 81
  decision to pivot, 142
  existential threats to, 98–99
  focusing through strategic
    visualization, 150
  partnership with Siemens, 89
  workforce skill growth, 85
Accenture's financial pivot
  Accenture Ventures investing
    organization, 114, 167
  Advanced Technology Centers,
    99
  Ambition 2020 plan, 100
  building own new core, 109
  focusing through strategic
    visioning exercises, 150
  Industry X.0 business unit, 100
Accenture's innovation pivot
  Accenture innovation centers,
    167–168
  Accenture's Innovation
    Architecture, 111, 112 (figure)

developing relationships
  throughout ecosystem, 182
diversification as aspiration
  management strategy, 179–180
innovation architecture, 111
joint venture with Apax Partners,
  110
launch of new practice areas in
  emerging disruptors, 100
managing innovation across all
  three lifecycle stages, 167
new approach to investing, 109
new business architecture, 109–113
new processes for acquiring and
  integrating acquisitions, 114–115
rapid expansion of highly
  specialized skills, 205
reallocation of resources, 109, 113
services business expansion, 99
speed-up of development work,
  99
Touchless Testing platform, 9, 99
Accenture's lifecycle management
  acceleration of growth in all three
    lifecycles, 103–104
  acquisition program expansion,
    106
  adaptation to continuous
    disruption, 102
  applying expanded growth and
    extra revenue, 103

Accenture's lifecycle management
    (*continued*)
  focus on needs of clients, 108
  innovation, major investments
    in, 102
  investment thinking reset, 106–107
  newer businesses, acceleration
    and expansion of investment
    in, 103
  older businesses, renewed
    investment in, 102–103
  shift to renewed investment, 108
  wise pivot in all three lifecycles at
    once, 104, 107
Accenture's people pivot
  Accenture Connected Learning,
    116
  adoption of advanced tools and
    techniques, 218–219
  broader range of career paths, 117
  creation of more flexible
    workplaces, 218
  diversification of workforce, 117
  influx of talent from acquisitions,
    205
  investment in training programs,
    116, 218
  juggling work styles and talent
    mixes, 217–218
Accenture's wise pivot
  Accenture Interactive, 119
  Accenture Labs, 167
  Accenture Research, 160, 167
  Accenture Studios, 167
  approach to innovation, 149
  being "truly human," 212
  Cloud First strategy, 182
  creation of model for prediction of
    sales volumes and velocity, 201

direct engagement with clients'
    customers, 99
integration of entrepreneurial
    leaders, 222–223
new consumer services and
    experiences, 108
obsession with continuing
    education, 192
results of, 118–120
substantial investment in employee
    development and reskilling, 205
use of cloud computing, 19
use of zero-based budgeting,
    134–135
workforce gene pool expansion,
    222
See also Accenture's financial
    pivot; Accenture's innovation
    pivot; Accenture's lifecycle
    management; Accenture's
    people pivot
Access, 148
Accolade, 126
Adidas, 31
AdSense, 149
AI. *See* artificial intelligence
Airbnb
  consumer-owned assets, 33
  as disruptor of hospitality
    industry, 24
  nimble IT infrastructure, 68
  regulation, 57–58
  Trapped Value Unlocked by
    Innovation, 35 (figure)
  users generate revenue for
    themselves, 80
  virtual business operations, 194
Airware, 52–53
Alibaba, 24, 34, 35 (figure), 36, 80, 88

AllLife, 76

Alphabet
  approach to innovation, 149
  diversification of revenue sources, 148
  focus on information collection, analysis, and curation, 149
  investments' relationship to company's core product, 148
  minimizing losses and risk, 148
  rapid pivots toward new, scalable products, 140
  speculative investments, 148

Amazon
  cloud platform of, 8, 68, 182, 207
  as disruptor of brick-and-mortar stores, 14–16, 24
  effect of General Data Protection Regulation on, 57
  internet-based streaming applications, 50
  investor relations, 55
  Kindle e-reader's success, 7, 242
  more investment in new technologies, 172
  online sales, 226
  success as book retailer, 7, 184

Amazon Prime Video, 124, 136

Amazon Web Services, 6, 8, 68, 182

Ambani, Mukesh, 195–196

Ambition 2020 plan, 100, 150

American Giant, 199

Anheuser-Busch InBev
  acquisitions of new product businesses, 135
  embrace of zero-based budgeting, 134–135
  expansion into adjacent beverage categories, 135
  focus on releasing trapped value in underserved markets, 134
  merger with SABMiller, 136
  renewed cost cutting, 134

Ant Financial, 24

Apax Partners, 110

Apple
  Apple Stores opening, 194
  Apple Watch sales, 58
  asset-smart strategy, 77
  customer service, 15
  e-commerce sales, 226
  as industry disruptor, 24, 124
  Steve Jobs' return as CEO, 54
  streaming services of, 124
  use of PARC ideas, 164

Arismore, 115, 205

artificial intelligence (AI), 22, 23, 83, 202, 219, 228–231

aspiration lever
  allocation of resources, 177
  analysis of trapped value, 177
  cannibalization of mature businesses, 182
  leveraging most successful products into the new, 184
  use of joint ventures and consortia, 183

asset-smart companies
  balancing ownership and leased assets, 76–77
  building learning algorithms, 77
  developing cloud computing services, 78
  increasing utilization of existing assets, 77
  predicting inventory needs, 78
  vehicle insurance companies, 77
  See also Apple

Athleta, 202
AT&T
 analog voice network shutdown, 207
 DirecTV acquisition, 207
 employee skills realignment, 209–210
 reskilling current employees, 210
 retraining of existing workforce, 86, 208–209
 Time Warner merger, 207
autonomous electric vehicles, 183

Baidu, 24
Bare Foods Co., 156
BCBG, 188
Beerman, Ross, 76
Benko, Cathy, 209
Bezos, Jeff, 55
Bharti Airtel, 195
big bang disruption, 24–25, 25 (figure), 26, 46, 97, 115–116, 124–125, 127, 150, 155, 160, 161–162, 172, 180, 181 (figure)
 e-commerce and, 178
 influencing reconfiguration, 150, 155
 product launch creating, 56
 technologies and, 27, 39, 49
 trapped value and, 27, 46, 141–142
Big Bang Disruption (Downes and Nunes) 24
Birla, Kumar Mangalam, 195
BlackRock, 79–80
blockchain, 22, 79, 100, 111, 232
Blue Apron, 54
Blue Ocean Strategy (Kim and Mauborgne), 29
Blue Point Brewing Company, 135

Bonobos, 225
Boomi, 223
Bosch Group, 88, 171, 172, 183
Boston Consulting Group, 137
broadband networks, 23, 36, 148, 232
Brown, Adrian, 69
Brown, John Seely, 164
Burke, Steve, 123
business makers, 221

CableLabs, 125
CaringBridge, 81
cash cows, 137–140
Caterpillar, 87
CB Insights, 160
CBS All Access, 124
chatbots, 217
Cheddar, 126
Chevron, 75–76
cloud computing
 advantages of, 78
 defined, 22
 flexibility of, 69
 internet of things (IoT), 23
 low-cost IT services, 21, 68
 use of for employee training, 205
 video and music-streaming, 136
Cloud Sherpas, 182
collaboration, 29, 72, 87, 91
Colson, Eric, 230
Comcast
 collaborations with companies invested in, 126
 core infrastructure upgrade, 125, 130
 core infused with new technologies, 128–129
 corporate venture capital use for early investment, 126, 130

DreamWorks Animation
acquisition, 123
focus on releasing trapped value
in pay-TV, 125
hyper-relevant strategy of
extreme customization, 131
iControl Networks acquisition,
126
internet access revenue, 125
Internet Essentials program, 125
investment in new technologies
and content, 123–124
investment to scale in the new,
126
nationwide network of Wi-Fi
access points, 126, 131
NBCUniversal assets purchase,
123, 128–129
pivot from analog to all-digital
distribution, 125
streaming services integration
with network, 129
telephone service migration to
mobile devices, 126
XI software platform, 125, 129
xFi digital dashboard, 125
Xfinity rebrand of bundled
distribution assets, 125
Competing for the Future (Hamel and
Prahalad), 103
compressive disruption, 25–27, 26
(figure), 46, 97, 115–116, 124–125,
127, 142, 150, 155, 160, 161–162,
172
influencing reconfiguration, 150,
155
technologies and, 39, 49
trapped value and, 46, 141–142
Concrete Solutions, 115

consumer level of trapped value,
33–34
corporate venture capital, 87, 114,
defined, 6, 18
strategy changes in, 160–161
creative destruction, 60
culture lever
adaptation to different work styles
and social values, 234
adaptation to more fluid
corporate culture, 231–232,
233–234
See also Estonia; Procter &
Gamble; Royal Philips; Walmart
CVS Pharmacy, 72–73

Daimler AG, as creator of
ecosystem to accelerate self-
driving innovation, 183
data-driven companies
best practices, 74–75
data analysis uses, 75
data hygiene practices, 74
data security, 74
information pollution, 74
new laws about data security, 74
prediction of future customer
demand, 73
robo-underwriting, 76
Daugherty, Paul R., 219
DayNine, 115
Defense Point Security, 205
Dell, Michael, 222–223
Dell computer company, 15, 223
Deutsche Telekom
changing acquisition and
management of talent, 216
development of AI solutions for
customer service, 217

Deutsche Telekom (*continued*)
  diversity in, 216
  quotas for number of women in
    management positions, 216
  training program for executives,
    215
  use of new technologies, 216
  work conditions, 216
Dickerson, Chad, 55
DiDi, 80
Digital Asset, 78–79
digital-first approach, benefits of,
    19–20, 64, 78
digital-first retailers, 15, 27
digital music distribution, 42–43
digital obsolescence, 48–49
digital payment systems, 29
Digital Services Factory, 168
digital technology, effect of on
    economy, 21
DirecTV Now, 124
Disney, 124
disruption
  big bang, 24–25, 25 (figure)
  compressive, 25–27, 26 (figure)
  constant cycle of, 40
  generating opportunity and risk,
    92
  rapid spread of, 48–49
  "shark fin," 24, 25 (figure)
The Dock multidisciplinary research
    and incubation hub, 111, 167
DocuSign, 126
Dollar General, 17
Dollar Shave Club, 126
Donovan, John, 209
Draw Something, 51
DreamWorks Animation, 123
Drucker, Peter, 60, 63

Duck Creek Technologies, 110
Dunn, Andy, 225

e-commerce, early, 26–27
eBay, 15, 34, 35 (figure), 80
Eddie Bauer, 188
Edge and Fog computing, 22
Elysian Brewing Company, 135
EMC Corp, 223
Enel
  creation of smart grid, 145
  deployment of fiber-optic cable
    throughout its network, 145
  embrace of many winning
    strategies, 147
  energy-management start-up
    acquisitions, 146
  installation of charging
    infrastructure throughout Italy,
    146
  investment in smart home and
    building energy management
    applications, 146
  launch of internet access
    business, 145
  migration of all data-processing
    activity to AWS cloud, 146
EnerNOC, 146
enterprise level of trapped value,
    30–31, 67
Estonia, 232–233
Etsy, 54–55, 80
extended reality software, 22

Facebook, 24, 56, 57
Fanning, Shawn, 43
FarmVille, 51
fast following, 87, 102
Fast Retailing Company, 187

figures
  Accenture's Innovation
    Architecture, 112
  Big Bang Disruption Phases
    of Market Adoption of
    Innovation, 25
  Compressive Disruption, 26
  Evolution of Big Bang Disruption
    at Nintendo, 181
  The New Wisdom of Future
    Growth, 127
  Nine Levers of a Wise Pivot, 155
  Releasing Trapped Value, 37
  Releasing Trapped Value in the
    Old, the Now, and the New, 106
  Technologies for Executing the
    Seven Winning Strategies, 66
  Technology Change Creates
    Trapped Value, 20
  Ten New Technologies, 22
  Three Stages of the S-curve, 105
  Trapped Value Unlocked by
    Innovation, 35
  Where Trapped Value Resides, 30
financial pivot
  asset-smart strategies, 195–198
  employee skills, 193
  fixed assets as liabilities, 193–194
  fixed assets as valuable assets, 194
  inventory-handling, 192–193
  managing key capital assets, 191
  sudden devaluation of physical
    infrastructure, 191, 192
  virtual business operations, 194
  See also AT&T; Comcast; Jio;
    Uniqlo
Financial Times, on Proctor &
    Gamble's "big intervention,"
    235

Fink, Larry, 79
FinTech Innovation Lab, 113–114
Fitbit, 88
Fjord, 152, 182
Flees, Lori, 174
flexibility, 20, 42, 91
Flipkart, 178, 225
Foot Locker, 203
Forbes magazine, on Stitch Fix's
    algorithms, 230
Fortune magazine
  on self-driving cars, 185
  survey of "America's Most
    Admired Companies," 171
  on transitioning talent, 211
Foster, Richard, 48
Frank, Elke, 216

GE Appliances, 175–176
genomic sequencing and
    manipulation, 23, 38
Gigster, 85
Gilmore, James H., 71
Girls Who Code, 117
GitHub, 6
Gmail, 149
GoFundMe, 81
Golden Road Brewing, 135
Google
  continued innovation of core
    products, 140–141
  as disruptor, 24
  as dominant provider of internet
    search, 171
  General Data Protection
    Regulation, effect of, 57
  innovative leadership at, 53–54
  as part of cloud revolution, 148, 182
Google+, 149

Google Cloud, 148
Google Fiber, 148
Google Glass, 148
Goose Island Beer Company, 135
Groupon, 50
Guess, 188
GV, 148

hackathons, 167, 176, 224
Haier Group Corporation
    combination of all seven winning
        strategies, 90–91
    embrace of social media, 62
    narrowing of trapped value gap,
        61–63
    Zhang's destruction
        of refrigerators with
        sledgehammer, 61
Haitz's law, 151
Hamel, Gary, 103
Hanjin Shipping Company, 193–194
Harvard Business Review
    on AT&T's employee retraining,
        209–210
    on reinvention, 134
    on zero-based budgeting, 134
Hastings, Reed, 8, 132
HBO Go, 124
HiSeq X, 38
Höettges, Timotheus, 213–214
holography, 67
Houzz, 126
How to Fix the Future (Keen), 233
HTC, 56–57
Huang, Jensen, 185
Hue LED lighting products, 150–151
Hulu, 50, 124
Human + Machine (Daugherty and
    Wilson), 219

human capital lever
    questions to consider, 211
    reskilling or retiring workers, 204
    See also AT&T
human-computer interactions,
    defined, 24
hyper-relevant organizations, 71–73

ID2020, 111
Idea Cellular, 195
iDefense, 115, 205
Illek, Christian, 215
Illinois Tool Works, decentralization
    of, 163–164
Illumina, 36–38, 37 (figure)
Ilves, Toomas Hendrik, 233
inclusive companies, 79–82
incubators, defined, 6
industry level of trapped value, 32–33
information pollution, 74
InnoCentive, 85, 91
innovation pivot
    centralization vs.
        decentralization, 164, 166–167,
        170
    control vs. autonomy, 170–171
    FirstBuild open innovation
        model, 175–176
    joint ventures and consortia, 183
    managing innovation across all
        three lifecycle stages, 167
    See also Alphabet; Anheuser-Busch
        InBev; GE Appliances; PepsiCo;
        Schneider Electric
innovation-sustainability balance, 45
internet companies, rise and fall of,
    139–140
internet of things (IoT), 22, 23, 62,
    73, 86, 201

internet shopping, 14–16
inventory management
    assessment of magnitude of
        demand, 200–201
    "catastrophic success," 199
    digital tools connected to online
        overstock sellers, 201
    IoT connecting parts of supply
        chains, 201
    lack of preparedness for
        catastrophic success, 199
    Nike, 202–204
    Nintendo, competition for
        components of Switch, 199–200
    timing of production, 200
    use of AI-driven optimization
        algorithms, 202
    use of technologies that simulate
        demand, 201
Invest Tech, 115
IONITY, 183

J. Crew, 188
Jet.com, 178
Jio (Reliance Jio Infocomm)
    construction of all-new mobile
        infrastructure, 196–197
    construction of cloud data
        centers, 195
    first mobile network based
        entirely on 4G LTE technology,
        195
    JioCinema, 196
    Jiophone, 196
    substantially lower prices than
        competitors, 197
    use of all four dimensions of
        trapped value, 196, 198
Jobs, Steve, 54, 164

Kahn, Barbara, 16
Karmarama, 182
Kay, Alan, 164, 171
Keen, Andrew, 233
KeVita, 156
Kim, W. Chan, 29
Kurt Salmon, 115

Laguarta, Ramon, 160
Lavallee, Marc, 166
leadership lever
    business runners and business
        makers, characteristics of,
        223–224
    leadership styles, 221
    See also Dell, Michael; Deutsche
        Telekom; Walmart
The Lean Startup (Ries), 49
learning boards, 116–117
LED technology, 150–151
Leffe beer, 135
Legere, John, 213–215
Leibherr, 61
Leonard Cheshire Disability, 81
LIDAR system components, 23
lifecycle stages of business, 2, 4–5,
    9, 101, 103–104, 105 (figure), 106
    (figure), 107, 127 (figure), 128, 166
    asset management across, 3, 98,
        147, 148, 209, 213, 220, 231, 232,
        243
    Comcast and, 126, 127
    Dell and, 222, 223
    Deutsche Telekom and, 215, 217,
        226
    Digital Service Factory, 169
    Enel and, 145, 147
    innovation throughout, 160, 166,
        171, 177

lifecycle stages of business
(*continued*)
 NVIDIA and, 185
 PepsiCo and, 160
 trapped value and, 18, 111
LinkedIn, 54–55
Liquid Studios, 112, 168
long-haul trucking disruption, 204
Lore, Marc, 173–174
Lucasfilm, 70–71
lululemon athletica, 202
Lutz, Bob, 144
Lyft, 126, 138

Mackevision, 119
MagicBands for Disney guests, 119
Maker Oats, 158
management mistakes
 anticipating customers who aren't
   likely to show up, 58–59
 creating capital structure built to
   fail, 51–53
 forcing innovators out of
   leadership roles, 53
 making the company too lean,
   49–51
 premature abandonment of older
   businesses, 131, 133
 premature IPOs, 54
 reliance on luck, 55–56
 serving regulators, not customers,
   57–58
market saturation speed, 50–51
maturity paradox, 17
Mauborgne, Renée, 29
McMillon, Doug, 224
Meeker, Mary, 24
MercadoLibre, 80
Mercedes-Benz, 86, 230–231

microbrewing or "craft beer," 133
microenterprises, 62, 91–92
microlending, 81
Microsoft
 acquisition of GitHub, 6
 "cloud first, AI-first mission," 6
 inclusive technologies, 82
 LinkedIn acquisition, 54–55
 as part of cloud-based ecosystem,
   89, 182
Microsoft Azure, 6
Milikin, Tony, 135
MindSphere, 89
ModCloth, 225
"moon shots," 172
Moore, Gordon, 20
Moore's Law, 20
Moosejaw, 225
Musk, Elon, 179

Nadella, Satya, 6, 82
Nanterme, Pierre, 65, 67, 100, 114, 167
Napster, 42, 43, 44
navigation apps, smartphone-based,
   24
NBCUniversal, 122, 123, 124, 129
near-perfect market information,
   47–48, 143
Netflix
 introduction of streaming service,
   8, 180
 production of original video
   content, 8–9, 133, 136
 revival of DVD service, 132
network powered companies
 collaboration, 87–88
 crowd engagement, 87
 early learner advantage, 87
 flexible ecosystems, 88

internet of things (IoT), 86
  smart products, benefits of, 86–87
  supply chains, 87
  wellness ecosystems, 88–89
new technologies, 2, 4–5, 22 (figure)
  more investment in, 172
  core infused with, 128–129
  investment in content and,
    123–124
  managers as advocates of, 65
  opportunities created by, 19
  overlooked opportunities for
    using, 28
  testing of potential applications
    using, 172–173
New York Times, on shopping, 16
New York Times Company, 165–166
Nextdoor, 82, 126
Niantic, 47–48
Nike
  focus on data collecting from
    customers, 203
  inventory control localization,
    203
  opening Nike by Melrose store,
    203
  retail partners reduced, 202
  robotic technology deployment,
    31
Nintendo
  pivoting from one core product
    to the next, 180, 181 (figure)
  trapped value gap closed ahead
    of market demand, 180
  as victim of near-perfect market
    information, 48
Nolan, Kevin, 175–176
Nooyi, Indra, 156–160
Nordstrom, 203

NVIDIA
  adaptation of GPU technology
    for future applications, 185
  development of solutions for
    specific industries, 184
  nurturing of GPU ecosystem, 185

Obama, Michelle, 156
OCTO Technology, 115
Oculus, 56–57
On-Demand Talent marketplace,
  236
Open Collective, 80
Oracle, 99, 182
OraLabs, 237

Palo Alto Research Center (PARC),
  164
people pivot
  approach to hiring and retaining
    talent, 217
  balancing cultures, 231, 234
  Deutsche Telekom's leadership
    style, 213–215
  human-machine collaborations,
    227–231
  leadership lever, 221–222
  See also Accenture's people pivot;
    Deutsche Telekom; Estonia;
    Procter & Gamble; Walmart
PepsiCo
  company's analysts, reassurance
    of, 157
  creation of nutrition products by
    scientists and designers, 157
  development of new core of
    healthier products, 156
  elements of centralization and
    decentralization of, 163

PepsiCo (*continued*)
  embrace of emerging global
    health consciousness, 159
  employees as part of social trend,
    157
  new expectations for risks and
    rewards of future innovation,
    158
  Nutrition Greenhouse, as external
    technology accelerator, 158
  opening The Hive internal
    technology incubator, 158
  PepsiCo Ventures Group strategy,
    158
  R&D spending tripled, 158
  reclassification of products, 157
  recruitment of innovation talent,
    158
  shift to being technology
    propelled and network
    powered, 159
Perot Systems, 223
petrochemical companies' unwise
  allocation of innovation
  resources, 179
Philips. *See* Royal Philips
Pine, B. Joseph II, 71
Pokémon Go, 47–48
portfolio pivot
  balanced portfolio, 149
  division of investment across all
    lifecycle stages, 147
  evaluation of current business, 150
  minimization of risk and losses,
    148
  vision of future, 148
  See also Alphabet; Royal Philips
positive externalities, 34
Postler, Rich, 235

Prahalad, C. K., 103
pretotyping, 168
Procter & Gamble, 235–236
Project Wing, 148
Pyhrr, Peter A., 134

quantum computing, 22
Qwikster, 132

regulatory restrictions, 25–26, 57
Reliance Jio Infocomm. *See* Jio
retailing
  brick-and-mortar stores, 14–15
  embrace of technology, 17
  evolution of, 16–17
Ries, Eric, 49
Roberts, Brian, 122
Roberts, Ralph, 122
robo-underwriting, 76
robot farming, 231
robotics, 22
Rogers, Everett, 24
Roku, 125
Rowland, David, 114
Royal Philips
  collaboration with Accenture's
    Technology Labs, 152
  cutting interest in Philips Lighting
    to less than 30%, 151
  development of technology for
    ALS patients, 152
  expansion of new core in health-
    care industry, 7
  LED companies acquisition, 7, 151
  Philips Lighting (now Signify), 151
  retirement of incandescent
    lighting business, 150
  spin-off of lighting business, 151
Rubin, Jason, 59

S-curves, 104–106, 105 (figure), 106 (figure)

Salesforce, 24, 68, 99, 182

Sällström, Björn, 83

Samsung, 56–57, 125

Santi, E. Scott, 163

SAP, 68, 89, 99, 182

scale, achieving, 6–7

Schaefer, Markus, 230

Schmidt, Eric, 53

Schneider Electric, 170
    creation of Digital Services
        Factory, 168
    planned IoT platform, 168–169
    product ideation to market
        delivery time shortened, 169
    putting customer at center of
        innovation process, 168

Seabury Group, 115

Sears' collapse, 194

seven wrong turns. *See* wrong turns

"shark fin" disruption, 24, 25 (figure)

Shoes.com, 225

Shun Guang, 90

Siemens, 89

Signify. *See* Royal Philips

SinnerSchrader, 115

Sky telecommunications company,
    122, 123

Slack, 126

Slate, review of sweatshirts, 199

Sleep Number, 88–89

Sling TV, 124

smart watches, 88

smartphone apps, 50

Snapchat, 54, 124

societal level of trapped value, 34,
    36, 38–39

SodaStream, 156

SoftBank Group, 213

Solomon, Russell, 42

SolutionsIQ, 115

Sony, 56–57

Spotify, 32, 38, 136

Sprint, 72, 213, 215

Standard & Poor's 500, on average
    company's life span, 48

Starace, Francesco, 147

Starbucks, 37 (figure), 38–39, 172

start-ups, excessive operating
    expenses of, 52

Stephenson, Randall, 211

Stitch Fix, 229–230

Strack Inc., 87

streaming services
    à la carte solutions, 124, 129
    as competition for pay-TV, 50
    Netflix, 8, 132, 133, 180
    Spotify, 32
    T-Mobile's Binge On, 214

Stubborn Soda, 158

T-Mobile, 214, 215, 217

talent rich companies
    human resource management, 84
    innovation training and
        mentoring, 83
    interconnection of humans and
        machines, 86
    learning new skills, 85–86
    proprietary and open talent
        platforms, 85
    talent development, 84
    toleration of growth and failure,
        85
    use of AI technologies, 83
    virtual labor exchanges, 84–85
    workforce, 82

taxicab companies, effect of mobile services on, 138–139

Taylor, David, 235

technologies, new, 22–23, 22 (figure)

technology debt, 67–69

technology disruptors, emerging, 22–23, 22 (figure)

technology-propelled companies
  CEOs, as technology boosters, 65
  conversion of older systems, 69
  leasing from cloud service providers, 68
  managers as new technology advocates, 65
  stimulating future innovation, 70
  technologies for, 66 (figure)
  technology debt, 67–69

10 Barrel Brewing, 135

Tencent, 24, 36, 37 (figure), 172, 180

Tesla, 32, 47, 58, 179

THQ, 59

3-D printing, 22

3M, 171

Tiffany, 17

TiVo, 50

Tower Records, 42–44, 45, 48, 51–52

Towergate, 69–70

Toyota's wise pivot to hybrid vehicles, 144–145

Toys "R" Us, 52

transportation companies, effect of regulation on, 138

trapped value
  advantages of, 13
  artificial constraints, 31
  in automotive industry, 32–33
  consumer preferences, 29, 64
  consumer surplus, 33

coordination costs, 32

defined, 13

failure to execute, 46

focus on earnings instead of innovative thinking, 45

focus on yesterday's customers, 45

on global scale, 28

in internet services, 33

levels of, 30–39, 30 (figure)

near-perfect market information, 47–48

operational inefficiencies, 18

out-of-touch professional management, 46

outdated infrastructure, 28, 31

overlooked opportunities for using new technologies, 28

reaching crisis point, 44

relationship with regulators, 46

technology debt, 67–69

trapped value gap, 20 (figure), 21, 24, 27–28, 29, 39, 40, 44–46, 53, 63, 101, 105, 109, 122, 125–126, 128, 132, 186, 223–224
  aspiration lever and, 177, 178
  asset management and, 186, 193
  control of, 137–138, 231, 237, 241, 243–244
  Google and, 141, 147
  Haier Group Corporation, 61–63
  Jio, 195
  LEGO and, 243–244
  Nintendo and, 180
  NVIDIA and, 185
  technologies and, 141–142, 161–162, 179, 180, 182, 193, 195, 206, 217, 231
  Tesla and, 179
  3M and, 171–172

Store No. 8 (Walmart) and, 174,
    178–179
Xerox PARC and, 164–165
trapped value, release of
    advantages of, 17, 37 (figure)
    constantly changing structure and
        strategy, 62–63
    defined, 18, 21
    by innovation, 35 (figure)
    opportunities created by new
        technologies, 19
    performance measurement, 64
    piggybacking off existing
        platforms, 36
    products and services consumers
        don't know they want, 34
    pursuit of innovation, 92
    Releasing Trapped Value in the
        Old, the Now, and the New, 106
        (figure)
    releasing value for others, 29
    superstars, 36–39
    technology change and, 20–21, 20
        (figure)
    by Tencent, Illumina, and
        Starbucks, 37 (figure)
    Three Stages of the S-curve, 105
        (figure)
    utilization of consumer-owned
        assets, 33
True Religion, 188
Twitch, 124
Twitter, 56

Uber
    allowing users to generate
        revenue for themselves, 80
    digital technology and, 138–139,
        194

as disruptor of transportation
    industry, 24, 68
effect of regulation on, 57–58
interest in self-driving cars, 183
nimble IT infrastructure, 68
as trapped value releaser, 33, 57
Under Armour, 202
Uniqlo
    attitude toward employees, 190
    automation using IoT technology,
        189
    becoming a digital-first business,
        189
    buying in bulk at low cost, 187
    "click and collect" strategy, 188, 191
    collecting real-time data on
        movement of merchandise, 189
    eco-friendly Jeans Innovation
        Center opened, 188
    financial pivot, 190–191
    improvement of customer service
        using cloud-based platform, 189
    investment in new warehouse and
        distribution systems, 189
    production of high-quality,
        fashionable, affordable
        clothing, 187
    production speed improvement,
        188
    pursuit of hyper relevance, 189
    stores opened in expensive
        premium locations, 188
    supply chain use of cloud-based
        platform, 189
    Tokyo store opening, 187
    use of technologies to improve
        supply chain, 188
    vertical integration of supply
        chain, 187

Universal Studios Florida theme
park, 123
Upwork Enterprise, 236
US airline industry deregulation,
143–144

value, trapped. *See* trapped value
value release. *See* trapped value,
release of
VMware, 223
Vodaphone Group, 195
Volvo, 83
Vox, 126

Walmart
acquisition of Jet.com and
Flipkart, 17, 224–225
compensation model pivot,
225–226
creation of Store No 8, 172–174
development of the capacity to be
first to market, 176
digital culture infused into
company's analog fabric, 173
e-commerce sales increase, 174
emphasis on more speed and less
bureaucracy, 226
leadership realignment, 225
plans to facilitate collaborations
to develop more disruptive
innovations, 174
streaming services in
development, 124
testing of potential applications
using many new technologies,
172–173
Walton family's support for pivot,
174
Walmart Labs, 173

Walton, Sam, 172
Waymo, 148
Waze, 148
WeChat, 36, 90, 180
Whole Foods Market, 172, 226
Williams, Evan, 53
Wilson, H. James, 219
winning strategies
asset smart, 76–79
combination of strategies, 90–93
data driven, 73–75
hyper relevant, 71–73
inclusive, 79–82
network powered, 86–89
talent rich, 82–86
technology propelled, 65–71, 66
(figure)
See also under each specific
strategy
Winthrop, Bayard, 199
wise pivot
assessment of approaching
disruptors, 143
balance and innovation in all
three lifecycles, 2, 160, 237
blend of existing core with
tools and techniques of most
successful disruptors, 237
constant reinvention, 2
culture lever, 227–237
decision to pivot, 142
elements of, 4
exploiting disruption, 3, 6
financial pivot levers, 192–193
growing profits in all lifecycles, 2
identifying and releasing trapped
value, 238
innovation pivot levers, 161–162
leadership lever, 221–227

managing core assets, 2, 98
new wisdom of future growth,
127–128, 127 (figure)
Nine Levers of a Wise Pivot, 155
(figure)
people pivot levers, 220–239
pivoting, importance of, 39–40
reacting quickly to disruption, 3
securing major mover advantage,
143
senior leadership changes, 176–177
starting point, 142–143
using portfolio of investments to
test and validate pivot, 143
See also financial pivot; innovation
pivot; people pivot
work lever
collaboration between machines
and humans, 24, 227–229
missing middle, 227–228
use of artificial intelligence,
228–231
Workday, 182
Wozniak, Steve, 164
wrong turns, 41, 60, 67, 92, 97, 147,
178, 180–181
anticipating customers who aren't
likely to show up, 58–59

creating capital structure built to
fail, 51–53
forcing innovators out of
leadership roles, 53
making the company too lean,
49–51
premature abandonment of older
businesses, 131, 133
premature IPOs, 54
reliance on luck, 55–56
serving regulators, not customers,
57–58
Wyse Technology, 223

X Development, 148
Xerox, failure to capitalize on PARC
innovations, 164

Yahoo, 53–54
Yanai, Tadashi, 186–189, 191
Yang, Jerry, 53
YouTube, 124
Yunus, Muhammad, 81

Zappos, 15
zero-based budgeting (ZBB), 134–135
Zhang Ruimin, 60–63, 91–92
Zynga, 51

about the authors

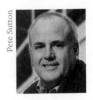

OMAR ABBOSH is group chief executive of Accenture's Communications, Media & Technology operating group. Previously, he was Accenture's chief strategy officer, responsible for overseeing all aspects of the company's strategy and investments, with management responsibility for Accenture Security, Accenture's Dublin Centre for Innovation (The Dock), Accenture's Ventures & Acquisitions, Industry Programs, Research, and Corporate Citizenship. He is a member of Accenture's Global Management Committee.

PAUL NUNES is the global managing director for thought leadership at Accenture Research. He leads the company in developing ground-breaking insights into technology and strategic business change. He is co-author of three books, *Big Bang Disruption: Strategy in the Age of Devastating Innovation, Jumping the S-Curve: How to Beat the Growth Cycle, Get on Top, and Stay There,* and *Mass Affluence: 7 New Rules of Marketing to Today's Consumers.*

LARRY DOWNES is a Senior Fellow with Accenture Research and an expert on developing business strategies in an age of disruptive innovation. He is the author or co-author of several books, including *Big Bang Disruption: Strategy in the Age of Devastating Innovation, The Laws of Disruption: Harnessing the New Forces That Govern Business and Life in the Digital Age,* and *Unleashing the Killer App: Digital Strategies for Market Dominance.*

ACCENTURE is a leading global professional services company providing a broad range of services and solutions in strategy, consulting, digital, technology, and operations. Combining unmatched experience and specialized skills across more than forty industries and all business functions—underpinned by the world's largest delivery network—Accenture works at the intersection of business and technology to help clients improve their performance and create sustainable value for their stakeholders. With approximately 469,000 people serving clients in more than 120 countries, Accenture drives innovation to improve the way the world works and lives.

Learn more at www.accenture.com.

PublicAffairs is a publishing house founded in 1997. It is a tribute to the standards, values, and flair of three persons who have served as mentors to countless reporters, writers, editors, and book people of all kinds, including me.

I. F. STONE, proprietor of *I. F. Stone's Weekly*, combined a commitment to the First Amendment with entrepreneurial zeal and reporting skill and became one of the great independent journalists in American history. At the age of eighty, Izzy published *The Trial of Socrates*, which was a national bestseller. He wrote the book after he taught himself ancient Greek.

BENJAMIN C. BRADLEE was for nearly thirty years the charismatic editorial leader of *The Washington Post*. It was Ben who gave the *Post* the range and courage to pursue such historic issues as Watergate. He supported his reporters with a tenacity that made them fearless and it is no accident that so many became authors of influential, best-selling books.

ROBERT L. BERNSTEIN, the chief executive of Random House for more than a quarter century, guided one of the nation's premier publishing houses. Bob was personally responsible for many books of political dissent and argument that challenged tyranny around the globe. He is also the founder and longtime chair of Human Rights Watch, one of the most respected human rights organizations in the world.

·　　·　　·

For fifty years, the banner of Public Affairs Press was carried by its owner Morris B. Schnapper, who published Gandhi, Nasser, Toynbee, Truman, and about 1,500 other authors. In 1983, Schnapper was described by *The Washington Post* as "a redoubtable gadfly." His legacy will endure in the books to come.

Peter Osnos, *Founder*